Tribal Justice

Tribal Justice

Twenty-Five Years as a Tribal Appellate Justice

Frank Pommersheim
University of South Dakota
School of Law

Carolina Academic Press
Durham, North Carolina

Library of Congress Cataloging-in-Publication Data

Pommersheim, Frank, author.
Tribal justice : twenty-five years as a tribal appellate justice / Frank Pommersheim.
pages cm
Includes bibliographical references and index.
ISBN 978-1-61163-665-9 (alk. paper)
1. Indians of North America--Legal status, laws, etc.--Cases. 2. Indian courts--United States. 3. Pommersheim, Frank. 4. Indian judges--United States--Biography. I. Title.
KIE110.P66 2015
347.73'28--dc23
[B]

2015021366

Carolina Academic Press
700 Kent Street
Durham, NC 27701
Telephone (919) 489-7486
Fax (919) 493-5668
www.cap-press.com

Printed in the United States of America

Dedicated to

All Tribal Judges
—past, present, and future—
with admiration and respect

Contents

Acknowledgments

This book, whatever its merits, rests on the shoulders of my many judicial colleagues during this past quarter century, as well as the many unacknowledged tribal appellate clerks working in the trenches to prepare and to advance the docket.

Without *all* of you, justice wavers, slips through the cracks, and is put at risk.

The list of individuals is too long to reprint without fear of unintended omissions, but you know who you are!

Tribal Justice

Introduction

From the City to the Prairie; From Outside Law to Inside Jurisprudence

It is almost impossible for me to imagine that when I was named to the Rosebud Sioux Supreme Court in 1987 I would still be serving on it twenty-seven years later. Harder to imagine still is the fact that I also would serve on six additional tribal appellate courts—namely the Cheyenne River Sioux Tribal Court of Appeals and the Flandreau Santee Sioux Tribal Court of Appeals in South Dakota, the Saginaw Chippewa Tribal Court of Appeals in Michigan, the Mississippi Band of Choctaw Supreme Court, the Grand Portage Chippewa Tribal Court of Appeals and Lower Sioux Tribal Court of Appeals in Minnesota.[1] During this quarter century of judicial service, I have also authored over 125 judicial opinions.[2]

Given the depth and breadth of my tribal appellate court service and related scholarship,[3] a number of people suggested that a book-length treatment of this experience might help to illuminate a particularly fertile and significant period of tribal court doctrinal and institutional development. It is thus the spirit of a

1. *See* LibGuide Index at http://libguides.law.usd.edu/content.php?pid=482397 for dates and length of service on each tribal appellate court. I have also recently been named Chief Justice of the newly formed Crow Creek Sioux Supreme Court. In addition to the Rosebud Sioux Supreme Court, I continue to serve on both the Cheyenne River Sioux Tribal Court of Appeals and the Flandreau Santee Sioux Tribal Court of Appeals.

2. *See* LibGuide Index for a complete list of opinions by court and subject matter. The LibGuide also includes the text of all 125 opinions.

3. *See* Selected Works of Frank Pommersheim for a bibliography of relevant scholarship (http://works.bepress.com/frank_pommersheim/).

case study detailing the evolution of a single tribal appellate justice's mind through time and place that animates this endeavor. This is a journey measured in the DNA of actual tribal court opinions and they constitute the heart of this book.[4]

This introduction provides a basic primer on tribal courts, including matters of institutional development and legitimacy. In addition, there is a discussion of a model of tribal court jurisprudence, which gives a thicker and more detailed description of the process of tribal appellate decision-making, as well as the nascent development of a tribal judging philosophy. There is even a relevant autobiographical snippet. In essence, I have attempted to provide a rich and complete picture of the institutional, doctrinal, and human factors that define modern tribal appellate courts.

The core of the text is a selection of complete and unedited tribal court appellate opinions. The cases in Part I are decisions concerning tribal court jurisdiction over non-Indians. These cases are followed by notes that discuss the fate of these decisions in the context of subsequent federal review. The cases in Part II provide a cross-section of decisions involving the basic civil and political rights of individuals subject to the authority of tribal government. Since these cases are not appealable to federal court, the note sections describe the reception of these cases within the tribe's own legal and political community. There is also a review and sampling of similar cases from other tribal courts. The conclusion reviews and tracks the accomplishments to date and the continuing challenges of the future.

A. From New York City to the Rosebud Sioux Reservation

The deepest journeys are seldom direct. When I finished law school in the late 1960s at Columbia in New York City, I had no interest in the practice or study of law. Three years of arid formalism without any encounter with justice left me high and dry. I was young enough to take affront. At the very last, I took my only 'job' interview and was selected for a new VISTA (Volunteers in Service to America) program to recruit 8–10 young law school graduates to work in the very rural 'bush' area of Alaska. The basic goal was to place young

4. To be clear, the opinions that appear in this book and LibGuide are the ones that I wrote. The one exception is *In the Matter of the Probate of Tasunke Witko a/k/a Crazy Horse*, *infra* pp. 234–37. These courts, of course, issued many, many other decisions that I did not write, but did participate in.

law graduates in Yupik, Inuit, and Athebaskan communities to provide basic (civil) legal services to Native people under the sponsorship of Alaska Legal Services, the statewide OEO (Office of Economic Opportunity) funded legal services program.

The experience was eye-opening—not so much from a legal point of view but more from a cultural point of view. The legal work was mostly routine, helping Native people obtain state (legal) recognition of indigenous 'adoption' practices, as well as navigating the ins and outs of many state and federal social services programs.

The cultural encounter was much more profound, especially to a young (non-Native) law school graduate, who was quintessentially urban and had never travelled west of the Mississippi River. Yupik culture was strongly communal, subsistence driven, spiritual (a hybrid of Russian Orthodox and indigenous beliefs), and welcoming. It was also riven by problems of alcohol, economic deprivation, and discrimination. I will always remember a local (state) magistrate, who was also a minister in the Moravian Church, informing me that the problems of local 'Eskimos' were a product of their 'inherent evil' as non-Christians.

As I was nearing the end of my two-year term of service, statewide discussion about the proposed Alaska Native Claims Settlement Act of 1979 (ANCSA)[5] was expanding into rural Native communities. Part of our job as VISTA volunteers was to 'explain' the particulars of this (proposed) complex statute. It was not easy to bridge the gulf between modern law and policy and rural, indigenous culture. The disconnect was profound. Most people in the Native communities along the Nushagak and Kuskokwim Rivers where I served had difficulty understanding corporate governance, land selection issues, and the potential loss of subsistence rights that surrounded the discussion of the proposed Act. These discussions made a lasting impression on me about the unique challenge of translating the language of contemporary law and policy in such a way so that it might be readily understood by local indigenous communities, especially in terms of its alleged 'benefits.'

I ultimately returned to New York City and worked at a storefront law office in East Harlem that was funded by the City of New York and a federal Model Cities Grant to provide consumer protection advice and representation to the poor. This was another valuable and instructive experience about the misuse of law to take advantage of the most vulnerable members of the community. I was also engaged in serious, non-violent resistance to the war in Vietnam.

5. 43 U.S.C. §1601 *et. seq.*

Despite this course of satisfying work and activism, fortuity intervened one more time. A friend of a friend contacted me about a job opening at a new college that was starting on the Rosebud Sioux Reservation in south central South Dakota. Sinte Gleska College (now Sinte Gleska University) was looking for someone with a law degree to teach and to develop some materials on treaties and tribal government.

I was offered the job. My wife Anne and I bought our first car (a 1973 Chevy Nova!) and drove from New York City to Rosebud, arriving on Labor Day in 1973. Our plans consisted of no more than thinking that it would be an interesting experience for a year or two. It turned out to be ten. I learned how to teach. I wrote two books, *Broken Ground and Flowing Waters: An Introductory Text with Materials on Rosebud Sioux Tribal Government*[6] and *Reservation Street Law: A Handbook of Individual Rights and Responsibilities*.[7] I made good friends. I found a place that helped me to grow, to mature, and to serve.

Sinte Gleska's philosophy emphasized the importance of faculty involvement in the community. As a result, I went to many community meetings, which were dispersed all over the three million-acre Reservation. I usually travelled with Stanley Red Bird, Chairman of the Board of Directors. I went to powwows, big and small. I went to the traditional ceremonies of Robert Stead, Frank Picket Pin, Art Running Horse, and Joey Eagle Elk. I stumbled and prayed in my own halting way. People prayed for me. The spirits (I was told) said I was doing good work. Stanley was always with me. Most of this daily experience just seemed ordinary to me. This is stuff you do on the Reservation, but part of it also went straight to my soul.

I also played hoops all over the Reservation. I was good. I had a wonderful jumpshot and was a terrific passer. I had played college ball. I was still an athlete of quality. Softball, too. I played in Indian-only fast pitch tournaments all summer long. I qualified through the unwritten—tribal common law—exception for non-Indian Reservation residents who were teachers. I played a mean first base and could hit well with two strikes. Sports provided solid, common ground and friendship across the racial divide, all the way from the Big Apple to the wide open prairie. We had a garden too. Things grew. A thousand flowers bloomed!

---

6. Frank Pommersheim, Broken Ground and Flowing Waters: An Introductory Text with Materials on Rosebud Sioux Tribal Government (Sinte Gleska College Press 1977).

7. Frank Pommersheim and Anita Remerowski, Reservation Street Law: A Handbook of Individual Rights and Responsibilities (Sinte Gleska College Press 1979).

There was darkness as well. Too many people died too often and too soon. Illness, violence, alcohol, and car wrecks took their toll. I attended too many wakes and funerals. Despite the intense sorrow, everyone was welcome, drunk or sober, friend or stranger. No one was rejected, no one turned away. I was often asked to speak without prior notice or invitation. I learned that I could do it.

Poverty was extreme, but not dehumanizing. Things were shared, especially food and material goods. A certain hope and endurance held sway. The traditional giveaways at graduations and funerals profoundly affected me. I saw the generosity of star quilts, honor songs, the extended hand. "It is better to give than to receive" was not just a quote from the Bible, but a cultural practice on the Reservation.

I learned about the importance of treaties and their centrality to sovereignty and dignity from traditional elders like Stanley Red Bird, Bill Menard, Ben Black Bear Sr., Christine Dunham, Isadore White Hat, and Dorothy Crane. They took me under their wing. I observed tribal government on a daily basis; struggling, often inept, even corrupt. Local tribal people also saw this and began to demand more. My students at Sinte Gleska were hungry to learn how to become more engaged tribal citizens and how to lead better, more productive lives. They drew me out of myself. They inspired me. One such student, Sherman Marshall, was in the very first class—Introduction to Sociology—that I taught at Sinte Gleska. He ultimately went on to graduate from law school and has served as the Chief Tribal Judge at Rosebud for the past thirty years, remaining a dear friend and colleague to this very day.

In return, I gave my best, the bond and dynamic of reciprocity. Day in, day out, just that life. I was quiet too. I could fit in without saying too much. I was just there. I didn't have any answers. That was good. Lakota people at Rosebud wanted information, feedback, connections, corroboration, even collaboration, but not answers. That worked for me.

After seven years as a teacher at Sinte Gleska College, I became the Director of Dakota Plains Legal Services, the statewide Indian legal services program funded by the federal government. In that capacity, I got a close look at the many difficulties that poor Native (and non-Native) people faced in tribal, state, and federal court. Poverty and race certainly skewed essential fairness and respect, even in tribal courts. It made me see that the beginning of justice was respect. Justice is not really possible unless judges and lawyers show respect to Indian litigants in both civil and criminal proceedings; not only respect for individuals, but institutional and cultural respect as well.

When I joined the faculty at the University of South Dakota School of Law in 1984, my contact with tribal people and institutions continued to grow. I brought my Indian Law students to the Rosebud Sioux Reservation to visit tribal court and spend an evening at the Tribal motel and casino. This is a legal practice and cultural experience that I have continued for more than twenty-five years. I know from both student evaluations and conversations with students that the Indian Law field trip is a powerful experience for many of them. Students are well-received and treated with respect. They have the opportunity to see a tribal court in session and share a meal in the courtroom. They experience Lakota generosity and the quest for fairness and justice. They see a beautiful landscape as the Little White River dips around the Grass Mountain Community down below Crazy Horse Canyon. They gamble at the Tribal Casino. These diverse and manifold interactions often break down the artificial barrier between different peoples and their institutions.

Other unexpected things happened when my friend and mentor Stanley Red Bird died. Tillie Black Bear, Stanley's granddaughter, told me that I was now an 'orphan' and that I needed family and relatives on the Reservation. In the Lakota way, Tillie arranged a *hunka* ceremony to make me (and another friend, Jerry Mohatt) a member of her extended family and *tiyospaye*—to make me a 'relative.'

I hesitate to mention this for fear of being misunderstood. It did not make me 'Indian' in any way, legal or otherwise, but it did make me a 'relative' with duties and responsibilities to my 'family.' While Tillie occasionally addresses me as her 'brother' in public settings, my status as a *hunka* relative remains little known. That seems best, though it has profoundly affected my understanding of who I am.

This autobiographical snippet is an inescapable part of what I bring to the bench, but it is no more than a very small part of the whole. Yet it remains true that any reliable and informative description of contemporary tribal courts and their jurisprudence must necessarily include an adequate understanding of the tribal people and communities and of the judges who sit on the bench.

Tribal court jurisprudence is inevitably made and developed by real flesh and blood tribal judges at both the trial and appellate level. It is therefore worth remembering that the competence and engagement of these judges is key to the realization of justice and fair play. My experience with tribal judiciaries throughout Indian country reveals a group of individuals with high levels of talent, commitment, and courage. This is of no small consequence, for there is an important nexus between the character of the judge and the quality of the judicial decision. As noted by Judge Noonan of the United States Court of Appeals for the Ninth Circuit:

> The connection is not mechanical. It is that you understand the judge much better if you understand the man.... [A]n American appreciation of the truth that the law a judge makes is a projection of values that are inescapably personal—even while the Judge labors to be impartial between the litigants and objective in his framing of the dispositive legal rule ...
>
> To see with the judge's eyes one should know where he comes from, what his experience has been, what his ideals and limits are.[8]

There must also be a complementary understanding of the institutional issues and forces that shape concerns for justice and the actual disposition of cases. Tribal appellate courts not only decide cases, but they also help to forge a unique tribal institution that reflects normative and cultural values. They hold justice in the balance.

The product of all these experiences was to give me a rich and informed understanding of local tribal people including their aspirations and their institutions. It was excellent 'training' for tribal appellate work. It gave me a personal and cultural context that enhanced my ability to help decide difficult cases with more than raw doctrine and law. Empathy is a dangerous but important word. It is often mistaken or confused with sympathy or condescension, but it is neither. Rather it is the ability to see how things look from another person or culture's point of view. It permits and encourages a larger framework of understanding within which to fit law, precedent, and doctrine. It does not mean favoritism or a predisposition that Indians and tribes always win.

B. A Model of Tribal Court Jurisprudence

Given the varied challenges of the two 'faces' of Indian law as 'offensive' nation building and 'defensive' resistance to state and federal threats to tribal institutions, especially tribal courts, it is worthwhile to consider the contours of a workable model of tribal court jurisprudence with which to respond. Such a model suggests idealized aspiration, not an absolute necessity attainable in

8. John T. Noonan, Jr., *Sitting in Judgment*, New York Times Book Review, June 21, 1998, §7, at 7 (reviewing the book Cardozo by Andrew L. Kaufman).

every case. It also provides a practical checklist of possibilities for tribal court judges who face the exigency of real, often staggering, caseloads, limited legal resources, and usually no law clerks at all. For these reasons, tribal court jurisprudence constitutes a pragmatic yet complex art. This model or paradigm[9] (there may well be others) contains the following parts:

1. Tribal court jurisprudence as craft;
2. Tribal court jurisprudence as culture;
3. Tribal court jurisprudence as narrative;
4. Tribal court jurisprudence as literacy primer;
5. Tribal court jurisprudence as 'the extended hand';
6. Tribal court jurisprudence as guide to the standards of review.

Ultimately, these pieces will be stitched together in their unique (tribal) patterns by the hearts and minds of real tribal judges doing their jobs day in and day out with their characteristic hard work and enviable commitment to render justice and fair play to the litigants that come before them.

1. Craft

The field of law invokes certain sets of practices and ways of thinking and speaking that make it a craft. It also constitutes a unique way of identifying and resolving legal disputes. The end product of such dialogue and "translation" is usually a judicial decision that summarizes, weighs, and resolves the competing arguments or claims.[10] The expectation is that the judicial decision will speak at least in part through the language or craft of law. In order to be credible to the legal community both on and off the reservation and to the larger society in general, tribal court decision-making must be convincingly rendered in the craft and analytical practices of legal reasoning. This does not mean that this requirement is preemptive or exclusive of other concerns, but only that it is necessary in a fundamental way. It is the yeast for the bread of legal conversation and discourse.

---

9. A fledgling discussion of this model appears in Frank Pommersheim, *What Must Be Done to Achieve the Vision of the Twenty-First Century Tribal Judiciary*, 7 Kan. J. L. & Pub. Pol'y 8 (Winter 1997).

10. *See id.* at 12–13. *See also* Frank Pommersheim, Braid of Feathers 74–79 (University of California Press 1995). [hereinafter Pommersheim]

2. Culture

The risk of craft standing alone in tribal court jurisprudence is that it will be seen to represent a kind of (dominant) mimicry and it will be perceived as inauthentic and merely imitative. The counterweight to an unhinged craft is the door of culture. Tribal culture provides a context for legal craft to be persuasive because it takes into account tribal history and tradition in the process of legal decision-making.[11] Too often legal decision-making and the legal system as a whole are seen as a purely formal system of rules and procedures that bear little relationship to the day-to-day life of people living on the reservation (or elsewhere for that matter). Sensitivity and awareness of (tribal) culture helps to insure that tribal court decision-making will not only be analytically sound, but also culturally informed. In many ways, craft and culture are the cornerstones for building a sturdy and enduring tribal court jurisprudence.[12]

3. Narrative

Tribal court decisions, both individually and collectively, tell a story about law, values, and culture. It is therefore critical for tribal court judges to be aware of the developing narrative and story their jurisprudence tells. How does it, for example, relate to the ongoing struggle to realize sovereignty and to vindicate particular values in unique human circumstances? Attention to narrative allows one to perceive more fully the meaning of tribal court jurisprudence not simply as the interplay of craft and culture but as something that reveals and explains a people to themselves and others. If law is a field of endeavor primarily for the mind and intellect, narrative is a way to the heart. Narrative is critical to tribal self-understanding not only in a cultural sense, but in a legal sense as well. This element of narrative in tribal court jurisprudence also connects pointedly with the "story telling" tradition that is central to many tribal traditions.

---

11. *See id.* at 107, 112–20. Note also the role of language in achieving change: "The importance of these poems of competing discourses lies in the poet's conviction that the person who owns the language owns the story, and that he who wishes to change the story must first change the language." HELEN VENDLER, SEAMUS HEANEY 126 (Harvard University Press 1998).

12. As noted by Professor Frickey, "This tension between uniformity and formalism versus uniqueness and contextualism (is) at the heart of federal Indian law theory." Philip P. Frickey, *A Common Law for Our Age of Colonialism: The Judicial Divestiture of Indian Tribal Authority Over Non-Members*, 109 YALE L. J. 1, 70 (1999). This tension also presents itself as a challenge in tribal court jurisprudence.

4. Literacy Primer[13]

Tribal court jurisprudence needs also to function, where it can, as a basic Indian law literacy primer in several different ways. First, since tribal court decisions often generate significant local tribal interest and discourse, it is helpful if such opinions contain background discussion about the nature of basic principles of Indian law and tribal sovereignty. Such descriptions often aid local understanding of important legal and cultural matters in the many cases that generate local interest. Because law—for better or worse—plays such an outsized role in reservation life, any background understanding is particularly advantageous to developing an informed and literate citizenry.[14]

Second, most recent United States Supreme Court jurisprudence in Indian law relative to tribal courts reaches back no further than *Montana v. United States*.[15] As a result, current Supreme Court decisions in Indian Law are re-

---

13. *See id. See also* Pommersheim, *supra* note 10, at 108–12; Frank Pommersheim, *Tribal Court Jurisprudence: A Snapshot from the Field*, 21 Vt. L. Rev. 7, 37–45 (1996). Note also these unique observations concerning narrative and language in the context of many indigenous cultures:

> The practical knowledge, the moral patterns and social taboos, and indeed the very language or manner of speech of any nonwriting culture maintain themselves primarily through narrative chants, myths, legends, and trickster tales—that is, through the telling of stories.

David Abram, The Spell of the Sensuous 181 (1996).

> The sense of being immersed in a sentient world is preserved in the oral stories and songs of indigenous peoples in the belief that sensible phenomena are all alive and aware, in the assumption that all things have the capacity of speech. Language, for oral peoples, is not a human invention but a gift of the land itself.

Id. at 263.

> It is a style of thinking then, that associates truth not with static fact, but with a quality of relationship.

Id. at 264.

> In contrast to the apparently unlimited, global character of the technologically mediated world, the sensuous world—the world of our direct unmediated interactions—is always local. The sensuous world is the particular ground on which we walk, the air we breathe.

Id. at 266.

14. *See* Frank Pommersheim, *Democracy, Citizenship, and Indian Law Literacy: Some Initial Thoughts*, 14 T.M. Cooley L. Rev. 457, 467–71 (1997); Frank Pommersheim, *Tribal Court Jurisprudence: A Snapshot from the Field*, 21 Vt. L. Rev. 7, 45 (1996).

15. 450 U.S. 544 (1981). For a significant elucidation of this point, *see also* David H. Getches, *Conquering the Cultural Frontier: The New Subjectivism of the Supreme Court in Indian Law*, 84 Cal. L. Rev. 1573, 1617 (1996).

markably truncated with little sense of the roots of tribal sovereignty and the sweep of Indian Law history from the colonial era onward. Again, tribal court jurisprudence can provide a valuable corrective to this pernicious historical and doctrinal amnesia. While there is no guarantee that reviewing federal courts—including the United States Supreme Court—will pay attention or even notice, any opportunity to educate and create dialogue needs to be seized.

Third, tribal courts do not have the luxury of assuming that other judges who read and review their decisions are adequately informed about tribal judicial descriptions of tribal law itself. Tribal courts, wherever possible, have to go that extra mile to explain basic tribal law and values. Without such efforts, it becomes all too easy for federal courts to avoid a genuine engagement with tribal court decisions.

Fourth, in a related but somewhat different vein, tribal court jurisprudence provides the opportunity for tribal courts to explain why some decisions of the Supreme Court and Circuit Courts are wrongly decided from the perspective of their own precedent and/or from the tribal court's understanding of its own law. None of this is meant to sound arrogant or presumptuous, yet the Supreme Court does seem to be further and further out of touch with its own historical precedents and its understanding of the law and capabilities of tribal courts. Tribal courts, where they can, need to assist the educable within the federal judiciary.

5. 'The Extended Hand'

While the Supreme Court appears to be retreating from its deference and solicitude toward tribal courts, tribal courts ought not reciprocate this indifference or hostility, but instead should remain poised with the 'extended hand' of respect and willingness to engage in judicial dialogue. Failure to do so will instill more, rather than less, federal jurisprudential chill and willingness to ignore, rather than engage, tribal court decision-making.

While such a proposal clearly requires a certain kind of judicial diplomacy that should be mutually shouldered by tribal and federal courts, the Supreme Court, whether inadvertently or not, has clearly stepped back from its own authoritative initiatives that were at the heart of the *National Farmers Union Insurance Cos. v. Crow Tribe of Indians*[16] and *Iowa Mutual Insurance Co. v. La-*

16. 471 U.S. 845, 857 (1985) (holding that parties must exhaust their tribal court remedies before challenging tribal court jurisdiction in federal court).

Plante[17] cases. Tribal courts ought not to follow suit, and where possible, should remind federal courts of the Supreme Court's own extended hand in *National Farmers Union* and *Iowa Mutual.*

6. The Standards of Review

In the immediate aftermath of *National Farmers Union* and *Iowa Mutual*, one of the primary questions addressed by federal courts was: What are the appropriate standards of review for the various kinds of findings a tribal court might make in the course of its own jurisdictional determination? The potential determinations are of three kinds: findings of fact, findings of tribal law, and findings of federal law. The consensus about the appropriate standard of review is as follows: tribal findings of fact are entitled to complete deference unless clearly erroneous; findings of tribal law are entitled to complete deference; and findings of federal law are reviewed de novo.[18] This is all well and good, but there are instances, perhaps increasingly so in a post-*Strate*[19] world, where lower federal courts may simply leapfrog the particulars of any review to the broad federal question about whether a tribal court has jurisdiction. This potentiality has been astutely pointed out by Professor Royster. As she notes:

> Tribal court adjudications involving non-member parties are thus messy affairs. Any given case may raise the issue of whether tribal court jurisdiction is proper as a matter of federal law. It may also raise the issue of whether tribal court jurisdiction over the nonmember is proper as a matter of tribal law, depending upon the wording and reach of tribal constitutional provisions and statutes. In addition, the case may raise the issue of whether tribal legislative or executive power over the non-member party is proper as a matter of federal law ...
>
> When a federal court on post-exhaustion review fails to conscientiously distinguish between those issues of federal law and tribal law, the result is not only doctrinal confusion but serious encroachment upon the proper role of the tribal courts.[20]

---

17. 480 U.S. 9, 16 (1987) (holding that exhaustion is required even in a diversity context: "[F]ederal policy supporting tribal self-government directs a federal court to stay its hand in order to give the tribal court a 'full opportunity to determine its own jurisdiction'.").

18. *See, e.g.*, Judith V. Royster, *Stature and Scrutiny: Post-Exhaustion Review of Tribal Court Decisions*, 46 U. Kan. L. Rev. 241, 254–66, 281 (1998). [hereinafter Royster]

19. Strate v. A-1 Contractors, 520 U.S. 438 (1997).

20. Royster, *supra* note 18, at 250–51 (citations omitted).

Tribal courts may seek to reduce the likelihood of such problems in the post-exhaustion review situation by doing two specific things in their opinions. First, tribal court opinions should accurately label their various determinations as such: findings of fact, findings of tribal law, and findings of federal law. Second, the opinions can explicitly make reference to Professor Royster's insight that findings of tribal law cannot willy-nilly be transmogrified into questions of federal law to permit de novo review that completely ignores a tribal court's interpretation of tribal law. This is a critical point. Failure to hue to this distinction means "tribal court jurisprudence cannot prosper."[21]

In the confusing, if not chaotic, post-*Montana* and post-*Strate* world, tribal courts face even greater responsibilities than ever in seeking to hold federal courts to their proper range of review rather than permitting them to exercise a free ranging de novo approach. If reviewing federal courts encounter tribal court decisions with clear findings and precise indications of the standards of review along with the admonition to "resist the temptation to turn tribal law issues into federal questions,"[22] it will provide a helpful guide to federal review and a salutary reminder to federal courts to respect tribal courts and not overstep their boundaries.

To be sure, this model of tribal court jurisprudence is comprehensive and broadly idealistic. Yet in the real world where the stakes are high and tribal resources may be quite limited, it is important to have something to look to for guidance and direction; something that is both functional and aspirational. The fateful consequences that increasingly characterize federal Indian law as the result of an increasingly illegitimate jurisprudential model ought not be reproduced in tribal court decision-making.

Any model of tribal court jurisprudence is inevitably carried out by real flesh and blood tribal judges at both the trial and appellate level. It is therefore worth remembering, as noted earlier, that the competence and engagement of these judges is key to the realization of any of the qualities set out in the model. In this light, the personal qualities of intellect, character, and commitment found in tribal judges are central components of tribal court jurisprudence. Without such individuals, no model of tribal court jurisprudence is sufficient to insure justice and fair play in Indian country.

---

21. *Id.* at 254.
22. *Id.*

C. The Process of Collaboration and Collegiality in Tribal Judicial Decision-Making

It has been my uniform experience in serving on several different tribal appellate courts during the past quarter century that there is a consistent and ongoing commitment to collegiality and lively deliberation and collaboration. Deliberations take as much time as necessary to give each justice the opportunity to identify and to speak to the issues. The deliberations are led and mediated by the Chief Justice. The discussions usually continue until the Chief Justice senses a consensus. Then he or she will articulate the consensus orally as to each issue and the resolution he or she discerns. If the other judges are in agreement, the Chief Justice will then usually summarize the overall result of the appeal—affirmed, reversed, remanded—to make sure that all the justices agree with the *disposition* of the case.

There is a strong—though seldom directly articulated—commitment to achieve unanimity in order to speak forcefully with a single, unified (judicial) voice. Over ninety-five percent of the cases in which I have participated have resulted in unanimous opinions. The actual writing of the opinion is usually assigned by the Chief Justice based on collegial commitment and the necessity to share the workload. With rare exceptions, the appellate courts on which I serve issue *per curiam* as opposed to signed opinions by particular justices.[23] This common practice has never involved much discussion. I understand this practice to be connected with collective modesty and a disinclination toward too much individualism.

The lead writer will always circulate the proposed opinion to the other justices for their comments and proposed revisions. My experience is that there is seldom, if ever, significant revision. Tribal appellate court opinions are not changed or modified to hold on to or to obtain a colleague's vote to join the opinion. This is just not the mindset of tribal appellate courts. Occasionally, different justices will write different parts of a particularly long and intricate opinion; however, in my judicial experience, this practice is quite rare.

---

23. As a result of this practice, all the opinions presented in this book as authored by myself must be taken on good faith that this is so.

D. Evolution of a Tribal Judging Philosophy

While little has been written to date about theories or approaches to tribal court judging—at either the trial or appellate level—I want to make an initial foray in this direction that focuses on my own judicial evolution and development. At some point, it is essentially disingenuous to say that you merely 'umpire' and neutrally apply the facts to the law as precedent requires.

The 'umpire' view is the stuff of mainstream legal education, but like much else in mainstream legal education, it bears little relationship to reality. This judging axiom has particular force in the tribal court context, where many tribal court judges, especially at the trial level, are recent law school graduates who are relatively young and likely still under the sway of the conventions of their law school education. Such youth often needs experience and reflection in order to connect more fully and adroitly with tribal legal and cultural reality.

This 'neutral' judicial model is also often advocated to ward off charges of partiality or favoritism of Indians over non-Indians or the tribe over its members. Such concerns are legitimate and quite real, but the 'neutral' approach has its own problems. It too often defaults to a vague and messy status quo and otherwise grants too much deference to narrow construction and interpretation with insufficient attention to history and context. This approach is further complicated by the fact that there are many, many cases of first impression in tribal appellate courts with little or no local tribal court precedent on point to guide or to frame the analysis. There is no guiding, easy to apply rule. Neither logic nor legal convention compels a particular result. Choices must be made.

If this is the Scylla of tribal court jurisprudence, there is also the Charybdis of making tribal court decisions with little or no reference to what tribal (or federal) law actually is. This approach 'creates' rather than analyzes or interprets law.[24] Knowingly or not, it claims too much and becomes excessive. It overreaches and is potentially destabilizing. There ought to be a responsive third way, and I believe there is. It involves a synthesis of craft, context, reason, and sensitivity to consequences.

This innovative approach may be highlighted and better understood by com parison to the contending views that exist within the federal court judging community. Recent work in this area by Judge Richard Posner of the Seventh Judicial Circuit Court of Appeals is most helpful and illuminating. He fruit-

24. Richard A. Posner, Reflections on Judging 219–24 (Harvard University Press 2013). [hereinafter Posner]

fully describes the two main contending judicial philosophies as the 'formalist' and 'realist' approaches.[25]

The character of legal formalism, for example, is captured in the slogan "the law is its own thing"[26] and more academically:

> The law as seen from the formalist perspective is a compendium of texts, like the Bible, and the task of the judge or other legal analyst is to discern and apply the internal logic of the compendium. He is an interpreter, indifferent or nearly so to the consequences of his interpretations in the real world. He is not responsible for those consequences; if they are untoward, the responsibility for altering them through a change in law falls to the "political branches" (as judges like to call the legislative and executive branches of government, thus distancing themselves from the taint of politics). On this view, judges who take into account the consequences of alternative interpretations are stepping outside law. Only the orthodox materials of legal analysis—statutes, constitutions, regulations, precedents, other legal documents—are law; all the rest is policy, or politics (or economics!). As one notable formalist has put it, impressively but opaquely, "formalism treats the law's concepts as pathways into an internal intelligibility." (footnotes omitted)[27]

Legal realism is:

> [H]arder to describe than legal formalism, because it is everything in legal thought and practice that is not formalism, ... The realist places emphasis on the consequences of judicial rulings, and in that regard is pragmatic but only if the realist considers systemic as well as case-specific consequences and thus avoids shortsighted justice—justice responsive only to the "equities" of the particular case—and is analytical and empirical rather than merely intuitive and political. Systemic consequences include the effect of a doctrine or decision on the predictability of law, on caseloads, on administrability, on the work of other branches of government (such as the legislative branch, which would be thrown into disarray if judges paid no heed to statutory language), and on reasonable expectations both private and public.
>
> ... The core of a defensible legal realism is the idea that in many cases, and those the most important, the judge will have to settle for a rea-

25. *Id.* at 4.
26. *Id.* at 4–5.
27. *Id.*

> sonable, a sensible, result, rather than being able to come up with a result that is demonstrably, irrefutably, "logically" correct. Law is not logic but experience, as Holmes famously put it. And experience is the domain of fact, and so the realist has a much greater interest in fact than the formalist, ... [28]

Put more simply, 'formalism' is primarily committed to the narrow abstraction of 'textual originalism':

> [W]hose votaries purport to "look for meaning in the governing text, ascribe to that text the meaning that it has born from its inception, and reject judicial speculation about both the drafters' extratextually derived purposes and the desirability of the fair reading's anticipated consequences." So all that judges have to do and all they should do when faced with an issue of statutory or constitutional interpretation is apply the relevant statutory or constitutional text to the facts of the particular case. The escape from empirical reality is then complete.
>
> In form, textual originalism is a celebration of judicial passivity; in practice, it is a rhetorical mask of political conservatism. At the other end of the political spectrum we encounter a freewheeling imaginative approach—one of rampant activism, so obviously unanchored as to be shunned even by liberal judges.[29]

'Realism' is more 'concrete' with its focus on facts and consequences, rather than the blind abstractions of 'formalism.'

All of this is necessarily mediated through 'interpretation.' No text or case is self-disclosing, and interpretation is necessary in order to arrive at a legal 'meaning' to apply to the facts and to decide a case. Cases in tribal court are often rife with unique issues of interpretation. To mention just a few, there are issues involving treaties entered into more than 150 years ago, tribal constitutions that were adopted more than seventy-five years ago with no reliable input from the tribal citizenry of the day, applying Supreme Court precedent that is no more than made up federal common law,[30] and discerning long ago tribal tradition and custom.[31] In this framework, I believe, 'original textualism' has almost nothing to offer, but pragmatic realism does, particularly with its concern for facts, context, and consequences in the real world.

---

28. *Id.* at 5–6.

29. *Id.* at 178–79 (internal footnotes omitted).

30. *See, e.g.*, Montana v. United States, 450 U.S. 544 (1981) and its progeny.

31. *See, e.g.*, Frank Pommersheim, *The Crazy Horse Malt Liquor Case: From Tradition to Modernity and Halfway Back*, 57 S.D. L. Rev. 42 (2012).

Some obvious caveats also pertain. Such a view does not license or encourage disregard for the text of tribal constitutions and statutes or the holdings of relevant Supreme Court cases. For original textualists, the text is the beginning and the end of the analysis. For pragmatic realists, the text is also the beginning, but it is not the end of analysis. There is additional concern for the 'quality' of the 'fit' of law with tribal history, culture, and practical consequences. In other words, pragmatic realism in tribal court jurisprudence often looks further back and further forward than the boundaries of original textualism.

There is also the 'reality' of the residue of colonialist jurisprudence that feels no compunction in adjusting or setting aside what tribes and tribal courts do, especially in regard to non-Indians. This is particularly glaring—even galling—when the most textual-originalist Supreme Court in the modern era routinely erodes tribal sovereignty without reference to any constitutional or statutory text. The Court just makes it up as it goes along and casts an ominous shadow over much tribal court decision-making.[32]

As noted elsewhere,[33] not only must tribal courts be able to earn federal court respect with craft and analytical rigor, but they also must be able to communicate successfully with the tribal public at large. This is another hallmark of pragmatic realism. Tribal court opinions should *not* add needless 'complexification' that further obscures the reality they are describing.[34] The law—lest we forget—is a human endeavor that ought not get stuck in its own jargon and bloated obfuscations.

Perhaps, active restraint is a key term or ingredient. Tribal appellate courts are often seen as sources of clarity and reason; necessary forums for the resolution of important legal questions. As a potential authority for both law and policy, there must be a willingness to go far, but not too far. Restraint with a true center of gravity; an anchor in what is necessary and what is possible.

Tribal courts must necessarily take all of this into account as best they can. While it certainly is no easy task, a pragmatic tribal realism offers the most thoughtful and reliable approach and reflects a truer sense of gravity. Perhaps the character Bazil Coutts in Louise Erdrich's novel *The Round House* says it best:

> These are the decisions that I and many other tribal judges try to make. Solid decisions with no scattershot opinions attached. Everything we do, no matter how trivial, must be crafted keenly. We are trying to

---

32. *See, e.g.*, Frank Pommersheim, Broken Landscape: Indians, Indian Tribes, and the Constitution (Oxford University Press 2009).

33. *See supra* notes 9–15 and accompanying text.

34. Posner, *supra* note 24, at 351–52.

> build a solid base here for our sovereignty. We try to press against the boundaries of what we are allowed, walk a step past the edge. Our records will be scrutinized by Congress one day and decisions on whether to enlarge our jurisdiction will be made. Some day. *We want the right to prosecute criminals of all races on all lands within our original boundaries*. Which is why I try to run a tight courtroom, Joe. What I am doing now is for the future, though it may seem small, or trivial, or boring, to you.[35]

I would lastly invoke Albert Camus, the French writer and activist. He makes for me a powerful point; all the more powerful for its counterintuitiveness. Camus notes that his own commitment to pursue justice in the face of so much injustice is nourished and buoyed by the beauty of his home ground. "In a word, the world's beauty, and not only its injustices, also demands our attention."[36] In Camus's case, his native Algeria, ravaged by poverty and colonialism, was the place of both sunlight and resolve. For me, the Rosebud Sioux Reservation is that 'home' place, that place of endless prairie beauty and wise struggle. That is why I can go on with resolve to render justice in each and every case I participate in. No matter the odds, engaged attention is the predicate of fairness and respect.

Reservation life (at Rosebud) is often besotted by tragedy but saved by (its) beauty and the dream of justice. Both the earth and the stars set deep in the night sky keep the darkness at bay. Yes, "to serve justice so as not to add to the injustice of the human condition, to insist on plain language so as not to increase universal falsehood, and to wager, in spite of human misery, for happiness."[37] Such is the call way out here on the prairie at the outer edges of Indian law and history.

This book and its complementary LibGuide provide an innovative blend of old fashioned text in the printing press tradition pioneered by Johannes Gutenberg (1395–1468) and the new wave of website technology in cyberspace. Those of you who know me will surely chuckle at the irony of a confirmed neo-Luddite at the cutting edge of anything more technologically advanced than pen and paper. Nevertheless, if you go to the University of South Dakota School of Law—Law Library Guides website (http://libguides.law.usd.edu/) and click the link for *Justice in Indian Country: 25 Years as a Tribal Appellate Justice*, you

35. Louise Erdrich, The Round House 229–30 (Harper and Row 2012) (emphasis in original).

36. Robert Zaretzky, A Life Worth Living 188 (Harvard University Press 2013).

37. *Id.* at 178.

will find a personal and jurisprudential introduction to this project, the complete texts of the 125 opinions that I have written, a link to my Selected Works site containing a bibliography of my Indian law scholarship, and even an embedded YouTube video of the reading of a few Buddha poems. As Buddha (probably) said,

Give more
eat less

It fills
you up

Part I

From Tribal Court to Federal Court

A. Background: The Bookends of *Montana* and *National Farmers Union*

The (potential) journey from tribal court to federal court is bracketed by two seminal Supreme Court decisions: *Montana v. United States*, 450 U.S. 544 (1981) and *National Farmers Union Insurance Cos. v. Crow Tribe of Indians*, 471 U.S. 845 (1985). *Montana* was decided in 1981 and *National Farmers Union* in 1985. *Montana* sets the (federal) substantive guidelines for determining tribal court subject matter jurisdiction concerning non-Indians and *National Farmers Union* sets the (federal) procedural guidelines for getting from tribal court to federal court in order to contest tribal court jurisdiction within the *Montana* framework.

The *Montana* case, with very little fanfare and even less authority, significantly reworked the analytical landscape for determining whether there is tribal court civil jurisdiction over non-Indians or non-Indian entities on fee land within the boundaries of a reservation. Prior to *Montana*, the conceptual approach to this problem was rooted in a constitutional and statutory framework. The framework recognized tribes as constitutional sovereigns, whose jurisdictional authority could only be limited through treaties or an express act of Congress.[1]

1. This authority (while itself questionable) is rooted in the Supreme Court's decision in Lone Wolf v. Hitchcock, 187 U.S. 553 (1903), which recognized a 'plenary power' in Congress to pass any and all legislation dealing with Indians and Indian tribes.

According to the preeminent Indian law scholar, Felix Cohen, this core formulation may be summarized as adherence to three fundamental principles:

> (1) An Indian tribe possesses, in the first instance, all the powers of a sovereign state. (2) Conquest renders the tribe subject to the legislative power of the United States and in substance terminates the tribe's external sovereignty, for example, its power to enter into treaties with foreign nations, but does not by itself affect the tribe's interior sovereignty, that is, its power of local self-government. (3) These powers are subject to qualification by treaties and express legislation of Congress, but, save those expressly qualified, full powers of internal sovereignty are vested in the Indian tribe and in their duly constituted organs of government.[2]

In the absence of such treaty or legislative activity, tribal jurisdictional authority was presumed to remain intact. This is the basic rule of *Williams v. Lee*[3] which was decided in 1959 and has never been overruled. The essence of *Williams v. Lee* was the recognition of the right of reservation Indians to make their own laws and be governed by them, which included the right to make laws governing the civil conduct of non-Indians and conferring jurisdiction on tribal courts to resolve any resulting disputes. In *Williams v. Lee*, the Court specifically noted the fact that the physical presence of a non-Indian engaging in commercial trade on the reservation was enough to create tribal court jurisdiction.

In other words, *Williams v. Lee* created a strong, near irrebuttable presumption, in favor of tribal court jurisdiction over non-Indians unless adjusted by Congress. *Montana*—without overruling, or in any way expressly limiting *Williams v. Lee*—went in the exact opposite (conceptual) direction and created a very strong presumption *against* tribal court jurisdiction over non-Indians, particularly for activities occurring on fee land.[4] This strong presumption, however, is *not* irrebuttable. *Montana* expressly articulated the

2. Felix Cohen, Handbook of Federal Indian Law 122–23 (1942 ed.).

3. 358 U.S. 217 (1959) (tribal, not state, court has jurisdiction over an action brought by a non-Indian store owner against a tribal member for goods sold on credit on the reservation).

4. This presumption against tribal court jurisdiction appeared to be tethered to the General Allotment Act and Crow Allotment Act because these statutes permitted non-Indians to become fee holders of land within the Reservation. *Montana*, 450 U.S. at 559. This statutory tether was subsequently abandoned in Nevada v. Hicks, 535 U.S. 353 (2001), when *Montana* analysis was extended to *all* land within the reservation.

test that must be satisfied in order to overcome the presumption against tribal court jurisdiction. This test is often referred to as the *Montana* proviso:

> To be sure, Indian tribes retain inherent sovereign power to exercise some forms of civil jurisdiction over non-Indians on their reservations, even on non-Indian fee lands. A tribe may regulate, through taxation, licensing, or other means, the activities of nonmembers who enter consensual relationships with the tribe or its members, through commercial dealing, contracts, leases, or other arrangements. A tribe may also retain inherent power to exercise civil authority over the conduct of non-Indians on fee lands within its reservation when that conduct threatens or has some direct effect on the political integrity, the economic security, or the health or welfare of the tribe.[5]

Almost all tribal court jurisprudence involving jurisdictional challenges by non-Indians turns on the analysis of whether either or both of the prongs in the proviso are satisfied. If the tribal appellate court rules 'yes,' the case will remain in tribal court, at least temporarily, for an adjudication on the merits. If the tribal appellate court rules that neither prong of the *Montana* proviso is satisfied, it will dismiss the case. The plaintiff will then have to find another forum in which to bring the claim.

The regime established by the 'pathmarking'[6] *Montana* case and its progeny[7] is an essential exercise of *judicial* plenary power, wherein the Supreme Court *substituted* its own common law jurisdictional analysis to replace the

5. Montana v. United States, 450 U.S. 544, 565–66 (1981) (citations omitted).

6. Strate v. A-1 Contractors, 520 U.S. 438, 495 (1997).

7. *Montana*'s progeny includes:

Strate v. A-1 Contractors, 520 U.S. 438 (1997) (state highways running through Reservations are to be considered fee lands for *Montana* analysis purposes); Brendale v. Confederated Tribes and Bands of Yakima Indian Nation, 492 U.S. 408 (1989) (non-Indian fee land on the reservation is subject to Tribal zoning if it is completely surrounded by Tribal trust land); South Dakota v. Bourland, 508 U.S. 679 (1993) (Federal government 'taken' lands on reservations are to be considered fee lands for *Montana* analysis purposes); Nevada v. Hicks, 535 U.S. 353 (2001) (*Montana* analysis applies to all land, including trust land, within a reservation); Atkinson Trading Co., Inc v. Shirley, 532 U.S. 645 (2001) (*Montana* analysis applies to tribal effort to tax non-Indians staying at non-Indian owned motel located on fee land within the reservation); and Plains Commerce Bank v. Long Family Land and Cattle Co., 554 U.S. 316 (2008) (no tribal court jurisdiction over discrimination claims involving the sale of fee land by a non-Indian bank). The Supreme Court held against tribal jurisdiction in all of these cases, with the single exception of a Tribe's right to zone non-Indian fee land located on part of the reservation completely surrounded by trust land.

previous constitutional and statutory framework. The Court in *Montana* never uses the term common law, never expressly limits or overturns *Williams v. Lee*, but somehow gets to a whole new place. A place where tribes and tribal courts are essentially presumed not to have authority over non-Indians on fee land, when prior to *Montana*, the exact opposite was true. This reversal of jurisdictional fortune creates significant pressure on tribal courts and severely challenges their dignity and integrity.

After there has been a final tribal appellate court ruling that there is tribal court jurisdiction—in most cases without any determination on the merits[8]—it creates the opportunity to continue the jurisdictional challenge in federal court. This is the procedure established by the *National Farmers Union* case.

National Farmers Union, decided four years after *Montana*, sets the *procedural*, as opposed to the substantive, guidelines for challenging tribal court civil jurisdiction over non-Indians. In distinction to *Montana*, the Supreme Court strikes a quite respectful note toward tribal courts. Instead of permitting non-Indians challenging tribal court jurisdiction to immediately jump into federal court, it requires non-Indians to "exhaust" tribal court remedies before carrying their challenge from tribal to federal court. The rationale for this approach is essentially twofold:

> We believe that examination should be conducted in the first instance in the Tribal Court itself. Our cases have often recognized that Congress is committed to a policy of supporting tribal self-government and self-determination. That policy favors a rule that will provide the forum whose jurisdiction is being challenged the first opportunity to

---

8. This is most often accomplished through the use of an interlocutory appeal from a tribal trial court to a tribal appellate court without any adjudication on the merits. Such an interlocutory appeal usually follows upon the trial court's denial of the defendant non-Indian's motion to dismiss for lack of subject matter jurisdiction. *See, e.g.*, 28 U.S.C. § 1292(b) for the federal rule concerning the parameters of interlocutory appeals:

> When a district judge, in making in a civil action an order not otherwise appealable under this section, shall be of the opinion that such order involves a controlling question of law as to which there is substantial ground for difference of opinion and that an immediate appeal from the order may materially advance the ultimate termination of the litigation, he shall so state in writing in such order. The Court of Appeals which would have jurisdiction of an appeal of such action may thereupon, in its discretion, permit an appeal to be taken from such order, if application is made to it within ten days after the entry of the order: *Provided, however*, That application for an appeal hereunder shall not stay proceedings in the district court unless the district judge or the Court of Appeals or a judge thereof shall so order.

> evaluate the factual and legal bases for the challenge. Moreover the orderly administration of justice in the federal court will be served by allowing a full record to be developed in the Tribal Court before either the merits or any question concerning appropriate relief is addressed. The risks of the kind of "procedural nightmare" that has allegedly developed in this case will be minimized if the federal court stays its hand until after the Tribal Court has had a full opportunity to determine its own jurisdiction and to rectify any errors it may have made. Exhaustion of tribal court remedies, moreover, will encourage tribal courts to explain to the parties the precise basis for accepting jurisdiction, and will also provide other courts with the benefit of their expertise in such matters in the event of further judicial review.[9]

This favorable disposition was further advanced in *Iowa Mutual Insurance Co. v. LaPlante*[10] in which the Court made it clear that "exhaustion" included "exhaustion" of tribal *appellate* court remedies. The Court further noted that "[t]ribal authority over the activities of non-Indians on reservation land is an important part of tribal sovereignty"[11] and "[t]ribal courts play a vital role in tribal self-government ... and the Federal Government has consistently encouraged their development."[12]

Despite these respectful notes, *National Farmers Union* is not without its own conceptual difficulties. The non-Indian challenge to tribal court civil jurisdiction was not grounded in any alleged violation of the United States Constitution or the violation of any federal statute. Therefore it became problematical as to what was the basis for federal court *jurisdiction* that did not assert any constitutional or federal statutory violation?

It appeared that there was no basis for federal "arising under" jurisdiction pursuant to 28 U.S.C. § 1331,[13] and thus there was no basis for the federal court to assess the parameters of tribal court civil jurisdiction over non-Indians. The Court nevertheless rescued itself from such jurisdictional misgivings by asserting that "arising under" jurisdiction was available because the extent of tribal court authority over non-Indians was a matter of federal common law.

---

9. 471 U.S. 845 (1985).
10. 480 U.S. 9 (1987).
11. *Id.* at 12.
12. *Id.* at 14.
13. 28 U.S.C. § 1331 provides: "The district courts shall have constituted original jurisdiction of all civil actions arising under the Constitution, laws, or treaties of the United States."

The Court's analysis in this regard was perfunctory and conclusory rather than probing and persuasive.[14]

No matter the misgivings, the procedural and substantive rules have been set. Tribal courts must proceed accordingly. Yet within the inner workings of tribal courts, the regime of *Montana* and its progeny creates significant burdens, tensions, and difficulties. They are threefold:

1. The unexamined common-law principles of *Montana* and *National Farmers Union* replaced a constitutional and statutory framework. These cases changed a generalized constitutional and statutory respect for tribal sovereignty into a particularized distrust and disrespect for tribal sovereignty especially in regard to non-Indians and the ability of tribes to engage in meaningful self-governance. These cases also impose a regrettable burden on tribal courts to show respect to federal precedent, when none is shown to them.
2. The common law regime of *Montana* and its progeny has made the issue of 'race' a core ingredient to determine *subject matter* (not personal) jurisdiction. The *Montana* framework applies *only* to non-Indians and thus creates significant *tension* in that tribal courts must apply 'special rules' that are 'race' based (*e.g.*, the *Montana* proviso) to one group of defendants (*i.e.*, non-Indians), but not to any group of Indian defendants. This reality often freights the usually prosaic assessment of subject matter jurisdiction with the subtext of 'race.' Why should tribal courts be placed in such an unenviable position to navigate these rough waters stirred and churned from afar?
3. The *Montana* rules create an aggravating and racially tinged asymmetry. There is one set of rules for non-Indians and another set of rules for Indians. This asymmetry troubles many tribal courts. How can you treat everyone fairly and equally when the Supreme Court mandates the opposite? It is not easy to obtain the balance so necessary for justice and fair play, when the Supreme Court has created "separate but equal" scales of justice for tribal courts.

The *National Farmers Union* exhaustion regime also unfairly burdens tribal judges and tribal courts in that they often become *defendants* in the federal proceeding. This occurs even in litigation that only involves private litigants. This is so because the non-Indian tribal court defendants want to enjoin the

---

14. *National Farmers Union*, 471 U.S. at 850–51.

tribal court proceedings while they pursue their federal relief and thus name the tribal judge and tribal court as defendants in their federal action. This is burdensome from both an efficiency and financial point of view. Tribal courts have to defend themselves in federal court. However unintended, such a result appears disrespectful, even condescending.

While much teaching and scholarship within the field of Indian law focuses on the *Montana–National Farmers Union* litigation in *federal* court, very little focuses on the analysis and thinking of the tribal court appellate opinions that are the necessary predicate for federal review. The following opinions and discussion seek to illuminate that predicate. None of this is meant to obtain undue sympathy or to make a special pleading, but rather to provide understanding of how it often looks from the *inside* of tribal courts. A voice, a text. The weight and gravity of what tribal courts actually say, but is so often occluded from ordinary view. The notes that follow each tribal court opinion will track and comment upon the 'review' of these decisions by the various federal courts.

Note: The opinions (including footnotes) that follow are reproduced exactly as they were filed with their respective courts and served on the parties. Minor errors of spelling, grammar, and punctuation have been corrected. *Infras* and *supras* in the opinions refer to page numbers in the original opinions and contain the book page numbers in parentheses.

B. The Cases

Estate of Tasunke Witko (aka Crazy Horse) v. Heileman Brewery

(Rosebud Sioux Supreme Court) (1996)

Rosebud Sioux Supreme Court
Rosebud Sioux Reservation
Rosebud, South Dakota

****

In the Matter of the Estate	*	
of Tasunke Witko, a.k.a. Crazy Horse,	*	
Seth H. Big Crow, Sr., as Administrator	*	#Civ. 93-204
of said Estate, and as a member and	*	
representative of the class of heirs	*	
of said Estate,	*	
Plaintiff/Appellant	*	Memorandum
vs.	*	Opinion
	*	and
The G. Heileman Brewing Co., The G.	*	Order
Heileman Brewing Co., d/b/a	*	
Hornell Brewing Co.; and Messrs.	*	
John Ferolito and Don Vultaggio,	*	
individually and d/b/a Ferolito,	*	
Vultaggio and Sons,	*	
Defendants/Appellees	*	
	*	

****

EN BANC before Chief Justice Greaves, Associate Justices Lee, Pommersheim, Roubideaux, Swallow,[1] and Zephier.

I. Introduction

Tasunke Witko, popularly known as Crazy Horse, is a revered nineteenth century (1842?–1877) Lakota political and spiritual leader who lived all of his life within the bounds of the Great Sioux Reservation[2] which included the pres-

---

1. Justice Swallow was unable to attend the oral argument due to inclement weather. As noted on the record at oral argument, Justice Swallow would (and did) participate in the deliberations of the Court after listening to an audio tape of the proceedings.

2. The Great Sioux Nation Reservation was created as part of the Fort Laramie Treaty of 1868. See Art. 2, 15 Stat. 635 (1868) and its original boundaries included all of present

ent day Rosebud Sioux Reservation.[3] Tasunke Witko was a person of great moral character who steadfastly opposed the use and abuse of alcohol products by his people.[4]

Mr. Seth J. Big Crow Sr., a member of the Rosebud Sioux Tribe and a resident of the Rosebud Sioux Reservation, is a direct descendant of Tasunke Witko. On March 4, 1993, he filed a petition for Letters of Administration in the Rosebud Sioux Tribal Court and was subsequently named as the Administrator of Tasunke Witko's estate on April 12, 1993.

The G. Heileman Brewing Company, Hornell Brewing Company, and John Ferolito and Don Vultaggio, the Defendants/Appellants herein, are the manufacturers, distributors, and marketers of various alcoholic (and non-alcoholic) drinking products including, but not limited to, the ornately packaged "The Original Crazy Horse Malt Liquor."[5] This particular product has been promoted,

---

day western South Dakota and parts of the surrounding states of Nebraska, Wyoming, and Montana. Of course, no western states existed in 1868 and the area was generally referred to by non-Indians and the Federal government as the Dakota Territory.

It is worth noting that neither the Fort Laramie Treaty of 1868 nor the Great Sioux Agreement of 1889 purport in anyway to divest the Rosebud Sioux Tribe of its sovereignty, much less the civil adjudicatory authority at issue in *this* case. On the importance of protecting treaty-based sovereignty, *see, e.g.*, Phillip P. Frickey, *Marshalling Past and Present: Colonialism, Constitutionalism, and Interpretation in Federal Indian Law*, 107 HARV. L. REV. 381 (1993).

3. The Rosebud Sioux Reservation was one of the six individual reservations created from the Great Sioux Nation Reservation as part of the Great Sioux Agreement of 1889. *See* Sec. 2, 25 Stat. 888 (1889).

4. *See* Affidavit of Plaintiff/Administrator Seth H. Big Crow Sr. (August 24, 1993) at paragraph 2. Specifically, "Crazy Horse basically led the fight to protect the Lakota people, their lands and culture from the avarice, alcohol, and disease which invaded the Great Sioux Nation."

5. Specifically:

> "12. That the front of the bottle bears a painted, black and white depiction of the profile of an Indian man facing left, wearing what is presumably an eagle feather bonnet.
>
> 13. That this malt liquor alcohol beverage is distributed for sale in a 40 oz. (1.18 liter) clear glass, antique whiskey-styled bottle bearing the following text on the front label, in black and white heat-treated paint:
>
> The Original CRAZY HORSE Malt Liquor (TM)
> SINCE MCMXCII
> DAKOTA HILLS LTD. (TM)
> This is the ultimate in Handcrafted
> Malt Liquor. Crazy Horse is brewed with 100%
> of the finest Malt Barley and Hops.

distributed, displayed for sale and sold from on or about March 17, 1992. Other alcoholic (and non-alcoholic) products of the Defendants/Appellees have been manufactured, promoted, and offered for sale prior to 1992. "The Original Crazy Horse Malt Liquor" has *not* been manufactured, advertised, or offered for sale in South Dakota or on the Rosebud Sioux Reservation. Other alcoholic beverages of the Defendant/Appellees such as "Old Style," "Schmidt," and "Special Export" are advertised and offered for sale in South Dakota and on the Rosebud Sioux Reservation.[6] Non-alcoholic beverages of the Defendants/Appellees such as "Arizona Iced Tea," "Arizona Mucho Mango Cocktail," and "Arizona

---

Fine Blend Lat No. 0690711
Forty Ounces
1 QT. 8 FL OZS 1.18 LITER
PRODUCT OF AMERICA

14. That along with an image of furtrapper mountain man, dressed in buckskin and furs, and holding a rifle, and with what is made to appear to be several beadwork designs of a presumably Northern Plains Indian motif, including symbols such as that of a "medicine wheel" deemed sacred in Lakota culture, the following text is printed on the back of the clear glass, whiskey-styled bottle, in white heat-treated paint:

CRAZY
<DAKOTA HILLS LTD.>
HORSE (TM)
The Black Hills of Dakota, steeped in the history of
The American West, home of Proud Indian Nations.
A land where imagination conjures up images of blue clad
Pony Soldiers and magnificent Native American Warriors,
A land still rutted with wagon tracks of intrepid pioneers.
A land where wailful winds whisper of Sitting Bull,
Crazy Horse and Custer.
A land of character, of bravery, of tradition.
A land that truly speaks of the spirit that is America.
Government Warning: (1) According to the Surgeon General women should not drink alcoholic beverages during pregnancy because of the risk of birth defects. (2) Consumption of alcoholic beverages impairs your ability to drive a car or operate machinery, and may cause health problems.
HORNELL BREWING CO., BALTIMORE, MARYLAND

15. That said forty (40) ounce bottles are distributed in twelve (12) bottle cases which also bear the distinctive markings proclaiming the name and purported image of Crazy Horse, symbolic designs, and the text "The Original Crazy Horse Malt Liquor," "CRAZY HORSE Handcrafted Malt Liquor" and "Dakota Hills Ltd." against a background of numerous irregular, rounded black patches of field suggesting perhaps a pinto horsehide."

Id. at paragraphs 12–15.

6. *Id.* at paragraphs 8–9.

Strawberry Punch Cowboy Cocktail" are also advertised and offered for sale in South Dakota and on the Rosebud Sioux Reservation.[7]

During the period of March—June 1993, there was written and oral communication between the parties and other concerned (non-party) Lakota individuals and groups about the alleged "insult and injury" of Defendants' actions and the likelihood of legal action if such activities of the Defendants/Appellees were not halted.[8]

No mutually agreed upon solution emerged from these various exchanges. As a result, the Estate of Tasunke Witko filed a lawsuit against the Defendants/Appellees in the Rosebud Sioux Tribal Court on August 25, 1993. An amended complaint was filed on September 22, 1993. The complaint and amended complaint assert five separate cause of action, namely, the knowing and willful tortious interference with customary rights of privacy and respect owed to a decedent and his family, the tortious interference with Plaintiff's property right commonly known as the "right of publicity," the negligent and intentional infliction of emotional distress on the heirs of the Estate through acts of exploitation and defamation, violation of the Indian Arts and Crafts Act,[9] and violation of the Lanham Act.[10] These claims were asserted—where applicable—under both tribal and federal law.

The Estate seeks wideranging relief including declaratory and injunctive relief, money damages, a written public apology, and culturally appropriate compensation such as "presenting the Estate one (1) braid of tobacco, one (1) four-point Pendleton blanket and one (1) racing horse for each State, Territory, or Nation in which said products have been distributed and offered for sale. On October 26, 1994, the Defendants/Appellees filed a motion to dismiss pursuant to Rule 12(b) of the Rosebud Sioux Rules of Civil Procedure.[11] A hear-

7. *See* Affidavit of Plaintiff/Administrator Seth J. Big Crow (June 27, 1994) at paragraph 5. *See also* Appellant's Brief at 8.

8. *See* Affidavit of Plaintiff/Administrator Seth H. Big Crow, *supra* note 4, at paragraphs 21 and 22. *See also* Appellant's Brief at 8.

9. 104 Stat. 4662 (1990), 25 U.S.C. §305 as amended (1994)

10. Sec. 43(a), 15 U.S.C. §1125(a) (1994).

11. "Every defense to a claim for relief in any pleading whether a Complaint, Counterclaim, Crossclaim, or Third Party Claim shall be asserted in the responsive pleading if one is required, except that the following defenses may at the option of the pleader be made prior to the filing of a responsive pleading by motion, namely, lack of jurisdiction over the subject matter, lack of jurisdiction over the person, insufficiency of process, insufficiency of service of process, failure to state a claim upon which relief may be grated, failure to join a party under Rule 19."

ing on Defendants' motion was held on June 27, 1994 before the Honorable Stanley E. Whiting, Pro-Tem Tribal Judge. No testimony was taken at this hearing. The motion was considered solely on the complaint(s), including affidavits and exhibits, and Defendants' motion to dismiss.[12]

On October 25, 1994 the Honorable Stanley E. Whiting granted Defendants' motion, issued a memorandum opinion, and dismissed the action for lack of jurisdiction. The trial court's opinion did *not* appear to distinguish between personal and subject matter jurisdiction. The Estate subsequently filed a timely notice of appeal. The Defendants filed no cross appeal. Pursuant to Rule 20 of the Rules of Procedure of the Rosebud Sioux Tribal Court of Appeals, the Court, on its own motion, ordered the appeal to be heard *en banc.*[13] Two amicus briefs were properly filed with this Court.[14] On March 29, 1996, oral argument[15] was heard before the *en banc* Court sitting at the University of South Dakota School of Law in Vermillion, South Dakota.

II. Issues

This appeal raises three significant—and occasionally overlapping—issues namely:

A. Whether the trial court applied the correct legal standard in deciding the Defendants' motion to dismiss;

B. Whether the trial court erred as a matter of law in its analysis of the issues of territorial, personal, and/or subject matter jurisdiction as they pertain to Plaintiff's causes of action sounding in tort, defamation, and the "right of publicity;" and

C. Whether the trial court erred as a matter of law in its jurisdictional analysis of the federal statutory causes of action asserted under the Indian Arts and Crafts Act and the Lanham Act.

---

12. Defendants did not apparently file an answer separate and apart from their motion to dismiss.

13. Rule 20, Rules of Procedure, Rosebud Sioux Tribal Court of Appeals provides:

> (a) When Hearing or Rehearing en banc will be Ordered. A majority of the Rosebud Sioux Appellate Justices who are in regular active service may order that an appeal or other proceeding be heard or reheard by the Court of Appeals en banc. Such a hearing or rehearing is not favored and ordinarily will not be ordered except (1) when consideration by the full court is necessary to secure or maintain uniformity of its decisions, or (2) when the proceeding involves a question of exceptional importance.

14. Amicus briefs of Professors Nell Jessup Newton and Joseph William Singer and Professors Oliver R. Goodenough and Nathan Bruce Duthu. *Id.* at Rule 21.

15. The oral argument and briefs of counsel for *both* sides were of the highest order and they are commended for their outstanding professional work provided to this Court.

III. Discussion

Each issue will be discussed in turn.

A. Legal Standard for Ruling on a Motion to Dismiss and the Appropriate Standard of Review.

The proper standard of review on questions of law concerning jurisdiction is *de novo*.[16] *See, e.g., Haisten v. Grass Valley Medical Reimbursement Fund*, 784 F.2d 1392 (9th Cir. 1986). Most unfortunately, the trial court's opinion does *not* articulate or indicate any legal standard it applied or used to guide its analysis on the motion to dismiss. This in and of itself likely constitutes reversible error. For purposes of analytical and conceptual clarity in the future, this Court provides and sets forth the necessary analysis. The proper standard and guidance in this regard are found in the case of *Lake v. Lake*, 817 F.2d 1416 (9th Cir. 1987).

In *Lake*, similar to the case at bar, the trial court decided the issue of jurisdiction based on affidavits and other written materials but without making adequate factual findings. In this case—complicated by the absence of any legal standard—the analytical groundwork set forth in *Lake* is therefore worth quoting in some detail:

> The district court decided the issue of its personal jurisdiction over Taylor on the basis of affidavits and written discovery materials: thus, the Lakes needed to make only a prima facie showing of jurisdictional facts in order to avoid the motion to dismiss. *Data Disc, Inc. v. Systems Technology Assocs., Inc.*, 557 F.2d 1280, 1285 (9th Cir. 1977). Because the court made no findings on the disputed facts, we review the materials presented *de novo* to determine if the plaintiff has met the burden of showing a prima facie case of personal jurisdiction. *Brand v. Menlove Dodge*, 796 F.2d 1070, 1072 (9th Cir. 1986). All factual disputes are resolved in the plaintiffs' favor. *Id.*; *Fields v. Sedgwick Associated Risks, Ltd.*, 796 F.2d 299, 301(9th Cir. 1986). Presenting a prima facie case of jurisdiction, however, does not necessarily guarantee jurisdiction over the defendant at the time of trial. The district court has the discretion to take evidence at a preliminary hearing in order to resolve any questions of credibility or fact that arise subsequent to this appeal. If such an event arises, plaintiff, being put to full proof,

16. This is a question of first impression for this Court and it adopts the prevailing *de novo* federal standard as both fair and reasonable. Neither of the parties contend otherwise.

> "must establish the jurisdictional facts by a preponderance of the evidence, just as he would have to do at trial." *Data Disc*, 557 F.2d at 1285.[17]

Therefore, on remand, if there are any *subsequent* questions of credibility or fact, the trial court has the discretion to take evidence at a preliminary hearing in order to resolve them. If such an event arises, as noted in *Lake*, Plaintiff must establish the jurisdictional facts by a preponderance of the evidence, just as he would have to do at trial.

Within the limits of the record before this Court, we will proceed to analyze the remaining jurisdictional issues engendered by this appeal in accordance with the *prima facie* standard in which all factual disputes are resolved in the Plaintiff's favor. This analysis will also identify and apply the appropriate substantive legal standard(s).

B. Jurisdiction

1. Territorial Jurisdiction

The Defendants/Appellees contend that the tribal court's jurisdiction is territorial[18] in nature and since they never entered the physical confines of the reservation, there can be no jurisdiction over them for their activities that took place outside the territory of the reservation. The argument is seriously misinformed. The law of the Rosebud Sioux Tribe is clearly to the contrary.

While the Constitution of the Rosebud Sioux Tribe asserts that its jurisdiction "shall extend to the territory within the original confines of the Rosebud Reservation boundaries,"[19] this declaration is meant to emphasis the *internal* territorial integrity of the Tribe's legal authority as a matter of tribal law. It is, for example, axiomatic in Indian law that federal courts have sometimes (perhaps even often) decided the result of tribal jurisdiction, at least, in part, on whether the land where the contested events occurred within the reservation was tribal or individual Indian trust lands or non-Indian land held in fee.[20]

---

17. *Lake*, 817 F.2d at 1420.

18. It does not appear that this issue was raised (it is *not* mentioned anywhere in the trial court's memorandum opinion) below and normally it could not be raised for the first time on appeal. However, jurisdictional issues are *never* waived and may be raised for the first time on appeal. *See, e.g.*, Deno v. Oveson, 307 N.W.2d 862 (S.D. 1981).

19. Art. II, Rosebud Sioux Tribe Constitution (1935).

20. *See, e.g.*, Montana v. United States, 450 U.S. 544 (1981), discussed *infra* at pp. 29–35 (pp. 48–51 here). Brendale v. Confederated Tribes and Bands of Yakima Indian Nation, 492 U.S. 408 (1989), and South Dakota v. Bourland, 508 U.S. 679 (1993). All of these cases in-

Clearly these land tenure distinctions within the reservation are not at issue in this case. The harm, if any, that the Plaintiff Estate suffered was on tribal or individual Indian trust land within the reservation.

The Rosebud Sioux Tribe does not limit its potential 'territorial' jurisdiction to the crabbed reading suggested by the Defendants/Appellees. The fact that the Tribe has a "long arm" statute set out at Rosebud Sioux Tribal Law and Order Code §4-2-7[21] indicates the Tribe's clear intent, consistent with notions of due process,[22] to assert jurisdiction over non-residents who, for example, commit tortious acts that have effects within the reservation.

2. Personal Jurisdiction.

It is this issue that appears to be at the heart of the trial court's decision. The trial court's memorandum decision focuses much of its attention on the "minimum contacts" analysis required under the due process guarantee. Yet its analysis is seriously flawed because it does not articulate any (much less the correct) legal standard applicable to a motion to dismiss, it applies some facts but ig-

---

volved federal statutes creating fee land on the reservation. There is neither a relevant federal statute nor fee land on the reservation involved in this case.

21. Rosebud Sioux Tribe Law and Order Code §4-2-7 (1989) provides:

4-2-7. Personal Service Off of Reservation—Acts Submitting Non-resident Persons to Jurisdiction of Court.

A. To the greatest extent consistent with due process of law, any person, whether or not a citizen, resident, or present on the Reservation, who in person or through an agent does any of the acts as enumerated in this Section, thereby submits said person or his personal representative to the jurisdiction of the Tribal Court as to any cause of action arising from doing any of the following acts within the Rosebud Indian reservation:

1. The transaction of any business;
2. The commission of a tortious act;
3. The ownership, use or possession of any property, real or personal;
4. Contracting to insure any person, property or risk;
5. The act of sexual intercourse within this Reservation;
6. Living in a marital relationship, notwithstanding the subsequent departure from this reservation, as to any action for divorce or separate maintenance so long as the petitioning party has continued to reside within the Reservation.

B. Only causes of action arising from acts enumerated herein may be asserted against a defendant in an action in which jurisdiction over him is based upon this Section.

Rosebud Sioux Tribal Ordinance 88-14, Civil Amendments of 1988.

22. *See* additional discussion *infra* at pp. 14–27 (pp. 39–47 here).

nores others without explanation, and it misapprehends and misapplies the appropriate due process standard. Each of these matters will be treated separately.

a) Motion to Dismiss Standard.

As noted above,[23] the proper standard to apply in the context of a motion to dismiss is that the Plaintiff needs to make only a *prima facie* showing of jurisdictional facts to avoid a dismissal and all factual questions are resolved in the Plaintiff's favor.[24] In light of the fact that all factual disputes are resolved in favor of the Plaintiff, it is both curious and fatal that some of what would appear to be the most relevant facts are not even mentioned in the trial court's memorandum opinion.

b) Relevant Facts.

The Plaintiff made numerous factual assertions in its complaint(s), affidavits, and exhibits that were not controverted by Defendants and even if they were, they would have to be construed in favor of the Plaintiff. However, these assertions were, apparently, simply ignored by the trial judge. These include, but are not limited to, the following: assertions that the Defendants continuously advertised and sold other alcoholic beverages such as "Old Style," "Schmidt's," and "Special Export"[25] in South Dakota and on the Rosebud Sioux Reservation; that the Defendants continuously advertised and sold other nonalcoholic beverages such as "Arizona Iced Tea," "Arizona Mucho Mango Cowboy Cocktail," and "Arizona Strawberry Punch Cowboy Cocktail"[26] in South Dakota and on the Rosebud Sioux Reservation; that Defendants made at least one telephone call to, and sent at least one package of allegedly defamatory materials to Plaintiff/Administrator on the Rosebud Sioux Reservation,[27] and that the Defendants' advertising label on each bottle of "Original Crazy Horse Malt Liquor"[28] specifically exalted and targeted the forum reservation which was the home of the decedent Crazy Horse and is the home of the Plain-

23. *See supra* note 17 and discussion at pp. 8–9 (pp. 35–36 here).

24. *Id.* This too is an issue of first impression with this Court and the general federal standard is adopted as fair and reasonable.

25. *See* Affidavit of Plaintiff/Administrator Seth H. Big Crow, *supra* note 4 at paragraphs 8–9.

26. *See* Affidavit of Plaintiff/Administrator Seth H. Big Crow, *supra* note 7 at paragraph 5. *See also* Appellant's Brief at 8.

27. *See* Affidavit of Plaintiff/Administrator Seth H. Big Crow, *supra* note 4 at paragraphs 26 and *supra* note 7 at paragraph 1C. *See also* Appellant's Brief at 10.

28. *See supra* note 5, at 3–4.

tiff/Administrator. There may be other relevant facts; this is merely a sampling. At this point, the issue, of course, is *not* whether these (or other) facts are ultimately true, but only assuming that they are true (as we must), do they make out a sufficient prima facie case to withstand a motion to dismiss? The answer lies in the application of these and other relevant facts to the applicable "minimum contacts" due process standard.

c) "Minimum Contacts" Due Process Analysis.

Due process exists as an individual guarantee against the federal government pursuant to the Fifth Amendment,[29] against state governments pursuant to the Fourteenth Amendment,[30] and against tribal government pursuant to the Indian Civil Rights Act of 1968,[31] and any tribal constitutional guarantee.[32] Normally, the strictures of the United States Constitution do not apply against tribes. *Talton v. Mayes*, 116 U.S. 376 (1896). Federal courts have also ruled that the substantive content of the due process clause and other guarantees of the Indian Civil Rights Act of 1968 need not exactly mirror that of the United States Constitution. *See, e.g.*, *Tom v. Sutton*, 533 F.2d 1101 (9th Cir. 1976) and *Wounded Head v. Tribal Council of Oglala Sioux Tribe*, 507 F.2d 1079 (8th Cir. 1975). And while this Court has no doubt that the traditional Lakota notions of due process that provide everyone the opportunity to be heard before making a decision are met in this case,[33] it is, nevertheless, necessary to also apply the federal due process "minimum contacts" analysis. This is so because as the Supreme Court announced in *National Farmers Union Insurance Cos. v. Crow Tribe of Indiana*, 471 U.S. 845 (1985) the proper extent of tribal court jurisdiction is ultimately a matter of federal (common) law and therefore as to matters of *jurisdiction*, federal standards—including "minimum contacts" due process analysis—are applicable.

There are essentially two issues involved in construing a long arm statute. These are whether the intent of the long arm statute is to maximize its possible jurisdiction, *and* if so, whether such assertions meet the requirements of due process. The former issue is decided solely by the local law of the forum and the latter by federal due process analysis. *Helicopteros Nacionales de Columbia v. Hall*, 466 U.S. 408 (1984).

---

29. U.S. Const. amend. V.

30. U.S. Const. amend. XIV.

31. 25 U.S.C. § 1302 (8) (1994).

32. Art. X, Sec. 3, Rosebud Sioux Tribe Constitution (1966).

33. *See, e.g.*, Thorstenson v. Cudmore, 18 I.L.R. 6051 (1991); Bloomberg v. Dreamer (Oglala Supreme Court Civ. App. 90-348 (1991)).

As to the former issue, it is clear that the intent of the tribal long arm statute is that its reach be co-existent with the federal due process clause. This is in keeping with the modern trend and the tribal commitment to provide a forum for all wrongs that have an impact on individuals residing on the reservation. The preamble to the tribal long arm statute which states, in relevant part, the intent of asserting jurisdiction "to the greatest extent consistent with due process of law" is unequivocal in this regard.[34] This interpretation of tribal law is not subject to federal review. As noted by the United States Supreme Court in *Helicopteros Nacionales de Colombia v. Hall*:

> It is not within our province, of course, to determine whether the Texas Supreme Court correctly interpreted the state's long arm statute. We therefore accept that court's holding that the limits of the Texas statue are coextensive with those of the Due Process Clause.[35]

The most recent hallmark decisions of the United States Supreme Court in the long arm context are *Calder v. Jones*, 465 U.S. 783 (1984) and *Burger King v. Rudzewicz*, 471 U.S. 462 (1985). Both of these cases make it clear that it is possible for a forum to assert personal jurisdiction over a defendant even

---

34. Rosebud Sioux Law and Order Code 4-2-7 (1989), *supra* note 21, at 12.

This is clearly in line with the modern trend. *See* for example the Restatement of Conflicts 2d (1971) § 37, which states in relevant part:

> "A state has power to exercise judicial jurisdiction over an individual who causes effects in the state by an act done elsewhere with respect to any cause of action arising from these effects unless the nature of the effects and of the individual's relationship to the state make the exercise of such jurisdiction unreasonable." *Id.* at 156.

Additionally, the Restatement advises that the usual interpretation of the phrase "commission of a tortious act within the states" is broad enough to cover "injuries within by acts from without a state":

> "Many states have enacted statutes which authorize the exercise of judicial jurisdiction under the circumstances stated in the rule. The prototypical statute is that of Illinois ... which, although it speaks only of "commission of a tortious act within this state," has been interpreted to confer jurisdiction on the Illinois courts in situations where a tortious act outside the States causes injury within the State.... States which adopted the Illinois language ... have generally followed the Illinois interpretation." *Id.* at 160.

35. Helicopteros Nacionales de Colombia v. Hall, 466 U.S. 408, 413 n.7 (1984). *See also* Duncan Energy v. Three Affiliated Tribes, 27 F.3d 1294 (8th Cir. 1994) and City of Timber Lake v. Cheyenne River Sioux Tribe, 10 F.3d 554 (8th Cir. 1993) in the context of federal court deference to tribal court determinations of tribal law. In addition, note specifically, the following: "The Tribal Court's interpretation of tribal law is binding on this court." *Hinshaw v. Mahler*, 42 F.3d 1178, 1179 (9th Cir. 1994).

when he has not physically entered or carried on business within the forum jurisdiction.

As the Supreme Court noted in *Burger King*, "The Due Process Clause protects an individual's likely interest in not being subject to the binding judgments of a forum with which he has established no meaningful 'contacts, ties, or relations.'" 471 U.S. 462, 471–72 (citing *International Shoe Co. v. Washington*, 326 U.S. 310, 319 (1945)). The *Burger King* opinion goes on to emphasize that a potential defendant may receive the necessary "fair warning" on which to condition jurisdiction if it has "purposefully directed" its activities at the forum and as a result it could have or should have foreseen being "haled" into that particular forum. In addition, the Court emphasized, "Moreover, where individuals 'purposefully derive benefits' from their interstate activities, ... it may well be unfair to allow them to escape having to account in other states for consequences that arise proximately from such activities." *Burger King*, 471 U.S. at 473–74. The *Burger King* Court found the necessary contacts of the Defendant who never physically entered or carried on business in the forum state of Florida.

In *Calder*, the actress Shirley Jones sued the writer of an allegedly defamatory article about her in California where Ms. Jones resided. The writer-defendant had never been in California. The Court found the necessary contacts to justify "in personam" jurisdiction over the defendant. It emphasized that defendant "knew" that Ms. Jones would suffer the "effect" of the defamatory statements in the forum state. The Court also noted that the vehicle for the defamatory article—*The National Enquirer* (not a defendant in the case)—had a substantial circulation in the forum state of California.

If the requirements of *Calder* and *Burger King* are integrated and harmonized, the key questions become, did the defendant engage in activities "purposefully directed" to the forum, did the defendant know the plaintiff would suffer the "effects" of defendant's activities in the forum, and was all of this reasonably foreseeable to justify "haling" the defendant into the forum's jurisdiction?

The trial court did not discuss this legal standard, but rather found *no* facts to support jurisdiction. The trial court stated, "[a]ctually, the facts established that Defendant made no contacts with the heirs of Crazy Horse or with the Rosebud Sioux Tribe Reservation." Slip Op. at 13. And again, "[f]urther, there are no contacts whatsoever by the Defendants with Plaintiff's [sic] in any manner." Slip Op. at 14. These factual conclusions are quite simply erroneous and unwarranted. The Plaintiff Estate made numerous factual assertions to the contrary (none of which were even contradicted by the Defendants) which must be assumed to be true for purposes of a motion to dismiss. *Lake*, 817 F.2d at 1420.

A reasonable cross-section of these facts has already been enumerated.[36] These facts include, but are not limited to: the advertisement and sale of other alcoholic and non-alcoholic beverages by the Defendants in South Dakota and on the Rosebud Sioux Reservation, the making of one telephone call and the mailing of one package of allegedly defamatory materials by a representative of Defendants to the Plaintiff/Administrator or his attorney on the Rosebud Sioux Reservation, and that the advertising label on "Original Crazy Horse Malt Liquor" bottles is specifically directed to the forum.

The trial court provided no explanation for ignoring these facts and it has therefore committed reversible error. Because the trial court made no findings on the facts—disputed or otherwise—we review the materials *de novo* to determine if Plaintiff has met the burden of showing a prima facie case of personal jurisdiction. *Lake v. Lake*, 817 F.2d 1416, 1420 (9th Cir. 1987).

We find that Plaintiff/Administrator has made a *prima facie* showing. Defendants are conducting business—albeit only with related non-offending alcoholic and non-alcoholic beverages—in the forum, and have made physical—admittedly limited—contact with the forum through the single telephone call and mailing of package of allegedly defamatory materials to the Plaintiff/Administrator or his attorney on the Rosebud Sioux Reservation. These physical and business activities satisfy traditional "minimum contacts" requirements.

In addition and in support of our conclusion, it is noteworthy to demonstrate how the Defendants want it both ways. In the advertising label affixed to each bottle of the "Original Crazy Horse Malt Liquor," Defendants clearly exalt and direct their activities to the forum. The label ornately proclaims:

> "The Black Hills of Dakota, steeped in the history of
> The American West, home of Proud Indian Nations.
> A land where imagination conjures up images of blue clad
> Pony Soldiers and magnificent Native American Warriors,
> A land still rutted with wagon tracks of intrepid pioneers.
> A land where wailful winds whisper of Sitting Bull,
> Crazy Horse and Custer.
> A land of character, of bravery, of tradition.
> A land that truly speaks of the spirit that is America."

Defendants demur to this reading claiming that they did not know there were any living descendants of Crazy Horse, much less living on the Rosebud Sioux Reservation at the time they began to market and sell the "Original Crazy Horse Malt Liquor." While it is true that the Rosebud Sioux Reservation is not

36. *Supra* notes 25–28.

specifically mentioned on the label, it is clearly subsumed within the phrase, "The Black Hills of South Dakota ... home of the proud Indian Nations." The professed East Coast ignorance may well have been true at the time the product first entered the market, but certainly it ended when Defendants were informed by the Plaintiff/Administrator (prior to instigating this lawsuit), other members of the Lakota Nation, and members of South Dakota's congressional delegation and others of their ongoing offensive conduct within the forum.[37]

---

37. Specifically, for example, see these statements of Defendants: "A socially-sensitive corporate citizen, Hornell is responsive to some, responsible Native American objections to marketing of the brand, that is, the deeply-held beliefs voiced by the Native Americans in States directly connected with the exploits of the man called 'Crazy Horse' (SD, ND, MN, NE, and MT)." (Plaintiffs' Exhibit E-1).

" 'We've said repeatedly', Ferolito continued, 'that we never intended an insult to Native Americans and we proved it by deliberately not marketing the brand in 14 States with large reservation [sic] and urban Indian communities. However, once we become aware of the concerns articulated by Mr. Her Many Horses, we realized that even though we had done everything according to the rules and regulations we had a responsibility to be sensitive to the feeling and the history of the Ogallala [sic] Sioux.' " (Plaintiff's Exhibit G). *See also* Appellant's Brief at 22.

See also the following chronology:

(i) March 1992—Hornell introduced Crazy Horse Malt Liquor in 14 states.

(ii) April 22, 1992—US Surgeon General Antonia Novello accused defendant Hornell of "insensitive and malicious marketing."

(iii) April 20, 1992—South Dakota senator Larry Pressler sent a letter to Hornell warning Hornell about its product and that the "defamation of this hero [Crazy Horse] is an insult to Indian culture."

(iv) April 27, 1992—Senator Tom Daschle wrote a similar letter to Hornell, expressing his displeasure.

(v) May 1992—Representative Pat Schroeder called a hearing to consider legislation to prohibit the use of the name Crazy Horse on alcoholic beverages.

(vi) July 1992—House passed a bill to approve the ban of the use of the name Crazy Horse on any alcoholic beverage.

(vii) July 1992—Instead of adopting House bill, Senate passed a resolution directing Hornell to meet with Sioux leaders and enter into a binding agreement abandoning the name Crazy Horse for its Malt Liquor.

(viii) Subsequently, Hornell officials met with Sioux leaders. Because those leaders insisted on a general ban of Indian names and symbols, Hornell broke off negotiations. Hornell public relations firm issued *Backgrounder: The Oglala Sioux Tribe vs. "The Original Crazy Horse Malt Liquor"* press release, with a caption foreshadowing the present lawsuit.

(ix) September 1992—Senate introduced legislation to ban the use of the name Crazy Horse on alcoholic beverages. Senator Adams rebuked Hornell for being "insensitive and disrespectful" to the Sioux's request to discontinue use of the name Crazy Horse.

(x) October 1992—P.L. 102-393. Statute to ban use of the name Crazy Horse was enacted and subsequently signed by President Bush.

Conduct, it may be noted, which has not been discontinued. For the *jurisdictional* importance of *ongoing* activity by a defendant with notice of the alleged wrongfulness of the conduct at issue, *see Beverly Hills Fan Co. v. Royal Sovereign Corp.*, 21 F.3d 1558 (Fed. Cir. 1994).

Despite this purposeful activity, Defendants have studiously avoided the actual marketing and sale of "Original Crazy Horse Malt Liquor" in Indian country in and around South Dakota including the Rosebud Sioux Reservation. Given the marketing and sale of similar—but non-offending—products in the forum, this avoidance appears to be the most cynical ploy. Defendants exalt and target the forum where it taps a likely vein of customers, but studiously avoid marketing and sale in the forum itself because their conduct is potentially offensive and tortious there. It seems wholly unlikely that the due process clause can be made to countenance such distortion and manipulation, and this Court holds that it does not.

These marketing activities of the Defendants are "purposefully directed" to the forum, with notice and knowledge of its potential adverse "effects" on the Plaintiff/Administrator within the forum. Potential harm is clearly foreseeable. The actions of the Defendants do *not* constitute "mere untargeted negligence." *Calder*, 465 U.S. at 789. These facts taken together clearly meet the requirements of *Calder* and *Burger King. See also Brainerd v. Governors of the University of Alberta*, 873 F.2d 1257 (9th Cir. 1989) in which the defendant was held subject to personal jurisdiction in a forum where his only contact was to re-

---

(xi) November 1992—Telephone and mail contact with Estate's attorney regarding rights to name and descendant opposition to label. (Big Crow Affidavit, June 27, 1994, Paras. 1 A. and B.).

(xii) March 1993—Letter from Estate to cease and desist. (Big Crow Affidavit, April 1, 1994, Paras. 27 and 28.).

(xiii) April 1993—First refusal of federal trademark application for labels by U.S. Patent and Trademark Office, citing unlawful use violation of Act of October 6, 1992, 102-393, and "because the mark consists of or comprises matter which may disparage or bring into contempt or disrepute Native Americans. Application Number 74/335913. In the Public Record of the U.S. PTO, Washington, D.C. (A second attempt under Application Number 74/606385 was also refused by the UI.S. PTO by letter sent in July, 1995, again on the grounds of Section 2(a)—Disparagement, "because the mark consists of or comprises matter which may disparage or bring into contempt or disrepute the renowned Oglala Sioux chief, warrior, and spiritual leader, Crazy Horse." In the Public Record of the U.S. PTO, Washington, D.C.)

(xiv) July 1993—Initial refusal of label approval/brand registration by Washington State Liquor Control Board. (Public Record)

Appellant's Brief at 23–24. *See also* these events (I-X) enumerated in Hornell Brewing Co., Inc. v. Brady, 819 F. Supp. 1227 (E.D.N.Y. 1993).

ceive two phone calls and respond to a letter. The defendant never physically entered the forum.

Similarly, in *VDI Technologies v. Price*, 781 F. Supp. 85 (D.N.H. 1991), the court held for jurisdictional purposes that a party commits a tortious act within the state when injury occurs in the forum even if the injury is the result of acts outside the state. This is also the case at bar.[38] In *VDI Technologies*, the court found personal jurisdiction over the defendant based *solely* on letters defendant sent to plaintiff's customers *outside* the forum because of defendant's knowledge of the likely harm to the plaintiff within the forum. Again, this closely parallels the case at bar. The Defendants were on notice that their ongoing tortious conduct was causing harm to the Plaintiff Estate within the forum. This case, like *VDI Technologies*, is one of purposeful effects, not unintended consequences. *See also Dakota Industries, Inc. v. Dakota Sportswear, Inc.*, 946 F.2d 1385 (8th Cir. 1991). Defendants may not escape accountability in the very forum they assiduously cultivate when it fits their purpose, but simultaneously seek to avoid because of the likely harm to accrue there.

The analytical horizon drawn from this line of cases is eminently reasonable and fully comports with the requirements of due process. We therefore find that the "minimum contacts" due process requirements—in the context of a motion to dismiss—are fully met in this case. More broadly, such a result comports with notions of reasonableness and fair play that are also embedded in the concept of due process, *Sinatra v. National Enquirer, Inc.*, 854 F.2d 1191 (9th Cir. 1978).

In sum, in assessing personal jurisdiction, the focus is on "the relationship among the defendant, the forum, and the litigation." *Shaffer v. Heitner*, 433 U.S. 186, 204 (1977). This analysis most often examines three elements, namely (1) that the nonresident defendant purposefully directs its activities toward the forum or its residents; (2) the claim must be one which arises out of or relates to the defendant's forum related activities; and (3) the exercise of jurisdiction must comport with fair play and substantial justice, i.e. it must be reasonable. *Haisten*, 784 F.2d at 1397. *See also Burger King*, 471 U.S. at 472–76.

As we have seen, the Defendants have purposefully availed themselves of the forum by advertising and selling other alcoholic and non-alcoholic beverages in South Dakota and on the Rosebud Sioux Reservation, by placing at

---

38. *See* Rosebud Sioux Tribe "long arm" statute, §4-2-7, *supra* note 21, at 12 that provides, in relevant part,

2. The commission of a tortious act…

least one telephone call to and sending one packet of allegedly defamatory material to the Plaintiff or his attorney on the Rosebud Sioux Reservation, and continually targeting the forum through each label affixed to a bottle of "Original Crazy Horse Malt Liquor" even after being informed by more than one non-party source of its offensiveness within the forum and elsewhere on Reservations in South Dakota.[39]

Jurisdiction, of course, may not be avoided by a lack of physical contact with the forum state or reservation. This is the central holding of both the *Burger King* and *Calder* cases. Nevertheless, a defendant may not be haled into a jurisdiction as the result of random, fortuitous, or attenuated contacts. *Burger King*, 471 U.S. at 479. In the instant case, none of the Defendants' conduct has been random or fortuitous or accidental. The contact is systematic and ongoing. It was clearly both proximate and foreseeable that Defendants would be haled into court on the Rosebud Sioux Reservation. Plaintiff's claim grows directly out of defendants' activities involved in the advertisement, marketing, and sale of both its offending and non-offending products.[40] It is significant to emphasize here that the alleged actions of the Defendants do not involve seeking to market a physically defective product—the classic products liability situation—within the forum, but rather a situation where Defendants are alleged to be intentionally causing harm to the personal or property (e.g. 'right of publicity') interests at the Plaintiff's place of residence and domicile as the result of the manufacturing, sale, and/or marketing of the "Original Crazy Horse Malt Liquor."

Finally, the exercise of a forum's jurisdiction must be reasonable and comport with fair play and justice. The burden on the Defendants to litigate in the tribal forum is minimal. They are all national corporations engaged in extensive interstate commerce. The scope of Defendants' resources and the nature of modern transportation and communication make any ensuing burdens in defending this lawsuit slight. The reservation forum is likely to be the most convenient for all parties, while it would be correspondingly difficult, both economically and geographically, for the Plaintiff to file his lawsuit in another forum far away from the reservation.

The local forum is also best situated to provide convenient and effective relief for the Plaintiff Estate should it prevail at trial on the merits. This is particularly significant in light of the fact that some of the causes of action asserted by the

39. *See supra* note 37, at 22–23. *See also* the chronological documentation set forth in Hornell Brewing Co., Inc. v. Brady, 819 F. Supp. 1227 (E.D.N.Y. 1993).

40. *See supra* note 37.

Plaintiff involve questions of tribal custom and tribal common law that, as questions of first impression, will not be readily discerned or easily answered in a state or federal forum at a substantial cultural and geographical remove from the reservation forum. The reservation forum is also the most efficient forum for this lawsuit because it has already dealt with the issue of jurisdiction (which is likely to arise in any forum) and because of its expertise in evaluating claims grounded in whole or in part in tradition, custom, and/or tribal common law. This is especially true in light of Justice Marshal's statement that, "[t]ribal courts play a vital role in tribal self-government ... and the Federal government has consistently encouraged their development."[41] Such support is particularly appropriate in this instance where the tribal court is uniquely capable to "provide other courts with the benefit of their expertise in such matters in the event of further judicial review." *National Farmers Union*, 471 U.S. at 856. Finally, the tribal forum has a well justified interest in the lawsuit as it alleges extensive and pervasive (tortious) harm that has accrued on the reservation against one of its residents.

3. Subject Matter Jurisdiction

The trial court also rested part of its decision to dismiss on its analysis of *Montana v. United States*, 450 U.S. 544 (1981). Slip Op. at 14–16. The trial court made no distinction in its opinion between personal and subject matter jurisdiction and the fact that *Montana* is a case about subject matter—not personal—jurisdiction. The trial court, despite observing that *Montana* was a case involving tribal jurisdiction over activities taking place on *fee* lands within the reservation, applied it to events that did *not* take place on fee lands and also, made a rather cursory and quite flawed analysis about the applicability of the two prongs of the *Montana* proviso.[42] It concluded "that *Montana* and its protégé [sic] does [sic] not grant jurisdiction to the Tribal court under the existing factual scenario." Slip Op. at 16. This conclusion is flat wrong.

---

41. Iowa Mutual Ins. Co. v. LaPlante, 480 U.S. 9, 14–15 (1987).

42. The proviso provides:

> To be sure, Indian tribes retain inherent sovereign power to exercise some forms of civil jurisdiction over non-Indians on their reservation, even on non-Indian fee lands. A tribe may regulate, through taxation, licensing, or other means, the activities of nonmembers who enter consensual relationships with the tribe or its members, through commercial dealing, contracts, leases, or other arrangements. [E.g.,] Williams v. Lee, 358 U.S. 217, 203. A tribe may also retain inherent power to exercise civil authority over the conduct of non-Indians on fee lands within its reservation when that conduct threatens or has some direct effect on the political integrity, the economic security, or the health or welfare of the tribe.

Montana, 450 U.S. at 565.

It is the opinion of this Court that *Montana* is inapplicable in the case at bar and even if it was, subject matter jurisdiction may properly be found under *both* of the Montana exceptions. Since *Montana* is often a key case employed both by tribal courts and reviewing federal courts when assessing the legitimate ambit of tribal court jurisdiction,[43] some review of that case—what it is and *not* about—is in order.

a) *Montana v. United States*

Montana v. United States is not a case—despite apparent conceptions to the contrary in some quarters—in which the Supreme Court assessed tribal court subject matter jurisdiction as a matter of either constitutional principles or federal common law. It is rather a case about statutory construction. In *Montana*, the Court assessed the jurisdictional implications of the creation of fee land within the Crow Reservation as a result of the General Allotment Act and the Crow Allotment Act. The Court found that *Congressional* authorization to alienate tribal lands had the necessary effect of limiting tribal sovereignty with regard to non-Indian activity on those fee lands. *Montana*, 450 U.S. at 1255–56.[44]

Therefore in the absence of a specific Congressional enactment, judicial decisions interpreting the reach of trial court jurisdiction are *properly* constrained. *See, e.g., United States ex rel. Morongo Band of Mission Indians v. Rose*, 24 F.3d 901, 906 (9th Cir. 1994) (*Montana* exceptions are "relevant only after the court concludes there has been a general divestiture of tribal authority over non-Indians by alienation of the land.").[45] More broadly, the Supreme Court has noted, "[c]ivil jurisdiction over such activities presumptuously lies in the tribal courts unless affirmatively limited by specific treaty provision or federal statute." *Iowa Mutual Insurance Co. v. LaPlante*, 480 U.S. 9, 18 (1987).[46]

---

43. *See, e.g.*, Duncan Energy v. Three Affiliated Tribes, 27 F.3d 1294 (8th Cir. 1994); Stock West Corp. v. Taylor, 964 F.2d 912 (9th Cir. 1990).

44. This interpretation itself seems a bit off the mark. The General Allotment Act and Crow Allotment Act do not purport to adjust tribal sovereignty or jurisdiction but rather to create property rights (and therefore certain protectable 'reliance interests') in non-Indians settling on the reservation, the result of which might be to insulate non-Indians in *some* cases from the reach of tribal jurisdiction. That is, the resulting (potential) limits on tribal jurisdiction are a collateral effect rather than the primary purpose of allotment legislation.

45. *See also* A-1 Contractors v. Strate, 76 F.3d 930 (8th Cir. 1996), for a different analysis.

46. The United States Supreme Court has had no post-*Montana* opportunity to go beyond its reasoning in *Montana*. Brendale v. Confederated Tribes and Bands of the Yakima Nation, 492 U.S. 408 (1989) involved construction of the same provisions of the General

Therefore the *Montana* decision is specifically limited to fee lands. To extend *Montana* to non-fee land and beyond the federal statutes involved in that case is to engage in *judicial law making* plain and simple. Federal authority in Indian law is primarily congressional and not judicial in nature. Courts—including federal reviewing courts—therefore need to hue to the proper limits of their authority.

In fact, this is exactly what the *Montana* Court itself did. When the Court turned its attention from tribal regulation of non-Indian activity on fee land to regulating the same conduct on tribal (and individual Indian) land, it did *not* examine that conduct through the *Montana* proviso, but rather summarily observed that "[t]he Court of Appeals held that the Tribe may prohibit nonmembers from hunting or fishing on land belonging to the tribe or held by the United States in trust for the tribe and with this holding we can readily agree." *Montana*, 450 U.S. at 557. If the *Montana* court itself did not apply the *Montana* proviso analysis to non-fee land, tribal and lower federal courts ought not.[47]

In the case at bar, the harm clearly occurs on individual and tribal trust land within the Rosebud Sioux Reservation and therefore *Montana* analysis is inappropriate. Neither of the parties contends that there is any other relevant federal statute that potentially bars the tribal court from asserting subject matter jurisdiction.

It is also pertinent to note that *Montana*-like analysis is properly limited to questions of tribal regulatory and legislative authority and not tribal court adjudicatory authority. The underlying question in *Montana* was whether the Crow Tribe could regulate (or legislate) concerning the right of non-Indians to hunt and fish on non-Indian land within the reservation. The Court answered that the Crow tribe could *not*. The Court did not in any way indicate that the tribal *court* would not be an appropriate forum to *adjudicate* a hunting issue that came up on the reservation.

The *Montana* Court did not make the legislative-adjudicatory distinction. Yet it is this implicit distinction that best explains the Supreme Court's subsequent decision in *National Farmers Union Insurance Cos. v. Crow Tribe of Indians*, 471 U.S. 845 (1985). In that case, the Supreme Court held that the tribal court did have adjudicatory jurisdiction in the first instance to hear a civil dispute, namely a tortious claim asserted by an Indian student against a non-

---

Allotment Act and South Dakota v. Bourland, 508 U.S. 679 (1993) involved construction of the federal Flood Control Act.

47. *See also* United States v. Wheeler, 435 U.S. 313, 322 (1978) (Indian tribes possess "inherent powers of a limited sovereignty which have never been extinguished.").

Indian school district resulting from a motorcycle accident that occurred on fee land owned and occupied by a state public school. The Court applied no *Montana* analysis. This would seem difficult to fathom *but for* the fact the case involved tribal *judicial* rather than *legislative* authority.[48] Since the case at bar involves the question of whether a tribal judicial forum is available to hear a tort case, just like the issue in *National Farmers Union*, and not whether the Tribe can regulate or legislate non-Indian conduct on fee land which was the issue in *Montana*, *National Farmers Union's* reasoning is more persuasive and provides yet another reason why *Montana* is inapplicable here.[49]

b) The *Montana* "Proviso"

Even if *Montana* were to apply to this case, both prongs of the famous 'proviso' are satisfied. In *Montana*, the Court stated that despite the presumption against tribal (regulatory) authority over non-Indians on fee land, there might nevertheless be tribal authority:

> To be sure, Indian tribes retain inherent sovereign power to exercise some forms of civil jurisdiction over non-Indians on their reservations, even on non-Indian fee lands. A tribe may regulate, through taxation, licensing, or other means, the activities of non-members who enter consensual relationships with the tribe or its members, through commercial dealing, contracts, leases, or other arrangements. [E.g.] Williams v. Lee, 358 U.S. 217, 223. A tribe may also retain inherent power to exercise civil authority over the conduct of non-Indians on fee land within its reservation when that conduct threatens or has some direct effect on the political integrity, the economic security, or the health or welfare of the tribe. *Montana*, 450 U.S. at 565.

Again, for purposes of emphasis, as discussed above, note the Court's use of the word 'regulate' rather than the word 'adjudicate.'

The Plaintiff/Administrator in this case alleges, among other things, that Defendants misappropriated the likeness of 'Crazy Horse' for their own commercial gain. It is significant to note in this regard that the trial court specifically recognized a "right of publicity" in the Plaintiff Estate. Slip. Op. at 11. In other words, the Defendants failed to enter into a 'consensual relation-

---

48. *See also* A-1 Contractors v. Strate, *supra* note 45 to the contrary and discussed *infra* at 35–36 (pp. 51–52 here).

49. Similar analysis is found in Iowa Mutual Ins. v. LaPlante, 480 U.S. 9, 18 (1987) ("[t]ribal authority over the activities of non-Indians on reservation lands is an important part of tribal sovereignty.").

ship' with the Plaintiff for use of the name and reputation of 'Crazy Horse.' This case is thus about, at least in part, the failure (caused by the Defendants) to have a consensual agreement. It therefore would seem an odd twist to say that Defendants' failure to enter into a consensual agreement which gives rise to the cause of action in the first instance could be used to defeat the Court's subject matter jurisdiction. Such reasoning would constitute the most arid formalism and insofar as the trial court so reasoned, it is hereby rejected.

Similarly, the trial court—without any analysis that this Court can discern—concluded that the second prong of the proviso was not satisfied. Slip Op. at 16. This unsupported conclusion is incorrect. The ability of the Rosebud Sioux Tribe to protect the 'health and welfare of the tribe' is directly implicated in this case. It is a touchstone of tribal 'health and welfare' to be able to provide a forum for the resolution of alleged harms suffered by tribal members (or any person) on the reservation. This is particularly, even glaringly, true in the context of allegations of the tortious interference with, and the misappropriation of, the image and reputation of a venerated cultural hero and political and spiritual leader. If the Tribe cannot successfully provide a forum in this dispute of wideranging individual and collective tribal import, *Montana* will have indeed run over its fee-lined banks and inundated the tribal jurisdictional landscape far beyond that which is justifiable. Confident that *Montana* was not so intended, we find the second prong of the process fully satisfied. And we repeat a cautionary refrain noted at the outset: this appeal and the current posture of this case are about jurisdiction—personal and subject matter—and the availability of a tribal forum. We are not concerned at this juncture about the substantive merit of Plaintiff's claims or his likelihood to prevail at trial.

c) *A-1 Contractors v. Strate*[50]

The Court also feels that it is necessary to make some observations about the *en banc* decision of the Eighth Circuit in *A-1 Contractors. A-1 Contractors* involved a non-Indian versus a non-Indian lawsuit resulting from a car-truck accident that took place on non-fee land on the Fort Berthold Reservation in North Dakota. In the original panel decision,[51] the court held (2 to 1) that

---

50. 76 F.3d 930 (8th Cir. 1996) (*en banc*). This case was decided after the briefs were submitted to this case though counsel for both sides made reference to it at oral argument.

51. No. 92-3359, 1994 WL 666051 (8th Cir. Nov. 29, 1994), *vacated*, 76 F.3d 930 (8th Cir. 1996) (en banc).

there was tribal court jurisdiction. The recent *en banc* decision vacated the prior decision and reversed, holding *Montana* analysis applicable even to disputes arising on non-fee land within the reservation and further found that neither prong of the *Montana* proviso was satisfied.[52]

As much of this Court's discussion suggests, *Montana* analysis is inappropriate in this case. And even if it is, both prongs of the proviso are satisfied. However, very little, if any, of *this* Court's reasoning and analysis appears in the *en banc* opinion of the Eighth Circuit and we are confident that if it did, that Court's decision would have been otherwise. Regardless of this speculation, this case is clearly distinguishable from *A-1 Contractors.* This case does *not* involve only non-Indians, but instead involves an Indian party seeking to vindicate personal and cultural injuries that clearly transcend the mere physical harms any 'garden variety' car accident might occasion. The Eighth Circuit's wide solicitude when only non-Indian parties are involved and its correspondingly quite attenuated understanding of apposite tribal interests in such circumstances are simply not applicable in the case at bar.

C. Jurisdiction Pursuant to Federal Statutes

The Plaintiff Estate has also asserted federal causes of action under the Indian Arts and Crafts Act, 25 U.S.C. §305 *et seq.* (1994) and the Lanham Act, 15 U.S.C. §1125(a) (1994). Neither of these statutes limit their jurisdiction to the federal courts. Nor is there any limitation in Tribal law to preclude tribal court jurisdiction as a matter of local law. The parties do not contend otherwise. In other words, there are no jurisdictional bars to the assertion of these federal statutory causes of action in tribal court.

The defenses by the Defendants to these two federal claims are matters of statutory interpretation as to the necessary elements that make up each cause of action. Each federal statutory claim will be treated in turn.

1. Indian Arts and Craft Act

The Indian Arts and Crafts Act was enacted to "protect Indian artists from unfair competition from counterfeiters."[53] The purpose of the Indian Arts and Crafts Act is not at issue in this case. What is at issue is whether an *in-*

52. *See A-1 Contractors, supra* note 50. A contrary decision on similar facts was reached in the Ninth Circuit. Hinshaw v. Mahler, 42 F.3d 1178 (9th Cir. 1994).

53. H.R. Rep. Nos. 400 (I & II), 101 St. Cong. 2d Sess. (1990), 1990 U.S.C.C.A.N. 6382, 6391).

dividual Indian has standing to initiate a lawsuit under the statute. The Defendants claim that the Plaintiff Estate lacks standing to bring a claim under the Indian Arts and Crafts Act. This argument is drawn from a plain meaning of the relevant statutory language and the supporting legislative history. Specifically, Defendants point to 25 U.S.C. § 305e(d)(1)[54] as a bar. Defendants allege that the structure of this section provides standing as follows: "A) by the Attorney General of the United States ... on behalf of an Indian who is a member of an Indian Tribe or on behalf of an Indian tribe or Indian arts and crafts organization;" or "B) by an Indian tribe on behalf of itself, an Indian who is a member of the tribe, or on behalf of an Indian arts and crafts organization."

Each of these sections permits lawsuits to be filed by representative parties. In A, the Attorney General is the representative party and in B, an Indian tribe is the representative party. In both A and B, the representative body may bring a lawsuit "on behalf of an Indian" or "on behalf of itself, an Indian who is a member of the tribe." There is no additional section that allows an Indian to bring a lawsuit in his or her *own* behalf. This reading is particularly reasonable in that B speaks of "an Indian who is a member of *the* tribe" (emphasis added) which clearly refers back to "an Indian tribe" as the representative party. Without this reading, the word *the* actually would be inappropriate and incorrectly used. We are not persuaded that it has been improperly used, but rather that it harmonizes with the structure of the standing provisions. There is no ambiguity to be resolved in Plaintiff's favor. In addition, as noted in the trial court's opinion, a contrary reading would not be consistent with the legislative history of the Act. Slip Op. at 19. Finally, the Plaintiff has indicated no case law suggesting a different result.

2. Lanham Act

The Plaintiff also alleges a cause of action against the Defendants based on the Lanham Act. Specifically, Plaintiff claims that the label affixed to each bot-

---

54. Section 305e(d)(1) provides:

(d) Persons who may imitate civil actions

(1) A civil action under subsection (a) of this section may be commenced—

(A) by the Attorney General of the United States upon request of the Secretary of the Interior on behalf of an Indian who is a member of an Indian tribe or on behalf of an Indian tribe or Indian arts and crafts organization; or

(B) by an Indian tribe on behalf of itself, an Indian who is a member of the tribe, or on behalf of an Indian arts and crafts organization.

25 U.S.C. § 305e(d)(1) (1994).

tle of "The Original Crazy Horse Malt Liquor" constitutes false advertising and false association in violation of § 43(a) of the Act as set forth at 15 U.S.C. § 1125(a). The definitions in the Lanham Act are to be construed broadly. *Smith v. Montoro*, 648 F.2d 602, 607 (9th Cir. 1981).

The trial court specifically recognized the Plaintiff's 'right of publicity' in the name of 'Crazy Horse.' Slip Op. at 11. Recognition of this right, with which we agree, clearly entails the potentiality of that right being infringed by the 'false advertising' or 'false association' of the Defendants. At this stage, the Plaintiff Estate has asserted that the actions of the Defendants involve both 'false advertising' and 'false associations' relative not only to "Crazy Horse" himself but also personal and tribal beadwork patterns or designs and sacred symbols. Amended complaint at 15–16. All of these items are potentially subject to commercial and non-commercial exploitation and loss. That is something to be developed at the trial on the merits. Neither side has cited to, or discussed, case law in the context of a *motion to dismiss* based on lack of standing under the Lanham Act. The Plaintiff has asserted, without contradiction, enough to survive a motion to dismiss. The standing issue may, of course, be revisited at trial.

IV. Conclusion

For all of the above stated reasons, the decision of the trial court is hereby reversed in part, affirmed in part, and remanded for prompt trial on the merits. Specifically, the trial court's findings as to personal and subject matter jurisdiction are reversed, as is its dismissal of the Lanham Act claim. The trial court's dismissal of the Indian Arts and Crafts Act claim is affirmed.

HO HECETU YE LO.
IT IS SO ORDERED.
Dated May 1, 1996.

Leroy Greaves Chief Justice	Patrick Lee Associate Justice	Frank Pommersheim Associate Justice
Ramon Roubideaux Associate Justice	Michael Swallow Associate Justice	Diane Zephier Associate Justice

Notes on *In the Matter of the Estate of Tasunke Witko (a/k/a Crazy Horse) v. G. Heileman Brewing Co.* (1996)

Prior to the tribal court litigation, this case was initially pursued in federal court by Hornell Brewing on First Amendment free (commercial) speech grounds because a federal statute prohibited the Bureau of Alcohol, Tobacco, and Firearms from granting a "certificate of label approval to any alcoholic product that used the name 'Crazy Horse' on any distilled spirit, wine, or malt liquor product." This provision was successfully challenged by Hornell Brewing as violative of (commercial) free speech.[1] With no federal ban prohibiting the marketing and sale of Crazy Horse Malt Liquor, tribal court litigation became inevitable.

The federal district court reversed the decision of the Rosebud Sioux Supreme Court on *Montana* grounds, but instead of dismissing the case, Judge Kornmann *remanded* the case back to the Rosebud Sioux Tribal Court for a more complete hearing on the jurisdictional facts.[2] Before the remand could be effectuated, both sides appealed to the Eighth Circuit. The Eighth Circuit quickly found that neither prong of the *Montana* proviso was satisfied. *Id.* at 1093. The Circuit panel found that the Tribal court non-Indian defendants did not engage in any on reservation activities, which is required under *Montana*. *Id.* at 1092.

Again, not unlike Judge Kornmann's opinion, despite the finding of no subject matter jurisdiction pursuant to the failure to satisfy *Montana's* (purported) predicate requirement of on reservation conduct by non-Indians, the court did engage in *Montana* analysis. It found (*not* surprisingly) that neither exception was satisfied. *Id.* at 1093. There was no "consensual relationship" between the Estate and any of the defendants. *Id.* In addition, there were insufficient effects on the health and welfare of the Tribe to trigger the second exception. *Id.*

The Eighth Circuit opinion ends rather abruptly, leaving a number of important issues hanging without complete explanation. For example, the court never analyzes whether the tribal court had (long arm) personal as opposed to subject matter jurisdiction over the defendants.[3] This is unfortunate in that

1. Hornell Brewing Co., Inc. v. Brady, 819 F. Supp. 1227 (E.D.N.Y. 1993).

2. Hornell Brewing Co. v. Rosebud Sioux Tribal Court, 133 F.3d 1087, 1090–91 (8th Cir. 1998) (note that Judge Kornmann's unpublished opinion could not be located and thus reference to it relies on the discussions of it in the Eighth Circuit's opinion).

3. As a technical matter, having decided that there was no subject matter jurisdiction, there was no necessity to analyze any other issue. *See, e.g.*, Ruhrgas AG v. Marathon Oil Co., 526 U.S. 574 (1999): "[t]here is no unyielding jurisdictional hierarchy. Customarily, a federal court first resolves doubts about its jurisdiction over subject matter, but there are circumstances in which a district court appropriately accords priority to a personal jurisdiction inquiry." *Id.* at 578.

Montana analysis is solely concerned with subject matter jurisdiction, yet its sole objective is to determine whether jurisdiction can be asserted over a particular non-Indian person or entity. The opinion suggests, potentially, that in Indian law, personal and subject matter jurisdiction over non-Indians are the same thing. Given that personal and subject matter jurisdiction are historically and conceptually quite distinct,[4] how can they potentially converge and meld in Indian law without any judicial identification or exegesis?[5]

The *Montana* framework appears ill-suited and ill-applied to the case at hand. Perhaps the court is suggesting, without actually saying so, that tribal courts are courts of limited or narrow jurisdiction and since *Montana* does not discuss or envision these facts of off-reservation actions causing harm on the reservation, the tribal court has no jurisdiction because it is beyond the parameters of *Montana*:

> On appeal, the tribal court also asserts that although Crazy Horse Malt Liquor was not sold on the Rosebud Sioux Reservation, it was advertised outside the Reservation and on the Internet (available to tribal members on the Reservation), and therefore, it had a direct effect upon tribal members. We find this contention specious.

Hornell Brewing Co., 133 F.3d at 1093.

4. Subject matter jurisdiction and personal jurisdiction are core inquiries:

> The Court of Appeals accorded priority to the requirement of subject-matter jurisdiction because it is nonwaivable and delimits federal-court power, while restrictions on a court's jurisdiction over the person are waivable and protect individual rights.... The character of the two jurisdictional bedrocks unquestionably differs. Subject-matter limitations on federal jurisdiction serve institutional interests. They keep the federal courts within the bounds the Constitution and Congress have prescribed. Accordingly, subject-matter delineations must be policed by the courts on their own initiative even at the highest level. *See Steel Co.,* 523 U.S. at 94–95; Fed. Rule Civ. Proc. 12(h)(3) ("Whenever it appears ... that the court lacks jurisdiction of the subject matter, the court shall dismiss the action.") ... ("If at any time before final judgment [in a removed case] it appears that the district court lacks subject matter jurisdiction, the case shall be remanded.") (citations omitted).
>
> Personal jurisdiction, on the other hand, "represents a restriction on judicial power ... as a matter of individual liberty." Ins. Corp. of Ireland v. Compagnie des Bauxites de Guinee, 456 U.S. 694, 702 (1982). Therefore, a party may insist that the limitation be observed, or he may forgo that right, effectively consenting to the court's exercise of adjudicatory authority. *See* Fed. Rule Civ. Proc. 12(h)(1) (defense of lack of jurisdiction over the person waivable); *Ins. Corp. of Ireland,* 456 U.S. at 703.
>
> These distinctions do not mean that subject-matter jurisdiction is ever and always the more "fundamental." Personal jurisdiction, too, is "an essential element of the jurisdiction of a district ... court, without which the court is "powerless to proceed to an adjudication." Employers Reinsurance Corp. v. Bryant, 299 U.S. 382 (1937).

Ruhrgas AG, 526 U.S. at 583–84. *See also* ERWIN CHEMERINSKY, FEDERAL JURISDICTION 269–70 (5th ed., 2007).

5. *Hornell Brewing Co.,* 133 F.3d at 1093.

In addition, the Court somewhat blithely informed the Estate that it "may assert these claims in federal district court."[6] On what basis? Certainly, the primary causes of action asserted by the Estate do not involve federal questions, and thus diversity jurisdiction is all that there is. Yet it would be problematic, especially in the context of the choice of law issue created by *Erie Railroad Co. v. Tompkins*.[7] In the context of *Erie*, the choice of law is always state law, seemingly required by the Rules of Decision Act.[8] Yet several of the causes of action claim to be based on tribal customary or common law. Do we need an exception to *Erie* and/or does the Rules of Decision Act not apply in this case?

The court also failed to address whether the Estate's claims under the Lanham Act were still viable in tribal court. This basic question of tribal court jurisdiction over federal causes of action was likely mooted by the Supreme Court's subsequent decision in *Nevada v. Hicks*.[9] There is also the converse issue. If the Lanham Act cause of action was filed in *federal* court, could the tribal causes of action be joined to that action pursuant to the supplemental jurisdiction statute of 28 U.S.C. § 1367? As a result of the avoidance of these prickly diversity and supplemental jurisdiction issues, much was left unresolved and hanging in the balance.

The Estate, apparently following the advice of the Eighth Circuit, subsequently filed its lawsuit against Hornell Brewing Company in federal district court in South Dakota.[10] In its complaint, the Estate asserted violations of privacy, the

---

6. *Id.*

7. 304 U.S. 64 (1938).

8. 28 U.S.C. § 1652 (2006) (originally enacted as § 34 of the Judiciary Act of 1789):

"The law of the several states, except where the Constitution of treaties of the United States or Acts of Congress otherwise require or provide, shall be regarded as rules of decision in civil actions in the courts of the United States, in cases where they apply." *Id.*

"Note that 'Civil actions' was substituted for the original 'trials at common law' to clarify the meaning of the Rules of Decision Act, in the light of the Federal Rules of Civil Procedure" (historical revision based on 28 U.S.C. § 725, Revised § 721 (1940). *Id. See also* Frank Pommersheim, *'Our Federalism' in the Context of Federal Courts and Tribal Courts: An Open Letter to the Federal Courts' Teaching and Scholarly Community*, 71 U. Colo. L. Rev. 123 (2000). Perhaps the Rules of Decision Act is inapplicable pursuant to its own limitation to "cases where they apply." *Id.*

9. 533 U.S. 353 (2001) (holding, in part, that tribal courts are not courts of general jurisdiction and therefore they do not have jurisdiction over federal causes of action).

10. Estate of Witko v. Hornell Brewing Co., 156 F. Supp. 2d 1092 (D.S.D. 2001). It is important to note that Heileman Brewing Company was not a named defendant in this lawsuit. Heileman Brewing Company had been acquired by SBC Holdings Inc., formerly Stroh Brewing Company, and was in active negotiations to settle with the Estate of Crazy Horse.

Indians Arts and Crafts Act,[11] the Lanham Act,[12] and the Federal Trademark Dilution Act of 1995,[13] as well as defamation, misappropriation and misuse of inheritable property rights, and negligent and intentional infliction of emotional distress.[14] Damages, as well as injunctive and declarative relief, were sought.[15]

True to form, the defendants filed a motion to dismiss for lack of personal jurisdiction.[16] While the court's opinion does not indicate the basis for federal jurisdiction, Judge Piersol applied the same basic analytical framework used by the Rosebud Sioux Supreme Court when it considered personal jurisdiction and reached the same result. The federal district court had personal jurisdiction over the defendants.[17]

Judge Piersol applied the "effects" test of *Calder v. Jones*,[18] finding that, "[h]aving spent thousands of hours in research and development of the product [Crazy Horse Malt Liquor] and its introduction into the marketplace, the defendants had to know that their actions were uniquely aimed at residents in South Dakota."[19] In addition, he found that in light of the purposefulness of defendants' actions, the fair play and substantial justice requirements of due process were also satisfied.[20] The defendants' claims that they were never physically in South Dakota and their product was never sold there were to no avail.[21]

---

11. 25 U.S.C. §305(d) (2006).

12. 15 U.S.C. §1125 (2006).

13. Pub. L. No. 104-98, 109 Stat. 985 (1996).

14. *Estate of Witko*, 156 F. Supp. 2d at 1094. The likely jurisdictional basis for these causes of action was diversity jurisdiction pursuant to 28 U.S.C. §1332 (2006). The more edgy approach would be supplemental jurisdiction, 28 U.S.C. §1367 (2006), when the tribal causes of action would be "supplemental" to the (federal) statutory causes of action. *See* Pommersheim, *supra* note 25, at 154–59.

15. *Estate of Witko*, 156 F. Supp. 2d at 1094.

16. *Id.*

17. *Id.* at 1101.

18. 465 U.S. 783 (1984).

19. *Estate of Witko*, 156 F. Supp. 2d at 1100.

20. *Id.* at 1100–01. Notice how the exact same reasoning of the Rosebud Sioux Supreme Court was rejected by the Eighth Circuit Court of Appeals. Unfortunately, the absence of the district court opinion prevents any review and analysis of Judge Kornmann's reasoning, insomuch as the Eighth Circuit opinion merely restates the opinion's conclusions. Note, however, that the Eighth Circuit opinion does indicate that Judge Kornmann rejected the Rosebud Sioux Supreme Court analysis of the second *Montana* exception because it was so broad "that the tribal courts would always have civil subject matter jurisdiction over non-Indians." *Id.* at 1093.

21. The lawsuit was dismissed by Judge Piersol in January 2004 because of a pending settlement. *Crazy Horse Malt Liquor Case to be Settled out of Court*, Wind River News, Jan. 15, 2004, at 5. No such settlement appears to have ever been finalized.

Heileman Brewing Co. took a different approach in dealing with the claims of Crazy Horse's Estate. This was the approach of respect and negotiated settlement. This conciliatory tact was adopted upon the acquisition of Heileman Brewing Co. by SBC Holdings Inc. (formerly Stroh Brewing Co.).[22] The settlement took place in a public event held on the Rosebud Sioux Reservation in South Dakota. The settlement involved the reading of a public apology by John Stroh III, chairman of SBC Holdings Inc. and a presentation by Mr. Stroh of thirty-two Pendleton blankets, thirty-two braids of sweetgrass, thirty two twists of tobacco, and seven thoroughbred horses to Mr. Seth Big Crow, administrator of the Crazy Horse Estate.[23] No money was involved.[24]

An attorney for the Estate said, "It's a step toward clearing the name for Crazy Horse and his descendants and restoring the spirit of Crazy Horse as a strong Indian leader."[25] An attorney for the brewery stated that his client "is thrilled it is able to resolve this matter in a way that is fair and more importantly, culturally significant to the Estate."[26] The settlement reflects a strong Lakota cultural sentiment that focuses on the concept that one ingredient of respect is the willingness to apologize and to seal the apology with a gift.[27]

The case did not come completely to an end with the settlement, but rather took another step forward by having to look back even further into Lakota tradition and custom. As the settlement aspect of the case concluded, another began. The Estate of Crazy Horse now held some (unique) property as a result of the settlement and likely would have to continue to make future decisions about the legacy of Crazy Horse, including the (potential) use of his name, as well as other questions concerning patrimony and inheritance. In essence, it was going to be necessary to determine who the (living) heirs of Crazy Horse were, and what the rules of descendancy were in 1877, when Crazy Horse died. The past is never past. It is always there. It comes full circle.[28]

---

22. Dennis Gale, *Brewer Settles Lawsuit with Horses*, AKRON BEACON JOURNAL, at C11 (April 27, 2001). [hereinafter Gale]

23. *Id. See also Brewer to Apologize to Indians*, CHICAGO TRIBUNE, at 3 (April 27, 2001); *Brewery Settles Crazy Horse Beverage Suit*, NEW YORK TIMES, at A14 (April 27, 2001).

24. Gale, *supra* note 22, at C11.

25. *Id.*

26. *Id.*

27. *See, e.g.*, LEWIS HYDE, THE GIFT: CREATIVITY AND THE ARTIST IN THE MODERN WORLD (Vintage, 2007) on the importance of gifts for establishing bonds of reciprocity.

28. *See, e.g.*, Frank Pommersheim, *The Crazy Horse Malt Liquor Case: From Tradition to Modernity and Halfway Back*, 57 S.D. L. REV. 42 (2012).

This probate action in Rosebud Sioux Tribal Court is ongoing[29] and is discussed *infra* 234–40 in the section on tribal court use of tradition and custom.

29. *Id.*

Plains Commerce Bank v. Long Family Land and Cattle Company, Inc.

(Cheyenne River Sioux Tribal Court of Appeals) (2004)

IN THE CHEYENNE RIVER
SIOUX TRIBAL COURT OF APPEALS

****

THE BANK OF HOVEN, NOW KNOWN	)	#03-002-A
AS PLAINS COMMERCE BANK,	)	R-120-99
Defendant/Appellant/Respondent	)	
vs.	)	MEMORANDUM OPINION
	)	AND ORDER
LONG FAMILY LAND AND CATTLE	)	
COMPANY, INC.—RONNIE AND	)	
LILA LONG,	)	
Plaintiffs/Respondents/Appellants.	)	
	)	

****

Per Curiam (Chief Justice Frank Pommersheim and Associate Justices Everett Dupris and Patrick Lee).

I. Introduction and Background

The facts in this case involve a series of complex commercial interactions between Ronnie and Lila Long, the Long Family Land and Cattle Company, Inc., Plaintiffs/ Respondents/Appellants (Longs), and Plains Commerce Bank (formerly Bank of Hoven), Defendant/Appellant/Respondent (Bank), dating back to 1989. Kenneth Long was a non-Tribal member whose first wife, Maxine Long, was a member of the Cheyenne River Sioux Tribe. Kenneth and Maxine owned approximately 2,230 acres of Dewey County real estate in fee simple as well as a house in Timber Lake. All of this real estate is located within the exterior boundaries of the Cheyenne River Sioux Reservation. All of this real estate was mortgaged to the Bank for loans to the Long Family Land and Cattle Company, Inc.

Upon the death of Maxine, Kenneth became the sole owner of the real estate in Dewey County. At the time of Kenneth's death on July 17, 1995, Mr. Long and the Long Family Land and Cattle Company owed the Bank approximately $750,000. Mr. Long's estate acting through Paulette Long, Kenneth's second wife and personal representative of the estate, conveyed the Dewey County real estate, as well as the house in Timber Lake, to the Bank in lieu of foreclosure. As a result of this conveyance on December 5, 1996, the Long Family Land and Cattle Company was given credit for $478,000 on its outstanding debt to the bank.

Ronnie Long is a member of the Cheyenne River Sioux Tribe and is the son of Kenneth Long. Upon his father's death, Ronnie inherited Kenneth's interest in the 2,250 acres of land in Dewey County on the Cheyenne River Sioux Reservation as well as his father's 49% interest in the Long Family Land and Cattle Company, Inc. The other 51% of the Company is owned by Ronnie and his wife Lila, who is also a member of the Cheyenne River Sioux Tribe. The Company has always been an Indian controlled company.

After Kenneth Long's death, employees of the Bank came to the Longs' land on the Cheyenne River Sioux Reservation to inspect it, as well as the cattle, hay, and machinery on the land. In addition, Bank officers met several times with the Longs, officials of the Cheyenne River Sioux Tribe, and Bureau of Indian Affairs employees. These meetings all took place on the Cheyenne River Sioux Reservation. All of these activities were directed to establishing a basis from which the Bank would provide new loans to Ronnie Long and the Long Family Land and Cattle Company, Inc. for their ranching operation on this land.

The Bank initially proposed that it would sell the land back to the Longs (which was conveyed to the Bank by the Long Estate) via a twenty year contract for deed. Upon the advice of counsel, in a letter to Ronnie Long dated April 20, 1996, the Bank withdrew this offer because of "possible jurisdictional problems." (Exhibit 4) The revised proposal of the Bank offered the Longs only a two-year lease and option within which to purchase and pay for the land in full.

The Lease with Option to Purchase included a purchase price of $478,000 for the land. The other features of the lease provided that annual Crop Reserve Program (CRP) payments to the Longs were assigned to the Bank and the right of the Longs to exercise their option to purchase for $478,000 at the conclusion of the lease period. Another document captioned "Loan Agreement" was signed by both the Bank and the Longs. It recited a series of debits and credits of the Longs to the Bank, and also stated that the Bank would request that the BIA increase the loan guarantee to 90% on note #98181, that the Bank would make an operating loan to the Longs in the amount of $70,000. The Bank also agreed to make another loan of $53,000 to pay off note #98809 of $17,000 with the balance of $37,000 to be used to purchase 110 cattle. Both the Lease with Option to Purchase and the Loan Agreement were signed by the Bank and the Longs on December 5, 1996.

Shortly thereafter, mother nature intervened with a vengeance during the horrific winter of 1996–97. As a result of the failure to provide the $70,000 loan and the implacable force of the brutal winter, the Longs lost 230 cows, 277 yearlings, and eight horses. The Bank did provide some additional loans that were quite modest. The Longs never recovered from these financial and weather-related blows and were unable to meet their outstanding debt to the Bank and were not able to exercise their option to purchase.

The Longs did not remove from the property in question at the expiration of the lease. The Bank began (state) eviction proceedings by sending a notice to quit to the Cheyenne River Sioux Tribal Court for service on the Longs. Service was apparently never effectuated. There was never any hearing or ruling by the state court. Without any order of eviction, and with the Longs remaining in possession of the land, the Bank nevertheless sold the land. On March 17, 1999, the Bank sold 320 acres to Ralph Pesicka for cash, and on June 29, 1999, the Bank sold the remaining 1,905 acres to Edward and May Jo Mackjewski on a contract for deed. None of these purchasers are members of the Cheyenne River Sioux Tribe.

The Longs then commenced an action in the Cheyenne River Sioux Tribal Court seeking a restraining order preventing the Bank from selling the real estate. The Bank's motion to dismiss for lack of subject matter jurisdiction was denied as was the Longs' motion for a restraining order against the Bank. The Longs subsequently amended their complaint to include several causes of action against the Bank that sought damages and other relief. The Bank counterclaimed seeking eviction of the Longs and damages. The Longs requested a jury trial on their claims. The Bank did not seek a jury trial on its counterclaim.

A two day jury trial was held on December 6 and 11, 2002. At the close of the Plaintiffs' case, Special Judge B.J. Jones dismissed Plaintiffs' claims that sought to void the contract, alleged fraud, failure of consideration, and unconscionability. The jury returned a verdict in favor of the Longs on their claims that the Bank breached the loan agreement, discriminated against the Longs based on their status as Indians, and acted in bad faith with regard to its dealings with the Longs. The jury awarded the Longs $750,000 along with prejudgment interest. Special Judge B.J. Jones determined that interest to be $123,131. The jury also found that the Bank did *not* use self-help remedies in an attempt to remove Plaintiffs from the land. A supplemental judgment was later entered permitting the Plaintiffs to exercise the option to purchase the 960 acres of the land they continued to occupy.

Both sides filed timely notices of appeal with this Court. Oral argument was heard on October 6, 2004.

II. Issues

This appeal involves seven (7) issues raised by the Defendant/Appellant/Respondent and two (2) issues of the Plaintiffs/Respondents/Appellants. They are:

A. Defendant/Appellant/Respondent

1. Whether the Cheyenne River Sioux Tribal Court lacked subject matter jurisdiction for a claim of discrimination against an off reservation bank.

2. Whether the trial court erred in failing to grant Defendant's motion for a directed verdict and judgment N.O.V. on the Plaintiffs' breach of contract claim.

3. Whether the trial court erred in failing to grant Defendant's motion for a directed verdict and judgment N.O.V. on Plaintiffs' separate cause of action based on bad faith.

4. Whether the trial court erred in failing to grant Defendant's motion for a judgment N.O.V. in that the damages awarded by the jury were excessive and controlled by passion.

5. Whether the trial court erred in not granting Defendant's cause of action for eviction against the Plaintiffs.

6. Whether the trial court erred in granting Plaintiffs' motion to exercise its option to purchase some of the real estate sold to Edward and Mary Jo Mackjewski under a contract for deed.

7. Whether the trial court erred in allowing pre-judgment interest on certain damages absent specific instructions to the jury.

B. Plaintiffs/Appellees/Respondents Longs and Long Ranch and Cattle Company, Inc.

1. Whether the trial court erred in its calculation of prejudgment interest.

2. Whether the trial court erred in permitting the Plaintiffs to exercise their option to purchase with regard to only part, rather than all, of the land described in the option to purchase.

Each issue will be discussed in turn.

III. Discussion

A. Defendant/Appellant/Respondent Bank

1. Jurisdiction

The Bank's jurisdictional claim is quite limited in scope and is best understood as involving two separate (but overlapping) legal contentions. As to scope, the Bank argues that the Cheyenne River Sioux Tribal court does not have jurisdiction over the Longs' discrimination claim. Bank's Brief at 6–9. This presumably forecloses any federal appeal under the *National Farmers Union* exhaustion doctrine of any other issue involved in this case save the jurisdiction claim relative to the discrimination cause of action. *See, e.g., National Farmers Union Insurance Cos. v. Crow Tribe of Indians*, 471 U.S. 845 (1985). The Bank's two legal arguments, while not drawn as sharply as they might be, assert that the trial court did not have jurisdiction over the discrimination claim because it is a *federal* claim barred under *Nevada v. Hicks*, 533 U.S. 353 (2002), and because no discrimination cause of action exists as a matter of Cheyenne River Sioux Tribal law. Each of these will be discussed in turn concluding with the pertinent jurisdictional analysis under *Montana v. United States*, 450 U.S. 544 (1981).

a. *Nevada v. Hicks* and Federal Causes of Action

The Bank alleges that Cheyenne River Sioux Tribal Court did not have subject matter jurisdiction over Plaintiffs' discrimination claim against the Bank. It is critical to note that the Bank does *not* challenge (on appeal) the general jurisdiction of the Cheyenne River Sioux Tribal Court over the lawsuit brought by the Longs against the Bank, but only against a single cause of action. Appellant's argument centers its claim on its reading of *Nevada v. Hicks*, 533 U.S. 353 (2002). More precisely, the Bank relies on *Hicks* for the limited proposition that tribal courts do not have jurisdiction over federal causes of action. Appellant's interpretation of *Nevada v. Hicks* in this regard is not incorrect, but it is inapposite. The Court in *Hicks* did hold that tribal courts do not have jurisdiction over a *federal* cause of action alleged under 42 U.S.C. § 1983.[1] The Bank argues by extension that tribal courts would have no jurisdiction over a discrimination claim grounded in 42 U.S.C. § 1981 (c). This is likely true, but misses the point. The Plaintiffs discrimination claim is based on a cause of action grounded in tribal, not federal, law.

Plaintiffs' amended complaint did not invoke 42 U.S.C. § 1981 or any federal statute as the source of the discrimination claim and the Bank did not seek to question the source of law for this claim through a motion to dismiss for failure to state a claim on which relief might be granted. In addition, there were no jury instructions provided to the jury on an alleged *federal* cause of

1. The Court's rationale for this holding that there was no congressional delegation of such authority to tribal courts remains unconvincing in light of Justice Stevens' observation that there is no congressional delegation to state courts yet it is unquestioned that state courts have 42 U.S.C. § 1983 jurisdiction. *See Nevada v. Hicks*, 533 U.S. at 402–03 (2002). (Stevens, J. dissenting).

action for discrimination. In fact, the Court in the *Hicks* case itself noted that *tribal* law is often a "complex 'mix of tribal codes and federal, state, and traditional law.'" 533 U.S. at 384–85.

In addition, the Court in *Hicks* concluded:

> that tribal authority to regulate *state officers* in executing process related to the violation, off reservation, of state [criminal] laws is not essential to tribal self-government or internal relations.[2]

The case at bar is not a criminal case, does not involve state officers, and did not take place off the Reservation. It is therefore totally inapplicable as to causes of action arising on the Reservation involving private individuals. The *Hicks* opinion limited its holding "to the question of tribal court jurisdiction over state officers" leaving "open the question of tribal court jurisdiction and nonmember defendants in general." 533 U.S. 358 n.2.

b. Discrimination Causes of Action Under Tribal Law

Notwithstanding its citation to *Nevada v. Hicks,* the Bank's claim is not really that the Tribal Court does not have subject matter jurisdiction over the discrimination claim, but rather there is no such cause of action under Tribal law. In essence, the Bank is claiming that the Longs' discrimination claim should have been dismissed not for lack of jurisdiction, but for a failure to state a claim upon which relief might be granted. This is especially evident in that the Bank's motion to dismiss was not directed to all of the Plaintiffs' claims, but was limited to the discrimination cause of action premised on the (erroneous) theory that it was being pursued as a federal cause of action under 42 U.S.C. § 1981. This more precise claim is also insufficient as a matter of law.

Private claims of discrimination based on status are recognized under federal and state statutes. *See, e.g.,* 42 U.S.C. 2000 (d), *et seq.* (2003), SDCL § 20-13-21 (2003). They are also recognized under the traditional (or common) law of the Cheyenne River Sioux Tribe.[3] While there is no express tribal ordinance

---

2. *Id.* at 364 (emphasis added).

3. Discrimination is prohibited under tribal customary law in much the same way that other injurious or tortious conduct is prohibited under the common law. While it is true that discrimination is frequently the subject of legislation, it is also actionable under the common law. The Supreme Court has long recognized that "an action brought for compensation by a victim of … discrimination is, in effect, a tort action." Meyer v. Holley, 537 U.S. 280, 285 (2003) (citing Curtis v. Loether, 415 U.S. 189 (1974)). In *Curtis,* the Court held that a claim for damages under the Civil Rights Act of 1968 "sounds basically in tort" and "is analogous to a number of tort actions recognized at common law." 415 U.S. 189, 195–196. The Court noted that, "[a]n action to redress racial discrimination may … be

creating a civil cause of action based on discrimination, there are nevertheless at least two other sources of tribal law that do recognize such a cause of action. They are tribal common law and the Cheyenne River Sioux Law and Order Code § 1-4-3 which confers jurisdiction on the trial court over claims arising out of "tortious conduct."

Since it is well understood that a claim based on discrimination essentially sounds in tort, jurisdiction over "tortious conduct" necessarily includes jurisdiction over Plaintiffs' discrimination claim.[4] In addition, there is basis for a discrimination claim that arises directly from Lakota tradition as embedded in Cheyenne River Sioux tradition and custom. Such a potential claim arises from the existence of Lakota customs and norms such as the "traditional Lakota sense of justice, fair play, and decency to others," *Miner v. Banley*, Chey. R. Sx. Tr. Ct. App., No. 94-003 A, Mem. Op. and Order at 6 (Feb. 3, 1995); and "the Lakota custom of fairness and respect for individual dignity." *Thompson v. Cheyenne River Sioux Tribal Board of Police Commissioners*, 23 I.L.R. 6045, 6048 (Chey. R. Sx. Tr. Ct. App. 1996). Such notions of fair play are core ingredients in federal and state definitions of discrimination. Therefore a tribally based cause of action grounded in an assertion of discrimination may proceed as a "tort" claim as defined in the Cheyenne River Sioux Tribal Code, as derived from Tribal tradition and custom, or even from the federal ingredients defined at 42 U.S.C. § 2000–2001.[5]

The core of the Longs' discrimination claim was based on the Bank's letter to the Longs dated April 26, 1996, (Exhibit 4, TR 106–07, 330) in which the Bank withdrew its offer to sell the land back to Longs on a twenty year contract for deed because it involved an "Indian owned entity" and related (but unidentified) "jurisdictional problems." The Bank's subsequent offer as contained in the lease with option to purchase required *full* payment within sixty

---

likened to an action for defamation or intentional infliction of mental distress," and further that "under the logic of the common law development of a law of insult and indignity, racial discrimination might be treated as a dignitary tort." 415 U.S. at 195–196, n.10. These are precisely the kinds of actions over which the tribal courts have jurisdiction. Under Tribal law, the courts "have jurisdiction over claims and disputes arising on the reservation." CRST By-Laws, Art. V, § 1(c), including claims arising out of "tortious conduct." Cheyenne River Sioux Tribal Code § 1-4-3. Cheyenne River Sioux Tribe's Amicus Brief at 14, n.3.

4. One kind of classical tort is the harm that results from the differential and invidious treatment of one individual by another individual or entity.

5. Note this last theory is *not* the pursuit of a *federal* cause of action in tribal court like the 42 U.S.C. § 1983 claim in *Nevada v. Hicks*, but that of a "borrowing" of federal law to stand in or amplify tribal law where it is necessary. *See, e.g.*, Cheyenne River Sioux Tribal Law and Order Code, Title VII Rule 1 (d).

days of the expiration of the two year lease. (Exhibit 7) It is also significant to recall that the land involved is fee land not trust land. While trust land does involve certain federal restrictions on alienability, fee land does not. The Longs contended that this adverse and differential treatment of them was based on their status as "Indians" and constituted discrimination, a question that was ultimately resolved in their favor by the jury verdict.

It is a testament to the vitality and dignity of American jurisprudence that it would most certainly shock the conscience if a claim of discrimination—especially one based on the disparity of treatment on account or race or status—would not be cognizable in state or federal court. In this vein, the Cheyenne River Sioux Tribal Court is no different from its federal and state brethren in its unwillingness to ignore claims of discrimination. In the area of discrimination, there is a direct and laudable convergence of federal, state, and tribal concern.

c. Jurisdiction under *Montana v. United States*

Since there is a discrimination cause of action under Tribal law involving fee land, the most relevant case for jurisdictional purposes therefore is not *Nevada v. Hicks* but *Montana v. United States*, 450 U.S. 544 (1981). In *Montana*, the Court held that tribal courts generally do *not* have jurisdiction over non-Indians involving matters that arise on fee land within the reservation. This presumption against tribal court jurisdiction is nevertheless subject to *Montana's* well-known proviso which states:

> [T]o be sure, Indian tribes retain sovereign power to exercise some forms of civil jurisdiction over non-Indians on their reservations, even on non-Indian fee lands. A tribe may regulate, through taxation, licensing or other means, the activities of members who enter consensual relationships with the tribe or its members, through commercial dealing, contracts, leases or other arrangements.... A tribe may also retain inherent power to exercise civil authority over non-Indians on fee lands within its reservation when that conduct threatens charities or has some effect on the political integrity, economic security, or the health or welfare of the tribe. 450 U.S. at 565–66 (citations omitted).

It is clear that the case at bar satisfies both prongs. This case is the prototype for a consensual agreement as it involves a signed contract between a Tribal member and a non-Indian bank. The contract deals solely with fee land located wholly within the exterior boundaries of the reservation. Fee land that was originally owned by the Longs, but owned by the Bank during the controverted events in this lawsuit. All bank loans in this matter were provided solely for the ranching operation by the Longs taking place on the Bank's land within the reservation. Numerous meetings of the Bank with the Longs, with Cheyenne River Sioux Tribal Officials, and Bureau of Indian Affairs personnel took place on the reservation, both when the land was owned by the Longs and subsequently when it was owned by the Bank.

It is somewhat misleading for the Bank to identify itself as an *off* reservation Bank, because it *owned* the land *on* the Reservation that is the subject of this lawsuit. As a result, the Bank is more accurately described as owning property and engaging in business activities *both* on and off the Reservation.

In addition, the case clearly involves the "economic security" of the Tribe in that the Cheyenne River Sioux Tribe (along with the Bureau of Indian Affairs) was a direct participant actively consulted by both the Longs *and* the Bank seeking economic data and support relevant to the cattle operation on the Longs' land. If the economic security of the Tribe was not involved, the Tribe would not have played such a large role in these events in seeking to support and advance the opportunity for Tribal members to succeed in their ranching operation on the Reservation.

2. Breach of Contract Cause of Action

Appellant Bank asserts that the Longs' breach of contract claim was improperly submitted to the jury, or if properly submitted to the jury, improperly decided by it because *no* contract existed as a matter of law or fact. In particular, the Bank contends that the key document captioned "Loan Agreement," which was prepared by the Bank and signed by both the Bank and the Longs on December 5, 1996 and recites, among other things, the Bank's commitment to provide two loans to the Long Land and Cattle Company, Inc. was not a contract at all. It was merely some kind of balance sheet that mainly recited a list of debits and credits relative to the real estate conveyed by the Long Estate to the Bank. In essence, according to the Bank, there was no consideration and hence no contract.

In the Bank's motion for judgment N.O.V. on this issue, Judge B.J. Jones decided against the Bank finding there was sufficient consideration when the "Loan Agreement" is considered as part of the Lease with Option to Purchase under the integrated document doctrine. These documents were contemporaneous, applied to the same subject matter, and were interrelated as to terms. *See Battery Steamship Comp. v. Refineria Panama S.A.*, 513 F.2d 735, 738 n.3 (2d Cir. 1975). Judge Jones had already adopted the integrated document doctrine in denying the Defendant's motion for summary judgment on its counterclaim for eviction, and it appropriately became the law of the case. This

Court now adopts the substance of this rule as appropriate law within this jurisdiction. In this view, it is reasonable to construe the Loan Agreement, along with the Lease with Option to Purchase, and find sufficient consideration provided by the Longs in their commitment to assign their CRP payments to the Bank. In addition, there is a commitment to continue the operation of their ranch in an attempt to pay off their debts to the Bank, without the Bank having to resort to legal action and the less than complete loan guarantees provided by the BIA.

The analysis set out by Judge Jones in his well-reasoned opinion of June 7, 2003 is persuasive. As noted above, there certainly was enough evidence submitted to the jury for it to have found adequate consideration. In reviewing a jury's determination on a motion for a judgment N.O.V., the South Dakota Supreme Court has established a reasonable standard of review, which this Court adopts. This standard directs the reviewing court to review the testimony and evidence in a light most favorable to the verdict or nonmoving party and then to decide without weighing the evidence if there is evidence which did support the verdict. *Matter of Estate of Holan*, 621 N.W.2d 588, 591 (S.D. 2000).

In sum, the application of the integrated documents doctrine is an appropriate legal standard within this jurisdiction. In addition, its legal elements of contemporaneity, similar subject matter, and interrelatedness of terms were also satisfied as a matter of law and there was a sufficient factual basis for the jury to find there was adequate consideration for a contract, and the Bank's failure to perform breached this contract.

3. Bad Faith Cause of Action

In a similar vein to the breach of contract claim, the Bank makes two contentions. First, that such a cause of action does not exist as a matter of law because it is subsumed in the breach of contract claim and second, even if such an independent cause of action does exist, there was insufficient evidence submitted to the jury to sustain a verdict upholding such a bad faith claim.

The question of law concerning a bad faith cause of action involves an issue of first impression within this jurisdiction. The trial court ruled that such a cause of action does exist within this jurisdiction and that it is one that is independent of any breach of contract claim. More precisely, it might be stated that the trial court ruled that the bad faith claim *derives from* but is *severable* and hence independent of the breach of contract claim. As Judge Jones stated in his order of June 7, 2003 on the post-trial motions, the heart of the breach of contract claim was the failure to *provide* the $70,000 loan, while the heart of the bad faith claim was the Bank's failure to follow through with its promise to seek an increase in the level of the BIA guarantee for several outstanding loans.

This statement of the governing law is reasonable and appropriate. While it appears that no other tribal court has addressed this issue, it is true that the rule articulated by the trial court is within the ambit of both South Dakota Law, *see, e.g., Garrett v. Bank West, Inc.*, 459 N.W.2d 833 (S.D. 1990) and the general rule as articulated in the *Restatement (Second) of Contracts* § 204 (1990), which states that every contract includes an implied covenant of good faith and fair dealing which prohibits either contracting party from preventing or injuring the other party's right to receive the agreed upon benefits of the contract.

The Bank's challenge to the sufficiency of the evidence in this issue is likewise rejected. Given the standard of review articulated in Part III.A.2 p. 11 (pp. 69–70 here), clearly there was sufficient evidence in the record concerning the Bank's failure to respond to the BIA's request for a more detailed application relative to potential increased loan guarantees from which the jury might conclude that the Bank acted in bad faith.

4. Excessive Damages Controlled by Passion or Prejudice

The jury awarded damages to the plaintiffs in the amount of $750,000. The Bank claims this was "excessive and controlled by passion and prejudice." (Bank's Brief at 16.) This conclusion remains just that, a conclusion unsupported by reason or law. Plaintiffs sought damages in the amount of $1,236,792 (Exhibit 23) and thus the award of $750,000 represents an award of only 60% of the amount requested. The trial judge also sustained a number of objections made by the Bank to the Plaintiffs' claimed damages and Exhibit 23 was changed accordingly. The Bank did not object, stating, "I have no objections with these changes," TR 308 and therefore the Bank waived any subsequent right to appeal. The absence of 'prejudice' is also further evidenced by the jury's rejection of the Longs' claim of improper self-help eviction by the Bank.

The Plaintiffs provided extensive evidentiary data and testimony relative to their damages. The Bank had the same opportunity. Given the appropriate standard of review in challenging a jury finding of fact as noted above, this Court cannot conclude that the jury award in this context lacked a sufficient factual predicate, even disregarding the Bank's waiver of this issue.

Ordinarily, this would conclude the Court's analysis of this otherwise legitimate issue, but for the Bank's decision to characterize the entire trial as "tainted":

> Once a claim for discrimination was allowed to be tried to the jury, where no one but tribal members could serve, the Bank could no longer obtain a fair trial. Allegations of racial discrimination by a non-member Bank located off the reservation *completely enflamed the jury.* They became incapable of rendering a fair and impartial verdict. The *race card tainted* the entire trial process. (emphasis added)

(Bank Brief at 23).

This rhetoric is itself inflammatory. At oral argument, counsel for the Bank admitted that he did not challenge any juror for cause, did not challenge the jury panel as a whole because it did not contain any non-tribal members, and perhaps most importantly, he did *not* request that the trial court use its discretionary power under Sec. 1-6-1(2) of the Tribal Code to "adopt procedures whereby non-enrolled Indians and non-Indians may be summoned for jury duty in cases in which one or more non-Indian parties are involved."

The Bank, apparently excusing its own ('benign') neglect of the issue at the trial, then twists it (somehow) to contend that the very existence of a discrimination cause of action was playing the 'race card.' The Bank's apparent 'solution' to this 'problem' is that claims of discrimination against non-resident Banks should not exist as a matter of tribal law. This asserts a rather extravagant privilege for the Bank that is presumably not available to others, especially Tribal members and the Tribe itself. Whether intended or not, this *is* the Bank playing its own 'race card,' which at a minimum is quite baffling and potentially quite disturbing in the context of seeking to maintain a fair and reasonable legal context for the necessary commercial transactions involving individual Tribal ranchers and business people and the banking establishment. Both Tribal members and the Bank need each other, and it is quite disheartening to have the Bank interject the potentially destabilizing 'race card' into these proceedings.

5. Eviction

The trial court dismissed the Bank's counterclaim for forcible entry and detainer against the Longs. The counterclaim was not tried to the jury as neither party requested it. The trial court rendered its decision after the jury verdict. It reasoned that based on its own previous decision that the loan agreement and the lease with option to purchase formed an integrated document and the jury's verdict that the Bank breached the contract, it could not render a favorable decision to the Bank on its counterclaim for eviction. The court's reasoning was that the jury finding that the Bank breached the contract (including the lease) effectively precluded any finding that the Longs had breached the lease or otherwise improperly held over and were subject to eviction.

In addition, the Bank made no attempt to comply with the Tribal Law and Order Code provisions for recovering the possession of real property set out §§ 10-2-1 – 10-2-8. § 10-2-6(6) specifically provides that when a tenant has held over for more than sixty days without any notice to quit by the landlord, the tenant shall have the right to remain in possession for a full year after the lease termination date. The lease between the Bank and the Longs ran from December 5, 1996 to December 6, 1998. The Longs held over but no notice to quit was served within the sixty days (i.e. February 5, 1999) and thus the Longs had the right to hold over to December 6, 1999. Indeed, the notice to quit was not served on the Longs until June 16, 1999. (Exhibit 20) The notice to quit described the Longs as still in possession of the entire 2,230 acres. Despite the fact that the Longs were legally in possession of this land as a matter of express Tribal law during this period, the Bank *sold* the land to two different purchasers in violation of the Longs' right to hold over and exercise their option to purchase under the original lease. (Exhibit 20). At no time did the Bank ever get an order from the tribal court removing the Longs from the land (TR 370).

6. Option to Purchase

The trial court granted partial relief to the Longs on this issue when it ruled that the Longs would be permitted to exercise their option to purchase the 960 acres they were currently occupying, but not the 960 acres that were sold to the Maciejewskis and the 320 acres sold to the Pesickas. The Bank asserts that the trial court in essence ordered (partial) specific performance be granted against the Bank, but that such a remedy was never sought by the Longs and that such a remedy is equitable in nature and not available in a breach of contract action which is an 'action at law' that does not authorize equitable relief. These statements constitute legal observations of a quite general kind and are not part of the positive law of the Cheyenne River Sioux Tribe.

In the instant case, the trial court attempted to strike a balance between law and equity and to secure fairness to both sides. The specific performance element involving the option to purchase involved land originally owned by the lessee and lost because of the inability to pay a significant debt to the Bank. The fact that the Longs were seeking to (re)purchase land that had been in their family for generations takes the case outside the realm of the formal law/equity distinction. In addition, Judge Jones was careful not to interfere with the property rights of the Maciejewskis and the Pesickas as good faith purchasers. The balance struck by the trial court is fair, reasonable, and violated no rule of Cheyenne River Sioux Tribal law.

7. Pre-Judgment Interest

The Bank objects to the award of pre-judgment interest.[6] Its essential argument—drawn primarily from South Dakota and California Law—is that prejudgment interest should only be awarded if the defendant knows or should have known based on reasonably accessible information what the amount owed was. This general observation however does not require a different result. It is routine in the West—including South Dakota—to calculate prejudgment interest on lost cattle based on their market value at the time of the loss. Deciding the date of loss—if contested—is a factual question to be resolved by the jury. Thus the method of awarding pre-judgment interest in this case conforms to the general practice throughout Western parts of the United States.

The Bank's claim is further undermined by the fact that it did not object to special jury interrogatory 6 or jury instruction 10a on the issue of the potential award of interest and it did not propose any special jury interrogatories of its own. Such failure ordinarily precludes raising the issue on appeal. *See, e.g., Alvine v. Mercedes-Benz of North America*, 620 N.W.2d 608 (S.D. 2001). In addition, the trial court adopted and accepted (to the penny) the Bank's proposed interest of $123,131.81 as opposed to the Plaintiffs' proposal of $453,698.

B. Plaintiffs/Respondents/Appellants Issues on Appeal

The Plaintiff Longs raise two issues on appeal, and they are the mirror images of the Bank's issues numbers six and seven, namely that trial court erred in *not* awarding Plaintiffs complete specific performance to (re)purchase *all* the land involved in the original lease and option to purchase, and the trial court erred in its calculation of pre-judgment interest to be awarded. Each issue will be discussed in turn.

1. Option to Purchase

The Longs contend that the trial court erred in its failure to permit the Longs to exercise its option to purchase all of their 2,225 acres rather than just 960 acres on which they effectively held over. The Bank had already sold 320 acres to Pesickas and 960 acres to Maciejewskis and Judge Jones decided the option to purchase would *not* apply to these parcels.

---

6. Pre-judgment interest is neither directly authorized nor prohibited by the Tribal Code. This might be an area where direct legislative guidance by the Cheyenne River Sioux Tribal Council would be beneficial, especially as to the rate of interest and the means of calculation of such interest.

In Judge Jones' supplemental judgment of February 18, 2003, he expressly stated:

> The court first notes that the tribal jury returned a verdict for the Bank and against the Plaintiffs on the Plaintiffs' claim that the Bank violated tribal law against self-help remedies when it sold certain parcels of the land the Plaintiffs had an option to purchase. The Court construes this to mean that the jury found that the sale of the land to the other parties was not done in violation of tribal law and the other defendants [i.e. the Pesickas and Maciejewskis] were good faith purchasers.

Counsel for the Longs does not state what the appropriate standard of review is, and more directly, why this legal determination of Judge Jones is wrong as a matter of tribal law.[7] Under these circumstances, Judge Jones' decision violated no rule of tribal law and balanced the equities in a most reasonable and fair manner.

2. Pre-Judgment Interest

The Longs contend that while the trial court was correct in submitting the question of whether to award pre-judgment interest to the jury (which answered in the affirmative), the trial judge erred in his calculations of the amount of pre-judgment interest to be awarded. The core of the Longs claim on this issue is that the trial judge should have adopted the South Dakota statute, SDCL §21-1-13.1, which sets a rate of 10% for pre-judgment interest. Working from this assertion, plaintiffs' counsel does what he regards as the necessary mathematical calculations and arrives at the figure of $453,698 (Respondents-Appellants Brief at 9).

There are several shortcomings in this line of argument. Counsel for the Longs does not identify what the appropriate standard of review is and whether the trial judge's mistake was one of law and/or fact. There can be no mistake of law because there is no express rate of interest specified in the tribal code and therefore any (reasonable) rate of pre-judgment interest would be an appropriate legal standard.[8] Judge Jones required that counsel for both parties submit proposals to him. Then Judge Jones accepted the Bank's proposal of

7. The discussion of Cheyenne River Sioux Tribe Law and Order Code Sec. 10-1-5 is inappropriate as it deals with the proposed sale of foreclosed property which is not involved in this lawsuit.

8. As noted above in footnote 6, *supra* at 16, the issue of pre-judgment interest including the specific rate of interest and method of calculation would greatly benefit form specific statutory guidance provided by the Cheyenne River Sioux Tribal Council.

pre-judgment interest in the amount of $123,131.81 based on a rate of 8.5%, the rate of interest identified in the lease with option to purchase to be charged the Longs if they exercised their option to purchase.

In addition to different rates of interest, the proposals of both parties used slightly different mathematical models of calculation based on the varying assessments as to the time of loss, value at the time of loss, and whether interest would be simple or compound. While these differences in approach lead to quite different final calculations, there is no demonstration by the Longs that these figures are clearly erroneous or arbitrary and capricious and therefore the amount of pre-judgment interest awarded by Judge Jones is affirmed.

Unfortunately, a final concern must be addressed. In his concluding summation to this Court, counsel for the Bank stated that a lot of banks and lenders were watching this case. While it seemed jarring and inappropriate at the time, it is even more so upon reflection. It is difficult to see the statement as merely some form of artless advocacy, but rather more as some kind of threat impugning the integrity of the Cheyenne River Sioux Tribe's judicial system, which this Court finds most offensive and unprofessional. Such statements must not be made again. Though it hardly needs repeating, the Court restates its commitment to fair play, the rule of law, and cultural respect for *all* parties who appear in the courts of the Cheyenne River Sioux Tribe.

IV. Conclusion

For all the reasons above stated, the decision of the trial court is affirmed on all issues.

Ho Hec'etu Ye Lo

IT IS SO ORDERED.

FOR THE COURT:

____

Frank Pommersheim
Chief Justice

Dated November 22, 2004.

Notes on *Plains Commerce Bank v. Long Family Land and Cattle Co., Inc.* (2004)

Upon the exhaustion of tribal court remedies, the Bank pursued federal relief. The decision of the Cheyenne River Sioux Tribal Court of Appeals was affirmed by the federal district court, 440 F. Supp. 2d 1070 (D.S.D. 2006), and by the Eighth Circuit Court of Appeals, 491 F.3d 878 (8th Cir. 2007). It was narrowly reversed by the Supreme Court in a 5–4 vote, 554 U.S. 316 (2008).

All of the lower courts readily discerned that there was a "consensual" (lease) agreement between the Long Family Land and Cattle Co. and Plains Commerce Bank. They further agreed that the Tribal prohibition against "discrimination" was a legitimate means of regulating the "activities" within the consent provision of *Montana v. United States.* Nevertheless, the Supreme Court managed to reconfigure and to narrow the reach of *Montana* by determining that *Montana* analysis did *not* apply to the sale of fee land on the Reservation by a non-Indian to an Indian. According to the Court, there simply was no tribal court jurisdiction in such matters. Interestingly, no such argument was made by either party—including the United States—at any stage of the proceedings.

Despite the unanimous view of the four courts below (four opinions, eight judges) that this case turned on a basic *Montana* analysis and that the sale of fee land was a quintessential consensual agreement, the U.S. Supreme Court with Chief Justice Roberts writing for the majority, said: "*Montana* does not permit Indian tribes to regulate the sale of non-Indian fee land."[1] Somehow, the Court concluded that the "activities" authorized by *Montana* for tribal regulation in the context of consensual agreements did not include the sale of fee land. It blinks both reality and the plain meaning of words to say that the sale of land is not an "activity" with regard to that land. Such a farfetched claim was not even mentioned by the petitioner in its brief or at oral argument.

This "new" and limited rule[2] was sharply criticized by Justice Ginsburg in her dissent. The dissent aptly noted that the majority opinion resolved the case "on a ground neither argued nor addressed below."[3] In addition, the majority's ruling appeared to diverge from the plain meaning of the *Montana* consensual agreement exception. Justice Ginsburg was nonplussed by the majority's

1. *Plains Commerce Bank*, 554 U.S. at 332.

2. There does not appear to be a single reported case involving the sale of fee land by a non-Indian to an Indian.

3. *Plains Commerce Bank*, 554 U.S. at 346 (Ginsburg, J., dissenting).

assertion that the sale of land was not a well-recognized "activity" within the ordinary sense of the word.[4]

The dissent also pointed out that "this case, it bears emphasis, involves no unwitting outsider forced to litigate under unfamiliar rules and procedures in tribal court."[5] The dissent was further perplexed by the notion that although the federal government and every state can make non-discrimination law in regard to contracts and land sales, tribes cannot.[6] In this regard, the dissent approvingly quoted the Cheyenne River Sioux Tribal Court of Appeals: "With regard to checks against discrimination, as the Tribal Court of Appeals observed, 'there is a direct and laudable convergence of federal, state, and tribal concern.'"[7]

The decision in the *Plains Commerce Bank* case in no way ended the litigation. Recall that the $750,000 jury verdict was a *general* verdict and therefore it was still the law of the case. At some point, the Longs will presumably move forward in Tribal court to enforce their judgment against the Bank. The effect, if any, of the dismissal of the discrimination claim on the amount of the judgment remains to be seen. Such an issue would be a question of first impression for the Cheyenne River Sioux Tribal Courts.[8] In addition, if the Longs continue to hold over on the land they occupy, the Bank could initiate state court eviction proceedings against them.

In the immediate aftermath of the decision, the *status quo* held sway. Plains Commerce Bank did not discharge its (remaining) indebtedness to the Long Family Land and Cattle Co., Inc. The Long Family held over on the land it occupied. Finally, in 2012, the Long Family Land and Cattle Co., Inc. filed an action in tribal court to pursue satisfaction of the remainder of its Tribal court judgment by enforcing the appeal bond on record with the court. Plains Commerce Bank went directly to federal court seeking to enjoin the tribal court

4. *Id.* at 347.

5. *Id.* at 346. The bank regularly filed suit in the tribal court in other cases and conceded jurisdiction to the underlying contract claims in this case. *Id.*

6. *Id.* at 350.

7. *Id.* at 351 n.3 (quoting App. to Pet. for Cert. A-55 to A-56). This was the *first* time in history that the Supreme Court, albeit in a dissent, *quoted* a tribal court opinion.

8. This very issue came up at oral argument before the U.S. Supreme Court. *See* Transcript of Oral Argument at 28–32, *Plains Commerce Bank*, 128 S. Ct. 2709 (2008) (No. 07-411, 2008 WL 1710923). Apparently, there is a circuit split about how to deal with the issue in the context of Rule 49(a) of the Federal Rules of Civil Procedure. *See, e.g.*, Gillespie v. Sears, Roebuck & Co., 368 F.3d 21 (1st Cir. 2004); McCord v. Maguire, 885 F.2d 650 (9th Cir. 1989).

proceeding. The District Court dismissed this action because of the failure to exhaust tribal court remedies as required by the *National Farmers Union* case.[9]

Ultimately, both parties agreed to a voluntary mediation and a settlement was signed by both parties in 2013. The settlement prohibits the disclosure of any of its terms.

This case is also unique in that it is the only *Montana*-like case to reach the Supreme Court in which there was an actual tribal (jury) trial on the merits. The lower courts, both tribal and federal, rejected various due process challenges by the Bank in regard to the makeup and composition of the all-Tribal member jury.

The due process claims consisted of three interrelated assertions, namely that the tribal appellate court should have been constrained to address the discrimination claim "under the federal law mentioned by the trial judge," that the Bank lacked proper notice "that it was facing a tribal rather than a federal claim for jurisdiction," and lastly that "it should not have been subject to liability for a tort that had not previously been recognized."[10]

The circuit panel found no violation of due process. Judge Murphy's opinion indicated that it is standard (federal and state) appellate practice to uphold a judgment on grounds not decided or discussed by the lower court so long as those grounds are supported by the record. It also indicated that there was no deficiency in notice or the opportunity to defend. The Longs never asserted a violation of federal law, the Bank never sought dismissal on grounds of vagueness, and the jury instructions made no reference to federal law.[11] Finally, Judge Murphy noted that although the discrimination claim was a case of first impression within the Cheyenne River Sioux Tribal Court system, such was the nature of (tribal) common law development:

> Tort law has historically developed incrementally in the courts. If the encouragement of tribal self governance through the development of legal institutions is to remain a federal priority, then tribal appellate courts must be given latitude to shape their own common law to respond to the cases before them, as our own courts have done over the centuries.[12]

---

9. 910 F. Supp. 2d 1188 (D.S.D. 2012).

10. Plains Commerce Bank v. Long Family Land and Cattle Co., 491 F.3d 878, 890 (8th Cir. 2007), *rev'd*, 554 U.S. 316 (2008).

11. *Id.* at 891.

12. *Id.* at 892 (citations omitted).

The Eighth Circuit Court of Appeals also pointed out that the Bank was not discriminated against by the Tribal court. There was no evidence of bias. The Bank made no attempt to request that non-Indian jurors be summoned as permitted under tribal law, challenged no individual Indian jurors for prejudice, and did not challenge the composition of the panel.[13]

There are some important lessons that stem from this part of the appeal. They include the recognition that tribal courts are entitled to incrementally shape their own tribal common law and the fact that some possibility for non-Indians to serve on civil jury cases involving non-Indians is a necessary ingredient in order for tribal court jurisdiction to be upheld. As is often the case, the Supreme Court ruling in *Plains Commerce Bank* appears fickle and askew, quite at odds with the basic legal reality encountered by the tribal court and lower federal courts.

13. *Id.*

Doe v. Dollar General Corp., Dolgencorp, Inc., and Dale Townsend

(Mississippi Band of Choctaw Supreme Court) (2008)

IN THE SUPREME COURT OF THE MISSISSIPPI BAND OF CHOCTAW INDIANS

No. CV-02-05

JOHN DOE, JR., A MINOR,)
BY AND THROUGH HIS PARENTS)
AND NEXT FRIENDS, JOHN DOE, SR.)
AND JANE DOE,)
Plaintiff/Appellee)
)
VS.) MEMORANDUM
) OPINION AND ORDER
DOLLAR GENERAL CORPORATION;)
DOLGENCORP, INC.; AND)
DALE TOWNSEND, INDIVIDUALLY AND)
JOINTLY AND SEVERALLY WITH)
DOLLAR GENERAL CORPORATION AND)
DOLGENCORP, INC.,)
Defendants/Appellants)

Per Curiam (Chief Justice Rae Nell Vaughn and Associate Justices Roseanna Thompson and Frank Pommersheim)

I. Introduction

The Plaintiff John Doe was thirteen years old in the summer of 2003. At that time, as a member of the Mississippi Band of Choctaw Indians Tribe and participant in the Tribe's Youth Opportunity Program, he was assigned to the Dollar General Store in the Choctaw Town Center in order to gain experience and to learn work skills. John's supervisor at Dollar General was Mr. Dale Townsend, a non-Indian adult, who resided outside the Reservation in Philadelphia, Mississippi.

During this time period, Dollar General was engaged in retail business at this store pursuant to a commercial lease wherein Dolgencorp, a non-resident foreign corporation, leased store space from Choctaw Shopping Center Enterprise, a wholly-owned entity of the Mississippi Band of Choctaw Indians. The leased premises are located completely within the exterior boundaries of the Mississippi Band of Choctaw Indian Reservation and are located on land owned by the Tribe and held in trust by the United States government for the benefit of the Tribe. In addition, at all relevant times herein, Dollar General possessed a valid Tribal business license, which permitted it to engage in commercial activities within the Choctaw Reservation. Such business license is required by § 14-1-3(1) of the Tribal Code.[1]

It is alleged, that during the time of John Doe's placement by the Tribe at the Dollar General Store, Mr. Dale Townsend made repeated and unsolicited sexual advances toward this minor. It is further alleged that these unsolicited advances caused substantial physical and emotional harm to John Doe. Subsequent to these events and on or about January 6, 2005, the minor John Doe, through his parents, John Doe Sr. and Jane Doe, brought a civil action against Mr. Townsend and the Dollar General Store in the Mississippi Band of Choctaw Indians Tribal Court. The lawsuit sought damages, including punitive damages, against the defendants for the alleged tort of (sexual) assault.

Prior to the filing of this lawsuit by the Plaintiff in early 2005, the Tribe, acting through its Attorney General's office, brought an action in the Tribal Court pursuant to § 20-1-2 of the Tribal Code, which sought to "exclude" Mr. Townsend from the Mississippi Band of Choctaw Indians Reservation. Mr. Townsend did not oppose the exclusion action and said exclusion order was signed by Judge Christopher Collins on September 22, 2003.

Subsequently, both Defendants filed a motion to dismiss the civil action for lack of subject matter jurisdiction. This motion to dismiss was denied in an oral opinion delivered by Judge Collins on July 28, 2005. This appeal followed. Oral argument was heard on November 16, 2007.

---

1. Section 14-1-3(1) of the Tribal Code provides:

> Any person who engages in any business or activity on reservation lands should apply to the commissioner for a permit to engage in and to conduct any business or activity upon the condition that the payment of tax accruing to the Mississippi Band of Choctaw Indians under the provisions of the Code shall take place, and shall keep adequate records of such business or activity as is required by the commission. Upon receipt of such permit, the applicant shall be duly licensed to engage in and conduct such business or activity. Said permit shall continue in force so long as the person to whom it is issued shall continue in the same business at the same location, unless revoked by the commissioner for cause.

II. Issues

This appeal raises four issues: namely whether this is a proper matter for an interlocutory appeal; what is the effect, if any, of the exclusion order on the Court's (personal) jurisdiction over defendant, Dale Townsend; whether there is proper subject matter jurisdiction over the lawsuit as a matter of federal law; and whether a claim for *punitive* damages against non-Indian defendants is foreclosed as a matter of federal (constitutional) law.

Each issue will be discussed in turn.

III. Discussion

A. Interlocutory Appeal

Whether a matter is a proper one for interlocutory appeal is governed solely by Tribal law. Such law is embedded in the Mississippi Band of Choctaw Tribal Code at §7-1-10(d)(1), which provides that an interlocutory appeal

> shall be granted only if the lower court has committed an obvious error which would render further lower court proceedings useless or substantially limit the freedom of a party to act and a substantial question of law is presented which would determine the outcome of the appeal.

It is clear to the Court that the necessary predicate of "obvious error" committed by the trial court is not satisfied in the instant case. Neither *Montana v. United States*, 450 U.S. 544 (1981) nor *Nevada v. Hicks*, 533 U.S. 353 (2001) (or any other case for that matter) establish any black letter rule that forecloses potential tribal court jurisdiction in this matter. These cases merely provide relevant tests to be applied to determine whether tribal court jurisdiction is appropriate in any particular instance. The facts in the instant case, as well as legal landscape of the Mississippi Band of Choctaw Indians Reservation, are readily distinguishable from both *Montana* and *Hicks* and thus there is no possibility of establishing "obvious error." For example, *Montana* involved a claim of jurisdiction over non-Indians for matters occurring on fee land and *Hicks* involved jurisdiction over *state* officials for actions that took place on trust land. Neither set of facts are analogous to those of the instant case. In fact, the Court in *Hicks* recognized as much, when it noted that "our holding in this case is limited to the question of tribal-court jurisdiction over the officers enforcing state law. *We leave open the question of tribal-court jurisdiction over nonmembers in general.*" *Id.* at 358 n.2 (emphasis added).

Despite this analysis, it is nevertheless true that there has been an inexplicable delay in hearing argument on the interlocutory appeal issue. As a result of this unaccounted for delay of more than a year, the Court finds that for reasons of judicial economy and in order to avoid further delay and potential (procedural) unfairness to the parties, the Court accepts the (interlocutory) appeal, because of its unique circumstances and procedural posture.[2]

B. Exclusion Order

Defendant/Appellant Dale Townsend argues that the exclusion order against him constitutes a 'waiver' of (personal) jurisdiction.[3] Mr. Townsend argues that such waiver results from actions by the Tribal court, but that cannot be so. Courts do not waive (personal) jurisdiction requirements. Thus there is a troubling oddity at hand and that is that a plaintiff in a lawsuit (John Doe) is subject to a claim that personal jurisdiction over the Defendant has been waived by a non-party (the Tribe).

While a plain reading of the text of the exclusion order appears to provide no exception to its categorical language which states "that the Respondent [Dale Townsend] be and he is hereby excluded from inside the boundaries of the Mississippi Band of Choctaw Indians Reservation lands," such a narrow reading may *not* be warranted in this instance. It would seem to defy both common sense and due process[4] for the Tribe to insist on the apparent absolute terms of the exclusion order it sought, which now potentially jeopardizes the right of a Tribal member to seek civil (redress) against a non-member for actions that took place on Tribal trust land within reservation boundaries. The fact that the exclusion order was entered more than one year previous to the filing on the complaint in this matter may well explain the Tribe's failure to seek any language of exception or limitation. Yet in order to avoid any misunderstanding on this issue and to provide due respect to a co-ordinate branch of Tribal government, the Court requests that the Attorney General's office inform this Court whether it does in fact insist on the absolute terms of the ex-

---

2. In other words, this part of the decision has no precedential value as to the general issue of what constitutes a meritorious interlocutory appeal under the Mississippi Band of Choctaw Indians Tribal Code.

3. Defendant/Appellant Dollar General contends that the exclusion order against Dale Townsend effects its interests as well because Mr. Townsend is a necessary and indispensable party to the proceeding against it.

4. *See* the Mississippi Band of Choctaw Indians Constitution at Art. X Sec. 1(h) which provides that the "Tribe shall not deny to any persons within its jurisdiction the equal protection of its laws or deprive any person of liberty or property without due process of law."

See also the Indian Civil Rights Act at 25 U.S.C. § 1302(8), which provides that "no Tribe shall deny to any person within its jurisdiction the equal protection of its laws or deprive any person of liberty or property without due process of law."

clusion order and is opposed to a limited exception to the exclusion order for the *sole* purpose of permitting Defendant Townsend to come onto the Reservation to defend this lawsuit or whether it is amenable to such a narrow exception. Such a limited exception to an exclusion order is clearly permitted under the Tribal Code. *See* §20-1-3(2).

C. Subject Matter Jurisdiction Under Federal Indian Law

The issue of the trial court's subject matter jurisdiction as a matter of federal Indian law principles involves the now familiar routine of parsing the entrails of the 'pathmarking' cases of *Montana v. United States*, 450 U.S. 544 (1981) and *Nevada v. Hicks*, 533 U.S. 353 (2001) and their application to the particular facts at hand in the instant case. Such analysis also requires an examination of this Court's opinion in *Williams v. Parke-Davis*, #1142-01 (2004) and its relevant jurisdictional analysis.

The basic 'rules' of the Supreme Court's decisions in *Montana* and *Hicks* are relatively straightforward. Tribal civil jurisdiction over non-Indian activities that take place on land within the reservation is appropriate *only* if the non-Indian activity satisfies either or both of the prongs of the well-known *Montana* proviso.

Originally, *Montana* analysis was only required when non-Indian activities took place on fee land within the Reservation. Subsequent cases[5] expanded the territorial reach of *Montana*, which culminated in *Hicks*' requirement that *Montana* analysis was always required, regardless of where the non-Indian activity took place. The *Hicks* case morphed *Montana's* primary concern with *place* into a primary concern with (non-Indian) *persons*, where place was still relevant, but not determinative or dispositive. *Hicks*, 533 U.S. at 360. Needless to say, this developing jurisprudence has neither constitutional nor statutory roots, but rather is the product of generally (unarticulated) judicial common law decisionmaking.

This common law approach appears to be guided not by the normal (federal) understanding that the primary role of common law decisionmaking is to fill gaps in the relevant substantive law,[6] but rather to vindicate a conscious judicial policy to significantly insulate non-Indians from civil accountability in tribal courts. This concern is manifest in both *Montana* and *Hicks*. In *Montana*, this was couched in language describing the fact that non-Indian settlers

5. *See, e.g.*, South Dakota v. Bourland, 508 U.S. 679 (1993) and Strate v. A-1 Contractors, 520 U.S. 438 (1997).

6. *See, e.g.*, Erwin Chemerinsky, Federal Jurisdiction 363–68 (5th ed. 2007).

on the Crow Reservation would never have envisioned being subject to tribal regulatory authority on fee land. *Montana*, 450 U.S. at 559–60. Likewise in *Hicks*, there was apparent concern to protect (non-Indian) state employees, who were legitimately carrying out state functions (*i.e.* executing a joint state-tribal search warrant) on the Reservation from accountability in tribal courts. *Hicks*, 533 U.S. at 364–65.

Such concerns, however questionable they might be, are not present in the instant case. Dollar General voluntarily signed a commercial lease with Choctaw Shopping Center Enterprise, a wholly-owned Tribal entity, and came on the Reservation for said commercial activities. The notion of surprise or lack of foreseeability so central to the Court's thinking in *Montana* and *Hicks* is simply not present in the instant case. Of course, these observations do *not* obviate the necessity of *Montana* analysis, but they do provide a relevant context in which to anchor and to evaluate the required *Montana* analysis.

1. *Montana* Analysis

Classic *Montana* analysis requires an inquiry as to whether the non-Indian activity at issue satisfies either or both of the prongs of the well-known *Montana* proviso, which provides:

> To be sure, Indian tribes retain inherent sovereign power to exercise some forms of civil jurisdiction over non-Indians on their reservations, even on non-Indian fee lands. A tribe may regulate, through taxation, licensing, or other means, the activities of nonmembers who enter consensual relationships with the tribe or its members, through commercial dealing, contracts, leases, or other arrangements. *Williams v. Lee, supra* at 223; *Morris v. Hitchcock*, 194 U.S. 384; *Buster v. Wright*, 135 F. 947, 950 (CAS); *see Washington v. Confederated Tribes of Colville Indian Reservation*, 447 U.S. 134, 152–54. A tribe may also retain inherent power to exercise civil authority over the conduct of non-Indians on fee lands within its reservation when that conduct threatens or has some direct effect on the political integrity, the economic security, or the health or welfare of the tribe. *See Fisher v. District Court*, 424 U.S. 382, 386; *Missoula County*, 200 U.S. 118, 128–29; *Thomas v. Gay*, 169 U.S. 264, 273.

Montana, 450 U.S. at 565–66 (footnotes omitted).

Clearly, the commercial lease between Dollar General and Choctaw Shopping Center Enterprise constitutes a consensual agreement, but does that consensual agreement include the plaintiff, an individual Tribal member, who is not a party to the agreement? The Supreme Court in both *Strate v. A-1 Contractors*, 520 U.S. 438 (1997), and *Atkinson Trading Co., Inc. v. Shirley*, 532 U.S. 645 (2001), cautioned against expansive interpretations as to the reach of consensual agreements. In this vein, Chief Justice Rehnquist used a pithy aphorism to note that "[a] nonmember's consensual agreement in one area this does not trigger tribal and civil authority in another—it is not 'in for a penny, in for a pound.'" *Id.* at 656. While hewing to this formulation, the unique facts in this case nevertheless justify a conclusion affirming Tribal court jurisdiction.

The alleged tort in this case took place on the leased premises that are subject of the consensual agreement and the individual tortfeasor was an employee, indeed the manager of the leased premises. Thus there is a considerable nexus between the alleged tort and the commercial lease. And in fact, the victim of this alleged tort was not a customer or private employee hired directly by Dollar General, but a Tribal minor placed at the store by the Tribe to receive job training. This fact tightens the nexus even further.

Indeed, it is reasonable to conclude that in addition to the consensual agreement embodied in the lease between Choctaw Shopping Center Enterprise, the wholly owned Tribal entity, and Dollar General, there is also an (unwritten) consensual agreement between the Tribe and Dollar General. The essence of such agreement being that when the Tribe places a Tribal minor with Dollar General for job training purposes, that it would be mutually understood that any issues relative to Dollar General's relationship to the minor regarding such things as training, wages, or potential harm would be resolved in Tribal court.

Such a reading is reinforced by the fact that Dollar General not only entered into a written lease with a wholly owned Tribal entity, but it also operated under a business license granted by the Tribe and required by Tribal law. Such a license is, of course, a quintessential consensual arrangement, which is necessary to engage in commercial activities on the Reservation. Such a business license presumably does *not* authorize (intentional) torts allegedly committed by the licensee's manager against a Tribal minor placed with the licensee for training and skill development. It strains credulity to somehow assert that the licensee is not accountable within the legal structure of the sovereign, who granted the license in the first instance, for an alleged wrong that took place at the very premises where the licensed commercial activities took place.

In this regard, for example, see the Eighth Circuit's decision in *Plains Commerce Bank v. Long Family Land and Cattle Company*, 491 F.3d 878 (8th Cir. 2007). In that case, the Court unanimously held that a non-Indian entity is subject to Tribal court jurisdiction for a *tort* that occurred in the context of a consensual commercial relationship:

> Here, the Tribe was doing just that and exercising its inherent authority. By subjecting the bank to liability for violating tribal antidiscrimination law in the course of its business dealings with the Longs, the Tribe was setting limits on how nonmembers may engage in commercial transactions with members inside the reservation. The fact that we are dealing with the common law of torts rather than a licensing requirement or other statutory provision makes no substantive difference here. Tort law is after all both a means of regulating conduct, *see, e.g,* W. Page Keeton, et al., Prosser and Keeton on Torts 25 (5th ed. 1984) (Prosser), and an important aspect of tribal governance.

Plains Commerce Bank, 491 F.3d 878, 887 (8th Cir. 2007).

Much of the above applies with equal force to analysis under the second prong relative to "direct effect on the political integrity, economic security, or the health or welfare of the tribe." The "health or welfare of the tribe" is certainly a function of the "health or welfare" of its individual members. If the Tribe cannot protect the "health or welfare" of its members by insuring the availability of a Tribal forum for disputes when it places a Tribal minor with a non-Indian commercial venture, who is on the Reservation *solely* as a result of a commercial lease with a Tribal entity, then this exception becomes essentially meaningless. It becomes no more than a bankrupt formalism. This Court believes otherwise. It believes that the Supreme Court in *Montana* meant this prong of its proviso to have potential consequences in the real world.[7] The Court considers the facts in this case to constitute such a real world situation.

2. *Parke-Davis* Analysis

Not only does the above *Montana* discussion support Tribal court jurisdiction in this case, said jurisdictional finding is also required by the Court's own precedent in the case of *Williams v. Parke-Davis*, C.A. 1142-01 (2004). In *Parke-Davis*, this Court found *both* as a matter of federal and Tribal law that the Tribal court had subject matter jurisdiction over a tort lawsuit brought by a Tribal member against a non-resident corporate entity, whose representative came

7. Note in this regard, Justice Ginsburg's statement in C & L Enterprises, Inc. v. Citizen Band Potawatomi Indian Tribe of Oklahoma, 532 U.S. 411, 422 (2001), relative to the enforceability of an arbitration clause that it "has a real world objective, it is not designed for regulation of a game lacking practical consequences."

onto the Reservation, and convinced Tribal officials to distribute the drug Rezulin at the Tribal pharmacy located on trust land.

The central facts in the case at bar are analogous to those in *Parke-Davis*. In both cases, the defendant specifically wanted to do business on the Mississippi Band of Choctaw Indians Reservation and made targeted efforts to do so. In both cases, the defendants were successful in such efforts. In *Parke-Davis*, Rezulin was distributed at the Tribal pharmacy. In the instant case, Dollar General obtained a written commercial lease to engage in business on leased Tribal land within the Reservation. In both cases, an alleged tort resulted from interaction between Tribal members and the business enterprise or its product. The result in *Parke-Davis* requires an affirmation of Tribal court jurisdiction in the case at bar.

As noted in *Parke-Davis*,

> Parke-Davis, it seems, would like to secure the benefits of doing business on the Reservation without any attendant responsibility. Such an asymmetrical approach by a party would clearly be impermissible in any state or federal situation and it should be no less so in a tribal situation. Respect and parity cannot be one-sided *for* the state and federal sovereign but *against* the Tribal sovereign.

Parke-Davis, Slip Opinion at 8.

D. Punitive Damages

Dollar General asserts that the fact that the plaintiff is seeking punitive damages raises federal constitutional issues relevant to the due process's proscription against 'excessive punishment.' Such a claim is both unwarranted and somewhat fanciful. As a general proposition, constitutional protections do not apply against Tribal governments. *See, e.g., Talton v. Mayes*, 163 U.S. 376 (1896). In addition, said proscription against 'excessive punishment' appears in both the Indian Civil Rights Act of 1986, 25 U.S.C. § 1302(8) and the Mississippi Band of Choctaw Indians Constitution at Art. X Sec. 1(h). As noted in *Santa Clara Pueblo v. Martinez*, 436 U.S. 49 (1978), no *federal* remedy is available in tribal civil matters, except in Tribal court:

> Tribal forums are available to vindicate rights created by the ICRA, § 1302 has the substantial and intended effect of changing the law which these forums are obliged to apply. Tribal forums have repeatedly been recognized as appropriate forums for the exclusive adjudication of disputes affecting important personal and property interests of both Indians and non-Indians.

Id. at 65.

IV. Conclusion

For all the above-state reasons, the (interlocutory) appeal is dismissed and the case is remanded[8] for immediate trial on the merits.

IT IS SO ORDERED.

FOR THE COURT:

____

Frank Pommersheim
Associate Justice

Dated: February 8, 2008.

Notes on *Doe v. Dollar General Corp.* (2008)

The decision of the Mississippi Band of Choctaw Supreme Court was affirmed by the federal district court, 846 F. Supp. 2d 646 (S.D. Miss. 2008), and the Fifth Circuit Court of Appeals, 732 F.3d 409 (5th Cir. 2014). This latter opinion was subsequently withdrawn and a new opinion, with minor revisions, was substituted, 746 F.3d 167 (5th Cir. 2014).

Both these federal courts found that the tort of sexual molestation arose directly from the consensual agreement between Dolgencorp and the Mississippi Band of Choctaw Tribe. The alleged sexual molestation by Dale Townsend, an employee of Dolgencorp, was committed against John Doe, a 13-year-old Tribal member, while Doe was assigned to the Dollar General Store pursuant to the Tribe's Youth Opportunity Program. This case is unique in finding that an actionable tort may be the foreseeable result of a "consensual agreement" and thus is jurisdictionally sound as a predicate for tribal court jurisdiction.

The Fifth Circuit noted that the tort alleged in this case was to be construed narrowly. The 'victim' was not a third party stranger to the consensual agreement but a Tribal 'intern' placed at the Dollar General Store pursuant to the specific agreement between the Tribe and Dollar General. In addition, the tort took place on tribal land that was the subject of a commercial lease between Dollar General and the Tribe. A lease that specifically referenced "[e]xclusive venue and jurisdiction shall be in the Tribal Court of the Mississippi Band of Choctaw." *Id.* at 10.

8. Note that no actual trial shall be scheduled until the Tribe's Attorney General's office has responded to its position on the "exclusion" order, discussed *supra* at 4–5 (pp. 84–85 here), and this Court has ruled on any potential modification of said order.

The Fifth Circuit expressly rejected any interpretation of *Plains Commerce Bank* that would have narrowed the scope of the *Montana* proviso by requiring consensual agreements to also directly "impact tribal governance and internal relations." *Plains Commerce Bank*, 554 U.S. at 334–35. Judge Smith's dissent took sharp issue with this view and contended that *Plains Commerce Bank*, indeed, narrowed further the already narrow reach of the *Montana* proviso.

A petition for rehearing *en banc* was denied, 732 F.3d 409 (5th Cir. 2013). A petition for a writ of certiorari in the Supreme Court of the United States was filed on June 12, 2014. On October 6, 2014, the Court requested the views of the United States (CVSG or call for the views of the Solicitor General). On May 11, 2015, the Solicitor General filed its brief on behalf of the United States arguing that both the tribal court and lower federal court decisions were correct and that certiorari should be denied. On June 15, 2015, the Supreme Court granted certiorari. 2015 WL 2473345.

Another aspect of this case is quite troubling from both a procedural and practical point of view. Both the federal district court and the Fifth Circuit agreed that the Tribal court did not have subject matter jurisdiction over the tort action against Dale Townsend inasmuch as Mr. Townsend did not have any consensual agreement with the Tribe. Thus, the plaintiff, according to the Fifth Circuit, would be forced to litigate his single tort claim in two different forums. One action in Tribal Court against Dollar General and Dolgencorp, one action (presumably) in state court against Mr. Townsend. This is grossly inefficient, fiscally burdensome on the parties, and invites the potentially vexatious issues of *res judicata*, collateral estoppel, and full faith and credit.

Such a fractured result does not connect with the real world, but only adds needless complexification to the already needlessly complex world of tribal court jurisdiction. Surely, Mr. Townsend, as an employee of Dollar General, should be considered to have a consensual agreement with the Tribe for jurisdictional purposes. There ought not to be different jurisdictional rules for employers and employees in the *Montana* context. Or is this, heaven forbid, too simple, too commonsensical? We shall see.

Flandreau Santee Sioux Tribe v. Sioux Falls Construction

(Flandreau Santee Sioux Tribal Court of Appeals) (2011)

IN THE FLANDREAU SANTEE SIOUX TRIBAL COURT OF APPEALS
FLANDREAU, SOUTH DAKOTA

FLANDREAU SANTEE SIOUX TRIBE,	)	
Plaintiff/Appellee	)	
v.	)	
SIOUX FALLS CONSTRUCTION	)	
COMPANY,	)	
Defendant/Third Party Plaintiff/	)	
Appellee	)	MEMORANDUM OPINION
v.	)	AND ORDER
FOX DRYWALL AND PLASTERING,	)	
INC.; S AND S BUILDERS, INC.;	)	
G&D VIKING GLASS, INC.; H&R	)	
ROOFING OF SOUTH DAKOTA, INC.	)	
Third Party Defendants/Appellants	)	
	)	

Per Curiam (Chief Justice Patrick Lee, Associate Justices B.J. Jones and Frank Pommersheim)

I. Introduction

Sioux Falls Construction Company, defendant/third-party plaintiff/appellee, entered into a contract with the plaintiff/appellee, Flandreau Santee Sioux Tribe, to serve as the general contractor and build an addition to the Tribe's Royal River Casino and Motel. Sioux Falls Construction entered into subcontracts with the four named third-party defendants/appellants.[1] At the conclusion of the project in March 2008, the Flandreau Santee Sioux Tribe, plaintiff/appellee, brought suit against Sioux Falls Construction in the Flandreau Santee Sioux Tribal Court alleging breach of contract, breach of warranty, deceit, and bad faith.

Sioux Falls Construction subsequently filed third-party indemnity and contribution actions against all the subcontractors as third-party defendants in the lawsuit brought by the Tribe. The subcontractors—as a single entity—

---

1. The fifth subcontractor, Gene Pollinger Construction, Inc., is not a party to this appeal.

filed a motion to dismiss for lack of subject matter jurisdiction. That motion was denied by Judge Sherman Marshall and an intermediate appeal was filed with this Court.

This Court considered the appeal—including oral argument—and filed its opinion and order on October 2, 2009 reversing and remanding the case for a more complete evidentiary hearing. On remand, Judge Marshall held the evidentiary hearing, received more evidence, and again, in a thoughtful, well-written opinion, denied the motion to dismiss.

A timely request for (another) intermediate appeal was granted by this Court. Oral argument was heard on May 23, 2011. All three parties—the Tribe, Sioux Falls Construction, and the (four) subcontractors—appeared and participated in oral argument.

II. Issue

The sole issue before this court, as it was in the previous intermediate appeal, is whether the Tribal court has subject matter jurisdiction over the dispute between the major contractor, Sioux Falls Construction Company, and the various subcontractors.

III. Discussion

A. Background and Textual Analysis

As agreed by all the parties to this lawsuit, there is no Supreme Court (or lower federal or tribal court) decision directly on point and thus the case is one of first impression in both federal and tribal jurisprudence. While all the parties acknowledge that the 'pathmarking'[2] case of *Montana v. United States*, 450 U.S. 544 (1981), provides the relevant analytical framework for deciding the jurisdictional issue, it is necessary to fully understand the factual and contractual particulars before proceeding to matters of application.

As this Court noted in its previous opinion, it is necessary for the "trial court to develop a complete a record as possible relative to the identity of the parties, the legal classification of the relevant landscape, and the nature of the interaction between the pertinent parties." (Slip Opinion at 3). Based on the evidence presented before Judge Marshall at the remand hearing, a number of salient facts have emerged. These include the following: the building project took place solely on trust land located within the exterior boundaries of the Reservation. The owner of the project—the casino and motel—is the Flan-

---

2. Strate v. A-1 Contractors, 520 U.S. 438, 445 (1997).

dreau Santee Sioux Tribe. The major contractor, Sioux Falls Construction, is a non-Indian corporation organized under the state laws of South Dakota and located less than forty miles away from the reservation. All the subcontractors are non-Indian corporations organized under South Dakota state law and located, like Sioux Falls Construction, in close proximity to the Flandreau Santee Sioux Reservation.

As to the particular knowledge of the subcontractors, Judge Marshall found that:

> Representatives from each of the subcontractors were called to testify. Each representative testified that they signed the subcontract and agreed to its terms and conditions and argued to be bound by its provisions. *Each representative testified that they knew that the project was construction work on the casino and noted that they knew it was owned by the Tribe. Each representative knew that the work to be performed was on land owned by the Tribe.* (Slip Opinion at 2) (emphasis added).

Weekly project meetings were also held on the project site. In sum, this project did not simply involve several non-Indian corporations performing work for another non-Indian corporation. Such a narrow and formal reading of the facts blurs the more basic reality of a significant commercial (building) project occurring on *trust* land within the reservation and involving *three* interlocking parties, namely the Tribe, as owner of the project, Sioux Falls Construction, as the major contractor on the project, and the various subcontractors. Without all *three* (knowing) participants, this construction project for the addition to the Tribe's Royal River Casino and Motel simply does not occur.

This common sense approach to the facts is verified by the subcontracts[3] themselves. The subcontracts—which are not signed by the Tribe—nevertheless include several key provisions that expressly reflect the tri-partite nature of this construction undertaking. Judge Marshall specifically enumerated the following provisions in his opinion:

> Article 2.3 provides "[t]he Subcontract Documents include this Agreement [and] the Owner-Design-Builder agreement ..." Article 3.1 provides that the Subcontractors assume toward the Design-Builder all the same obligations, rights, duties, and remedies that the Design-Builder assumes toward the Owner. Article 3.2 required the Subcon-

---

3. All five subcontracts are identical form contracts used in the commercial construction business.

> tractors to initiate claims against the Owner for like claims by the Design-Builder. Article 8.3.1 provides "[u]pon acceptance of the Subcontract Work by the Owner … [and evidence of fulfillment of the subcontract] the Design-Builder shall incorporate the Subcontractor's application for final payment…." Article 11.4 requires that disputes between Design-Builder and Subcontractors that involve disputes between the Design-Builder and Owner shall be decided in the same forum. Article 12.1 provides "[t]his agreement shall be governed by the law in effect at the location of the project."
>
> (Appendix of Appellant's Brief at 3–4).

These provisions, individually and collectively, indicate the pervasive presence and reliance on the interlocking rights and responsibilities of all *three* parties. Article 2.3 incorporates the master agreement between the owner (Flandreau Santee Sioux Tribe) and the Design-Builder (Sioux Falls Construction), Article 3.1 describes the 'obligations, rights, duties, and remedies' of the subcontractors to the Design-Builder as *identical* to those of the Design-Builder owed to the Owner, Article 3.2 requires the Subcontractors to use their best efforts to hire local workers, *i.e.* tribal members,[4] Articles 5 and 10 permit the subcontractors to initiate claims against the Owner for like claims by the Design-Builder. Given that the Tribe may only be sued in Tribal court for activity occurring on Tribal trust land, any action by either the Design-Builder or subcontractor could only be brought in Tribal court.[5]

As argued by the appellants, there is the likelihood of a totally counterintuitive, if not bizarre, situation. That situation being while the subcontractors may *only* sue the Owner-Tribe in tribal court, the Owner-Tribe could not sue the subcontractors in tribal court,[6] or that while the Design-Builder, Sioux Falls Construction, could only sue the Owner-Tribe in tribal court, it could not sue the subcontractors in tribal court. This seems, to use Justice Scalia's phrase, 'nonsense upon stilts.'[7]

---

4. This is often a Tribal regulatory matter that is referred to by the acronym TERO (Tribal Employment Rights Ordinance).

5. *See, e.g.*, NELL JESSUP NEWTON, ED., COHEN'S HANDBOOK OF FEDERAL INDIAN LAW §§7.02–7.03 (2005 ed.).

6. Presumably, according to appellants, because there would be no consensual agreement between them and the Tribe adequate enough to satisfy the *Montana* test.

7. Sosa v. Alvarez-Machain, 542 U.S. 692, 743 (2004): "In Benthamite terms, creating a federal command (federal common law) out of 'international norms,' and then constructing a cause of action to enforce that command through the purely jurisdictional grant of the ATS, is nonsense upon stilts."

In essence, the appellant subcontractors assert that this *is* the quagmire of federal Indian law and it cannot be avoided by a 'forum selection clause' that confers subject matter jurisdiction that does not otherwise exist. While such an assertion is the most basic of black letter truisms,[8] it is a truism that is not at issue in this case.

This case is not about forum selection clauses, but whether there are sufficient "consensual relationships with the tribe or its members, through commercial dealings, contracts, leases or other arrangements"[9] to support tribal court (adjudicatory) jurisdiction. In this analytical rubric, a forum selection clause is not an assertion of *law*, but a *fact*—indeed only one of many—that is evidence of "consensual relationships" established through "commercial leasing ... or other arrangements."

B. *Montana v. United States:*[10] Background and Application

It is absolutely dead on, that in matters of tribal court jurisdiction (especially involving non-Indians) the application of the now classic *Montana* proviso is the most significant analytical necessity required by the Supreme Court. The proviso reads:

> To be sure, Indian tribes retain inherent sovereign power to exercise some forms of civil jurisdiction over non-Indians on their reservations, even on non-Indian fee lands. A tribe may regulate, through taxation, licensing, or other means, the activities of nonmembers who enter consensual relationships with the tribe or its members, through commercial dealing, contracts, leases, or other arrangements. *Williams v. Lee, supra*, at 223; *Morris v. Hitchcock*, 194 U.S. 384; *Buster v. Wright*, 135 F. 947, 950 (CAS); *see Washington v. Confederated Tribes of Colville Indian Reservation*, 447 U.S. 134, 152–54. A tribe may also retain inherent power to exercise civil authority over the conduct of non-Indians on fee lands within its reservation when that conduct threatens or has some direct effect on the political integrity, the economic se-

8. *See, e.g.*, Ark. Blue Cross & Blue Shield v. Little Rock Cardiology Clinic, 551 F.3d 812, 816 (8th Cir. 2009) ("It is a verity that federal courts are courts of limited jurisdiction. Parties many not enlarge that jurisdiction by waiver or consent."); Seymour v. Colville Confederated Tribes, 3 CTCR 40, 6 CCAR 5, ¶39 (Colville Confederated Tribal Court 2001) ("As a general rule, consent to jurisdiction cannot defeat lack of subject matter jurisdiction.").

9. Montana v. United States, 450 U.S. 545, 565 (1981).

10. 450 U.S. 545 (1981).

> curity, or the health or welfare of the tribe. See *Fisher v. District Court*, 424 U.S. 382, 386; *Williams v. Lee, supra*, at 220; *Montana Catholic Missions v. Missoula County*, 200 U.S. 118, 128–129; *Thomas v. Gay*, 169 U.S. 264, 273). *Montana*, 450 U.S. at 565–66.

This axiom of federal Indian law was specifically noted by this Court in our earlier decision in this case:

> This [Montana] test has remained at the core of jurisdictional analysis in Indian law. Twenty-five years of subsequent Supreme Court adjudication in this area has, unfortunately, proved rather unilluminating. Every significant case—*Strait v. A-1 Contractors*, 520 U.S. 438 (1997); *Nevada v. Hicks*, 538 U.S. 353 (2001); *Atkinson Trading Co. v. Shirley*, 532 U.S. 645 (2001); and most recently *Plains Commerce Bank v. Long Family Land and Cattle Company, Inc.*, 128 S.Ct. 2709 (2008)—appears to turn on the *unique* mix in each case of the nature of the parties—*i.e.*, whether Indian or non-Indian, the nature of the land involved, whether on trust or non-trust land, and the nature of contact between the parties involved. No reliable rule has emerged from the intense, case specific jurisprudence of the Supreme Court. This Court nevertheless distills from relevant precedent an analytical rubric that requires the trial court to develop a complete record as possible relative to the identity of the parties, the legal classification of the relevant landscape, and the nature of interaction between the pertinent parties. (Slip Opinion at 3).

Before proceeding to the actual analysis, a broad review and restatement of *Montana* is particularly instructive and helpful in the instant case. *Montana* is essentially a tribal regulatory case in which the Supreme Court held that the Crow Tribe had complete regulatory authority over *all* individuals—Indians and non-Indians—in the context of hunting or fishing on *trust* land within the reservation. Specifically, the Court stated:

> The Court of Appeals held that the Tribe may prohibit nonmembers from hunting or fishing on land belonging to the Tribe or held by the United States in trust for the Tribe, 605 F.2d, at 1165–66, and with this holding we can readily agree. We also agree with the Court of Appeals that if the Tribe permits non-members to fish or hunt, it may condition them entirely by charging a fee or establishing bag and release limits. *Montana*, 450 U.S. at 557.

The language clearly stands for the proposition that tribes have the *regulatory* authority to determine the terms and conditions on which non-members may enter onto tribal lands to engage in various activities. This observation is relevant to the case at bar in that it clearly authorizes the Flandreau Santee Sioux Tribe to set the terms and conditions for contractors and subcontractors who perform commercial (construction) work for the Tribe on trust land within the Reservation.

Although it appears from the record in this case that the Tribe has enacted no formal regulations in the commercial (construction) arena, all the evidence presented, including the express position asserted by the Tribe in its brief,[11] is that the Tribe expected all legal matters relative to this three way commercial endeavor to be settled in Tribal court. Such a position is commonsensical as a matter of law and policy relative to fairness, efficiency, and the orderly administration of justice. Anything to the contrary would seem so extraordinary and confounding as to require an express regulation or agreement that the Tribe disclaimed jurisdiction.

In fact, the subcontracts themselves support the Tribe's position. For example, the subcontracts directly incorporate and reference the Owner (Tribe)—Designer/Builder (Sioux Falls Construction) agreement, Article 2.3; directly reference subcontractor liability to the Owner (Tribe) "for all loss, cost, and expense attributable to any acts of commission or omission of the subcontractors," Article 3.29; and most significantly, provide that the subcontractors shall suspend or terminate work immediately upon the Owner's (Tribe's) instruction, Articles 10.3 and 10.4. These last provisions are most significant in that they expressly recognize the ability of the Owner/Tribe to *regulate* the subcontractors and order them to immediately suspend or terminate work. This is case specific Tribal regulatory authority of the highest order.

To put it another way, it is fair to say that *Montana* creates a rule in favor of tribal jurisdiction in all matters that occur on trust land and directly involve the Tribe and a (rebuttable) presumption that disfavors tribal jurisdiction over matters occurring on non-trust land and in which the Tribe is not directly involved. *See, e.g., Strate v. A-1 Contractors*, 520 U.S. 438 (1997), *Nevada v. Hicks*, 533 U.S. 353 (2001), and *Atkinson Trading Company v. Shirley*, 532 U.S. 645 (2001), and most recently *Plains Commerce Bank v. Long Family land and Cattle Company, Inc.*, 554 U.S. 316 (2008). While all of these cases held against tribal jurisdiction, none of them occurred on tribal trust land (except *Nevada v. Hicks*) and none of them directly involved the tribe as a party.

11. Flandreau Santee Sioux Tribe's Brief at 8–19.

Strate involved a tort action that took place on a state highway running through the Fort Berthold Reservation in which the Tribe was a 'stranger' to the accident between the plaintiff and defendant non-Indians.[12] This is not the case at bar. *Hicks* expanded the fee land analysis of *Montana* to include trust, indeed all, land within the reservation,[13] but expressly noted that its holding was "limited to the question of tribal-court jurisdiction over state officers enforcing states laws."[14] This is not the case at bar. *Atkinson* involved a Navajo Tribe occupancy tax applied to non-Indians staying in a non-Indian owned motel located on fee land within the Reservation.[15] This is not the case at bar. *Plains Commerce Bank* involved the sale of fee land within the reservation between two non-Indians.[16] This is not the case at bar. Tribal jurisdictional interest is at its highest when an event takes place on trust land and directly involves the Tribe. This is the core of *Montana* and this *is* the case at bar.

While not cited by any of the parties, the most relevant decision to the case at bar is *Williams v. Lee*, 358 U.S. 217 (1959) which expressly held that in a dispute between a non-Indian store owner and a Navajo customer, state court jurisdiction was inappropriate. This is very analogous to the case at bar as the appellant subcontractors assert that state court is the appropriate forum for a commercial building dispute that occurred on Tribal trust land in which the Tribe is the owner of the project. While it is true that a narrow *part* of the particular dispute in the instant case involves a non-Indian design/builder and its non-Indian subcontractors, the lawsuit as a whole involves the Flandreau Santee Sioux Tribe as plaintiff and Sioux Falls Construction as a defendant and the subcontractors as third-party defendants.

Williams v. Lee held that state jurisdiction was inappropriate when an Indian was a defendant even if the dispute did not take place on trust land. As discussed *supra* pp. 3–4 (pp. 93–95 here), the instant case has even more facts that point to tribal jurisdiction. These elements taken as whole fully meet the *Williams* test that:

> There can be no doubt that to allow the exercise of state jurisdiction here would undermine the authority of tribal courts over Reservation affairs and hence would infringe on the right of Indians to govern

12. *Strate*, 520 U.S. at 457.

13. *Hicks*, 533 U.S. at 360.

14. *Id.* at 358 n.2 ("We leave open the question of tribal-court jurisdiction over nonmember defendants in general.").

15. *Atkinson*, 532 U.S. at 648–49.

16. *Plains Commerce Bank*, 554 U.S. at 320.

> themselves. It is immaterial that respondent is not an Indian. *Williams*, 358 U.S. at 223.

As a result, this case likely should be disposed of on non-*Montana* grounds. Given the vagaries of modern Indian law involving non-Indians, this, unfortunately, seems quite unlikely.

This more complete consideration of *Montana* and *Williams v. Lee* serves to inform and guide a more reliable application of the crucial test articulated in the well-known *Montana* proviso quoted *supra* p. 6 (p. 112 here). Again:

> To be sure, Indian tribes retain inherent sovereign power to exercise some forms of civil jurisdiction over non-Indians on their reservations, even on non-Indian fee lands. A tribe may regulate, through taxation, licensing, or other means, the activities of nonmembers who enter consensual relationships with the tribe or its members, through commercial dealing, contracts, leases, or other arrangements. *Williams v. Lee*, *supra*, at 223; *Morris v. Hitchcock*, 194 U.S. 384; *Buster v. Wright*, 135 F. 947, 950 (CA8); see *Washington v. Confederated Tribes of Colville Indian Reservation*, 447 U.S. 134, 152–54. A tribe may also retain inherent power to exercise civil authority over the conduct of non-Indians on fee lands within its reservation when that conduct threatens or has some direct effect on the political integrity, the economic security, or the health or welfare of the tribe. See *Fisher v. District Court*, 424 U.S. 382, 386; *Williams v. Lee*, *supra*, at 220; *Montana Catholic Missions v. Missoula County*, 200 U.S. 118, 128–29; *Thomas v. Gay*, 169 U.S. 264, 273).

The key factors in the application of *Montana* in this case, as noted previously, include the following:

1) That the construction project was performed on Tribal trust land located within the exterior boundaries of the reservation;

2) That the construction project directly involved the Tribe as owner of the project;

3) That the subcontracts expressly recognize the (regulatory) authority of the Owner/Tribe to order the subcontractors to immediately suspend or terminate work on this construction project;

4) That the subcontracts directly reference and incorporate the Owner/Tribe-Design Builder/Sioux Falls Construction Agreement;

5) That both the Design-Builder, Sioux Falls Construction, and the subcontractors are named defendants (or third-party defendants) in the Tribe's lawsuit involving work performed for the Tribe on Tribal trust land;

6) That all defendants including the third-party defendant subcontractors knew they were performing work for the Tribe on the Tribe's trust land on the Reservation;

7) That the subcontracts expressly identify the direct liability of the subcontractors to the Owner/Tribe;

8) That all the subcontractors manifested (written) consent and willingness for disputes to be resolved in a single forum; and

9) That no other forum except the Tribal court has authority over *all* the disputes involved in this lawsuit.

IV. Conclusion

For all of the above-stated reasons, the decision of the trial court is affirmed and it is remanded for an immediate trial on the merits.[17]

IT IS SO ORDERED.

Dated this 8th day of August, 2011.

FOR THE COURT:

____

Frank Pommersheim, Associate Justice

Notes on *Flandreau Santee Sioux Tribe v. Sioux Falls Construction* (2011)

This case—still ongoing—has had a most curious journey after the initial decision by the Flandreau Santee Sioux Tribal Court of Appeals. Not unexpectedly, pursuant to the 'exhaustion' doctrine, the subcontractors appealed to federal court seeking declaratory and injunctive relief.

The federal court not only ruled against the subcontractors on the merits of their challenge to tribal court jurisdiction, but also denied their bid for injunctive

17. In the previous appeal, the parties were asked to consider the possible relevance of *Gustafson v. Granite Re, Inc.*, No. 07-004 (Turtle Mountain Ct. 2007) to these proceedings. A close reading indicates that this case is only of marginal utility. The Turtle Mountain Court of Appeals said yes to Tribal court jurisdiction over Granite Re, a knowing bonder of the Tribe, but no to Tribal court jurisdiction over Goldleaf Financial, an unknowing guarantor of the bonder, who knew nothing of the Indian character of the building project. The subcontractors in the instant case are more deeply implicated in the Tribe's construction project. They are direct participants, knowingly engaged in brick and mortar activities performed for the Tribe on Tribal trust land.

relief to prohibit the tribal court from proceeding with a disposition on the merits. *Fox Drywall & Plastering, Inc. v. Sioux Falls Construction Co.*, 2012 WL 1457183. Injunctive relief, a staple of 'exhaustion' practice, is routinely pursued and granted. It is a basic necessity. Without it, there would be no bar to the tribal court proceeding to try the case on the merits. Obviously, the non-Indian parties do not want to be litigating on two different fronts—in tribal court on the merits and in federal court on subject matter jurisdiction.

Yet the granting of injunctive relief—as this case demonstrates—ought not to be assumed. Judge Schreier applied the standard four part test from the *Dataphase Sys., Inc. v. C.L. Systems, Inc.*, 640 F.2d 109 (8th Cir. 1981). The moving party must make the familiar four-part showing before the court issues a preliminary injunction: (1) the threat of irreparable harm to the movant, (2) the balance between the harm and the inquiry that granting the injunction will inflict on the other parties, (3) the probability the movant will succeed on the merits, and (4) the public interest.

The extensive opinion of Judge Schreier found that the subcontractors had "not shown that they have a fair chance of prevailing on the merits." *Id.* at 10. This was so as this dispute was, at heart, a routine construction contract dispute involving the Tribe, the primary contractor, and the subcontractors to perform work for the Tribe on trust land. This was a quintessential, consensual agreement pursuant to *Montana.* Judge Schreier also found that the subcontractor would not likely suffer irreparable harm; the balancing of harms did not favor the subcontractor; and the public interest would not be advanced by an injunctive ruling. In sum, the subcontractors did *not* satisfy any of the four elements relevant to obtaining preliminary relief and its motion for same was denied. Judge Schreier repeatedly cited the opinion of the Flandreau Santee Sioux Tribal Court of Appeals with approval. *Id.* at 10–12. Judge Schreier's opinion is an apt and powerful example of the importance of well-crafted and analytically persuasive tribal court opinions.

The case was then sent back to Tribal court for a presumed resolution on the merits. Yet the case took another bizarre twist. Instead of proceeding to the jury trial requested by both the Tribe and Sioux Falls Construction, the case headed into the netherworld of motions for the appointment of referees and a trial to the court instead of a jury trial. The resulting confusion and misdirection eventually came back to the Flandreau Santee Sioux Tribal Court of Appeals for clarification and resolution.

This resulted in another lengthy opinion, which returned the case to its jury trial status and clarified the role of the referee (not referees) in this process. The Court further expressed its concern over the seeming interminable delay, five years of litigation without any adjudication on the merits, even describing the case as the Reservation answer to Charles Dickens' novel *Bleak House*. The full text of this opinion may be found at http://libguides.law.usd.edu/content.php ?pid=482397.

In sum, the record of federal 'review' for these cases looks like this.

1. *Estate of Tasunke Witko (aka Crazy Horse) v. Heileman Brewing*

   The decision of the Rosebud Sioux Supreme Court was reversed by the federal district court and the federal district court's decision was (unanimously) affirmed by the Eighth Circuit Court of Appeals, 133 F.3d 1087 (8th Cir. 1998).

2. *Plains Commerce Bank v. Long Family Land and Cattle Co.*

   The decision of the Cheyenne Rivers Sioux Tribal Court of Appeals was upheld by the federal district court, 440 F. Supp. 2d 1070 (D.S.D. 2006), and the federal district court decision was (unanimously) affirmed by the Eighth Circuit Court of Appeals, 491 F.3d 878 (8th Cir. 2007). This decision was reversed by the Supreme Court in a 5–4 vote, 554 U.S. 316 (2008).

3. *Doe v. Dollar General Corp.*

   The decision of the Mississippi Band of Choctaw Supreme Court was upheld by the federal district court, 846 F. Supp. 2d 646 (SD Miss. 2008), and the federal district court decision was affirmed by the Fifth Circuit Court of Appeals in a 2–1 decision, 746 F.3d 167 (5th Cir. 2014). A writ of certiorari has been granted by the Supreme Court. 2015 WL 2473345.

4. *Flandreau Santee Sioux Tribe v. Sioux Falls Construction, Inc.*

   The decision of the Flandreau Santee Sioux Tribal Court of Appeals was upheld by the federal district court, *Fox Drywall & Plastering, Inc. v. Sioux Falls Const. Co.*, 2012 WL 1457183. No further federal review was sought. The case was remanded to the Flandreau Santee Sioux Tribal Court of Appeals for a disposition on the merits. The Tribal trial court decision on the merits is still pending.

A cautious inference emerges. The lower federal courts are more likely to fully engage the grist of facts and what tribal courts actually do and say than the Supreme Court. The Supreme Court prefers to engage its own preconceptions about tribal courts and its own predilections regarding the (judicial) fate of non-Indians. Of course, this sample of cases is not statistically significant, but that's not the point. The point has to do with respect and engagement, not pointless abstraction and the boundless application of unacknowledged federal common law.

Other Federal Court Cases Involving Montana *Analysis*

As the above cases indicate, there has been some (though admittedly limited) lower federal court success in satisfying the *Montana* proviso and upholding tribal court jurisdiction over non-Indians. This record of limited success is replicated elsewhere. *See, e.g., Water Wheel Camp Recreation Area, Inc.*, 642 F.3d 802 (9th Cir. 2011), upholding tribal court jurisdiction over an eviction action brought against a non-Indian lessee of tribal land. The circuit court's opinion found tribal court jurisdiction appropriate, while eschewing the need for any *Montana* analysis:

> In this instance, where the non-Indian activity in question occurred on tribal land, the activity interfered directly with the tribe's inherent power to exclude and manage its own lands, and there are no competing state interests at play, the tribe's status as landowner is enough to support regulatory jurisdiction without considering *Montana*. Finding otherwise would contradict supreme court precedent establishing that land ownership may sometimes be dispositive and would improperly limit tribal sovereignty without clear direction from Congress.
> *Id.* at 814.

Other federal cases finding tribal court jurisdiction appropriate include: *Amerind Risk Management Corp. v. Malaterre*, 585 F. Supp. 2d 1121 (D.N.D. 2008), upholding tribal court jurisdiction over a tort action against a non-member insurance company for claims arising directly from insurance contract with the defendant; *Smith v. Salish Kootenai College*, 434 F.3d 1107 (9th Cir. 2006), upholding tribal court jurisdiction based on consent in a non-commercial context. There are, of course, many more federal cases to the contrary; holding that tribal courts, do not have jurisdiction over non-Indians or non-members. See the excellent compilation and discussion in Sarah Krakoff, *Tribal Civil Jurisdiction over Nonmembers: a Practical Guide for Judges*, 81 Colo. L. Rev. 1189 (2010).

Given the fact that the range of permutations as to parties, place, and activity remains exceptionally large, cases dealing with the issue of tribal court jurisdiction over non-Indians will continue to abound. This state of affairs is yet more evidence of the ongoing necessity to produce persuasive and well-crafted tribal court opinions. Evolving tribal court jurisprudence must continue to rise to meet these challenges.

Part II

From the People to Tribal Court and Back to the People and the Community

A. Background: Individual Civil Rights and Rights of Political Participation

Tribal courts have become the premier local forum for the recognition and resolution of individual civil and political rights on the reservation. This is the essential legacy of *Santa Clara Pueblo v. Martinez*, 436 U.S. 49 (1978). Prior to *Santa Clara Pueblo*, federal courts were the preferred forum for the resolution of individual civil and political rights in Indian country pursuant to the Indian Civil Rights Act of 1968.[1]

---

1. 25 U.S.C. § 1301-03. These rights are enumerated at 25 U.S.C. §§ 1302(a)–(f):

(a) In general

No Indian tribe in exercising powers of self-government shall—

(1) make or enforce any law prohibiting the free exercise of religion, or abridging the freedom of speech, or of the press, or the right of the people peaceably to assemble and to petition for a redress of grievances;

(2) violate the right of the people to be secure in their persons, houses, papers, and effects against unreasonable search and seizures, nor issue warrants, but upon probably cause, supported by oath or affirmation, and particularly describing the place to be searched and the person or thing to be seized;

(3) subject any person for the same offense to be twice put in jeopardy;

(4) compel any person in any criminal case to be a witness against himself;

(5) take any private property for a public use without just compensation;

Santa Clara Pueblo slammed the federal courthouse door shut. It ruled that there was no implied federal cause of action under the ICRA. Federal courts were

---

(6) deny to any person in a criminal proceeding the right to a speedy and public trial, to be informed of the nature and cause of the accusation, to be confronted with the witnesses against him, to have compulsory process for obtaining witnesses in his favor, and at his own expense to have the assistance of counsel for his defense (except as provided in subsection (b));
(7) (A) require excessive bail, impose excessive fines, or inflict cruel and unusual punishment;
(B) except as provided in subparagraph (C), impose for conviction of any 1 offense any penalty or punishment greater than imprisonment for a term of 1 year or a fine of $5,000, or both;
(C) subject to subsection (b), impose for conviction of any 1 offense any penalty or punishment greater than imprisonment for a term of 3 years or a fine of $15,000, or both; or
(D) impose on a person in a criminal proceeding a total penalty or punishment greater than imprisonment for a term of 9 years;
(8) deny to any person within its jurisdiction the equal protection of its law or deprive any person of liberty or property without due process of law;
(9) pass any bill of attainder or ex post facto law; or
(10) deny to any person accused of an offense punishable by imprisonment the right, upon request, to a trial by jury of not less than six persons.

(b) Offenses subject to greater than 1-year imprisonment or a fine greater than $5,000
No tribal court may subject a defendant to a term of imprisonment greater than 1 year but not to exceed 3 years for any 1 offense, or a fine greater than $5,000 but not to exceed $15,000, or both, if the defendant is a person accused of a criminal offense who—
(1) has been previously convicted of the same or a comparable offense by any jurisdiction in the United States; or
(2) is being prosecuted for an offense comparable to an offense that would be punishable by more than 1 year of imprisonment if prosecuted by the United States or any of the States.

(c) Rights of defendants
In a criminal proceeding in which an Indian tribe, in exercising powers of self-government, imposes a total term of imprisonment of more than 1 year on a defendant, the Indian tribe shall—
(1) provide to the defendant the right to effective assistance of counsel at least equal to that guaranteed by the United States Constitution; and
(2) at the expense of the tribal government, provide an indigent defendant the assistance of a defense attorney licensed to practice law by any jurisdiction in the United States that applies appropriate professional licensing standards and effectively ensures the competence and professional responsibility of its licensed attorneys:
(3) require that the judge presiding over the criminal proceeding—
(A) has sufficient legal training to preside over criminal proceedings; and

only available for the limited (federal) habeas corpus relief set out at 25 U.S.C. § 1303.[2] All other basic political and civil rights litigation against tribal governments was directed back to tribal courts, along with a basic and limited waiver of tribal sovereign immunity. The Court specifically noted: "Tribal forums are available to vindicate rights created by the ICRA, and § 1302 has the substantial and intended effect of changing the law which these forums are obliged to apply."[3]

All of a sudden tribal courts became the sole forum in which to litigate basic civil and political rights cases. This shift in the importance from being largely ignored to being impossible to ignore was seismic. As Bob Dylan noted, "Tie yourself to a tree with roots, you ain't going nowhere."[4] *Santa Clara*

(B) is licensed to practice law by any jurisdiction in the United States;

(4) prior to charging the defendant, make publicly available the criminal laws (including regulations and interpretative documents), rules of evidence, and rules of criminal procedure (including rules governing the recusal of judges in appropriate circumstances) of the tribal government; and

(5) maintain a record of the criminal proceeding, including an audio or other recording of the trial proceeding.

(d) Sentences

In the case of a defendant sentenced in accordance with subsections (b) and (c), a tribal court may require the defendant—

(1) to serve the sentence—

(A) in a tribal correctional center that has been approved by the Bureau of Indian Affairs for long-term incarceration, in accordance with guidelines to be developed by the Bureau of Indian Affairs (in consultation with Indian tribes) not later than 180 days after July 29, 2010;

(B) in the nearest appropriate Federal facility, at the expense of the United States pursuant to the Bureau of Prisons tribal prisoner pilot program described in section 304(c) of the Tribal Law and Order Act of 2010);

(C) in a State or local government-approved detention or correctional center pursuant to an agreement between the Indian tribe and the State or local government; or

(D) in an alternative form of punishment, as determined by the tribal court judge pursuant to tribal law.

(e) Definition of offense

In this section, the term "offense" means a violation of a criminal law.

(f) Effect of section

Nothing in this section affects the obligation of the United States, or any State government that has been delegated authority by the United States, to investigate and prosecute any criminal violation in Indian country.

2. Habeas relief would therefore not be available in most cases involving individual civil and political rights because no detention or loss of liberty is involved.

3. *Santa Clara Pueblo*, 436 U.S. at 65.

4. Bob Dylan, "You Ain't Going Nowhere," *The Basement Tapes* (Columbia Records, 2014).

Pueblo upped the ante and advanced the status of tribal courts. It gave tribal courts *Marbury v. Madison*, 5 U.S. 137 (1803), like status as the sole arbiter of the meaning and content of the ICRA's substantive guarantees, as well as any analogous guarantees recognized in Tribal constitutions, statutes, or traditional law.

Unlike the exhaustion regime under *National Farmers Union*, there is no way to get into federal court to review or to challenge tribal court decisions in the civil and political rights arena. Tribal court appellate decisions are final and unreviewable in federal court. This is an exceptionally powerful recognition of tribal sovereignty. For this very reason, there is a concomitant burden on tribal courts to insure that such rights have meaningful substantive content and reliable procedural contours. Tribal courts must also be sensitive to not go too far by authorizing relief that impairs the ability of tribes to function and carry out the responsibilities of governance.

This regime requires a delicate balance. It provides a legal platform for both Indians and non-Indians[5] to challenge the (potential) excesses of tribal government. Yet the ICRA creates no express remedy against tribal government. Most tribal courts have understood permissible relief to include declaratory and injunctive relief, but *not* monetary damages. Monetary damages against the tribe are available only if they are expressly authorized by tribal statute, such as a tribal tort claims act.

Increasingly, there is also a parallel set of civil rights guarantees that are to be found within tribal constitutions and ordinances. In such instances, tribal courts must often decide whether such guarantees are identical or merely similar (or even dissimilar) to those available directly through the ICRA. Such issues often surface in the context of cases of first impression brought in tribal court.

This is especially true in the context of what remedies are available. For example, should the right to counsel guarantee in the Rosebud Sioux Tribal Constitution also include the ineffective assistance of counsel standard as set out in the *Strickland v. Washington*, 466 U.S. 668 (1984) case? Should the exclusionary rule apply in tribal search and seizure cases? Should the same remedies be available under the ICRA? Does *Miranda*, 384 U.S. 436 (1966), apply in the tribal court context? The Rosebud Sioux Supreme Court case of *Rosebud Sioux Tribe v. Luxon*[6] provides the answers to some of these questions from a particular Tribe's constitutional and the ICRA perspective.

---

5. Despite the title of the statute, the '*Indian* Civil Rights Act of 1968,' its guarantees pertain to all 'persons.' 25 U.S.C. § 1301.

6. *Infra* pp. 203–11.

In the political rights arena of voting, running for office, referendum, and political reapportionment, tribal appellate courts often lean heavily on the due process and equal protection guarantees of the ICRA and similar guarantees in tribal constitutions. In many of these cases, the question is not about the existence of the right (*e.g.*, voting, referendum, redistricting), but its implementation within due process procedural guarantees and the non-discriminatory parameters of equal protection. Such diverse cases as *Snowden v. Saginaw Chippewa Tribe*[7] involving disenrollment and *Woods v. Cheyenne River Sioux Tribal Council*[8] involving reapportionment vividly illustrate these challenges.

The opinions in the following cases are therefore the final word for that particular tribe. They did not go to federal court. The only questions that remained were those of implementation. Would the tribe make the necessary changes? Would it abide by the decision? In each of these cases, the answer was yes. These post-decision actions necessarily advanced the legitimacy of tribal courts and helped to advance political stability and to secure the integrity of certain individual rights. The notes after each opinion track the issues of change and implementation. The notes also provide additional discussion of similar cases decided by other tribal courts.

Read on.

---

7. *Infra* pp. 110–20.
8. *Infra* pp. 176–85.

B. The Cases

Enrollment and Disenrollment

Snowden v. Saginaw Chippewa Tribe

(Saginaw Chippewa Tribal Court of Appeals) (2005)

IN THE APPELLATE COURT
OF THE
SAGINAW CHIPPEWA INDIAN TRIBE OF MICHIGAN

William A. Snowden &	)	Case No: 04-CA-1017
Robert Hinmon, *et al.*	)	
	)	
Plaintiffs-Appellants,	)	MEMORANDUM OPINION
v.	)	AND ORDER
Saginaw Chippewa Indian	)	
Tribe of Michigan,	)	
Defendant-Appellee.	)	

Appearances: Riyaz A. Kanji for the Plaintiffs-Appellants, and
C. Bryant Rogers for the Defendant-Appellee

Before: Carey N. Vicenti, Chief Justice; Michael Petoskey, Associate Justice; and Frank Pommersheim, Associate Justice

By Frank Pommersheim, Associate Justice, for a unanimous Court.

This case came before this Court upon a Notice of Appeal tendered by William Snowden and Robert Hinmon, *et al.* from a decision entered by the Community (Trial) Court. This Court accepted the appeal and set the matter for oral argument. Having fully considered the arguments, briefs, and the record below, this Court now enters a modified judgment in favor of the Plaintiffs-Appellants, William Snowden and Robert Hinmon, *et al.*

I. Introduction and Background

For the past decade, if not longer, the Saginaw Chippewa Indian Tribe has been embroiled in extensive political and legal conflict over issues of membership. While the cause of these disputes is deeply rooted in various *federal*[1] moves

1. These include, for example, federal certification at various times of potentially underinclusive base rolls for membership, as well as limiting the opportunity for enrollment

relative to membership, it has been left to the Tribe to resolve these often painful issues. This case is one example. It focuses on the issue of disenrollment.[2]

The consolidated cases in this appeal grow out of an attempt by the Tribe to disenroll two deceased Tribal members, Malinda Hinmon and Mary Lee (Tipkey) Snowden and their descendants. The descendants include two members of a prior Tribal Council, as well as a former Chief Judge of the Tribal Court.

On August 9, 2001, final administrative decisions were made under the authority of the Peters Tribal Council stripping Malinda Hinmon and Mary Lee (Tipkey) Snowden (who were both deceased by that time) of their membership. These proceedings did *not* provide any of the meaningful elements of due process. As a result, the descendants of Ms. Hinmon and Ms. Snowden sought judicial review of these disenrollment decisions in Tribal Court.

When a new Tribal Council, generally referred to as the Kaghegab Tribal Council, was elected, it pursued a different approach to the issue of disenrollment. It established a new Office of Administrative Hearings (OAH) and authorized the Office, *inter alia*, to rehear cases in which disenrollment decisions had been previously made. On June 20, 2003, the Kaghebab Council and the Hinmon and Snowden descendants filed with the Tribal Court joint motions asking the Community Court to vacate the adverse actions taken against Malinda Hinmon and Mary Lee (Tipkey) Snowden and to remand the cases to the OAH for new hearings. However, the parties also asked the Tribal Court to first resolve the predicate question of the extent of the Tribal Council's authority to initiate disenrollment proceedings within the limits of the Tribal Constitution.

---

by requiring the inclusion of the limited eighteen month window for descendary enrollment set out in the 1986 Saginaw Chippewa Tribal Constitution. *See, e.g.*, Saginaw Chippewa Tribe Constitution at Art. III Sec. 1(c).

2. The complementary issue in the area of membership is that of enrollment. *See, e.g.*, *Bryant v. Saginaw Chippewa Tribal Clerk*, Case No. 04-CA-1016 (decision pending). The case at bar and the *Bryant* case are complementary, but they are not identical or symmetrical. Both cases are about the cultural and legal aspects of membership and belonging, but they are about different aspects of that process and the application of different standards. The *Bryant* case is about enrollment. This case is about disenrollment. The *Bryant* case involves review of the trial court's *individualized* determination of the enrollment eligibility of twenty-six named plaintiffs. The case at bar involves *no* review of any determination whether to disenroll a particular individual, but rather is an appeal requesting that this Court determine the *Tribal* constitutional standard as to the *implied substantive* grounds, if any, for possible disenrollment. Both cases—one in the concrete, one more generally—involve Tribal constitutional adjudication and interpretation.

Both parties agreed that resolution of the Tribal constitutional question was pivotal to the entire issue of disenrollment. On June 20, 2003, the Community Court entered an order vacating the disenrollment decisions against Malinda Hinmon and Mary Lee (Tipkey) Snowden and remanded these cases for new administrative hearings but retained jurisdiction to first rule on the scope of the Tribal Council's constitutional authority to disenroll.

After a hearing in the Community Court, Judge Patrick Shannon issued a short four page decision on December 10, 2003 that ruled in favor of the Tribal Council.[3] The decision recognized extensive Tribal Council constitutional power to disenroll. This appeal followed. Oral argument was heard before this Court on May 15, 2004.

II. Issue

This appeal raises a single issue, namely, whether the Tribal Council's power to disenroll currently enrolled members is limited to the narrow grounds *expressly* identified in the Tribal Constitution, and if not, what are the Tribal constitutional boundaries in establishing (substantive) grounds for disenrollment.

III. Discussion

This case is not just about the meaning of the Saginaw Chippewa Tribal Constitution of 1986, but it is also a story about a People and a Tribe enmeshed in the coils of an unknowing and meddlesome Bureau of Indian Affairs and Federal Government. This destabilizing federal force is amply demonstrated in the history leading up to the adoption of the first Saginaw Chippewa Tribal Constitution in 1937. The Saginaw Chippewa Tribe of Michigan came into specific *legal* existence as a result of the Indian Reorganization Act (IRA) of 1934 and the adoption of the first Tribal Constitution in 1937. As is well known, the thrust of the IRA was to encourage tribes to formally adopt the Act through a tribal referendum[4] and then adopt a constitution as provided by Sec. 16 of the Act,[5] as well as a business charter, as provided in Sec. 17 of the Act.[6]

Many local Tribal leaders and people were interested in the possibilities offered by the IRA. In fact, even before the referendum on the IRA itself, a Busi-

---

3. The Community Court's decision on the meaning of the Constitution is reviewed *de novo* by this Court. This is a core ingredient of appellate review. The Community Court's opinion in this case rests mostly on conclusionary observations without detailed analysis.

4. 25 U.S.C. §478.

5. 25 U.S.C. §476.

6. 25 U.S.C. §477.

ness Committee headed by Elijah Elk was established to meet with various Tribal communities and to begin drafting a Tribal constitution. The work of this committee resulted in a (draft) constitution that was sent to Secretary of Interior Harold Ickes on Nov. 27, 1934 for his approval.[7]

The draft constitution is noteworthy in several respects that are directly pertinent to this litigation. The proposed constitution's preamble began, "We, the members of the Saginaw, Swan Creek, and Black River Bands of Chippewa Indians."[8] The proposed Tribal Council recognized four districts—three of which were outside the boundaries of the Isabella Reservation—three representatives from Mt. Pleasant (*i.e.* Isabella Reservation), three from Bay City, one from Caro, and three from Hubbard Lake.[9]

Action on this proposed Constitution was slowed as a result of BIA Commissioner John Collier's direction to Elijah Elk that no action could be taken until the formal referendum to accept the IRA took place.[10] As a result, energy shifted away from the draft constitution toward developing a list of eligible voters to vote in the IRA referendum. The list that was compiled by Tribal individuals and BIA special agent George Blakeslee contained the names of many Tribal people living outside the boundaries of the Isabella Reservation. The referendum was held on June 17, 1935 and included at least two off reservation voting places.[11] The referendum passed.

With the successful referendum accomplished, attention returned to the Constitution itself. The Tribe's desire to include all of its communities within its constitution—even those communities outside the Isabella Reservation—met strong resistance from Assistant Commissioner of Indian Affairs, William Zimmerman. Commissioner Zimmerman took the position that a tribe could only organize under the IRA if it had a reservation and its only members could be tribal people residing on the Reservation.[12]

With this dubious interpretation at the forefront of his review of the proposed Constitution, he changed the preamble to read, "We, the Indians residing on the Isabella Reservation it the State of Michigan."[13] In addition, he

7. Charmaine Benz, Ed., *Diba Jimooyung: Telling Our Story* 92 (2003).

8. *Id.*

9. *Id.*

10. *Id.*

11. *Id.*

12. *Id.* at 92–93.

13. *Id.* at 92; *see* Preamble, 1937 Constitution of the Saginaw Chippewa Indian Tribe of Michigan.

changed the proposed Tribal Council representation to require all council members be elected from within the Reservation,[14] and required that all Tribal members *reside* on the Reservation.[15] Commissioner Zimmerman further advised the Tribe that subsequent to the referendum to accept the constitution, the Tribe could "adopt" those individuals living off the reservation.[16] In fact, this "adoption" language appears in Sec. 2 of Art. III—Membership of the 1937 Constitution.

All these "recommendations" were accepted by the Business Committee and incorporated in the proposed Tribal Constitution that was voted on and accepted by Tribal members on March 27, 1937. Unfortunately, the 1937 Constitution—whatever its intent—sowed the seeds of membership confusion and discontent that yielded the bitter harvest at the core of this most challenging, even heartwrenching, litigation about the cultural and legal aspects of tribal belonging.

The shortcomings of the membership provisions of the 1937 Constitution were apparent from the beginning. The problems caused by severe land loss, conflicting allotment procedures, and artificial residency requirements virtually insured a confusing, inconsistent approach to enrollment. This flawed and inadequate patchwork approach was capped by Congress' insistence that as part of the settlement of the Saginaw Chippewa Tribe's successful land claim against the United States that a new Tribal Constitution—approved by Congress—be adopted by a vote of the members of the Saginaw Chippewa Tribe. The Constitution so adopted by majority vote was the Saginaw Chippewa Tribal Constitution of 1986, which contains the membership and other relevant sections at issue in this case.

The most essential ingredient of tribal sovereignty is the ability of tribes "to maintain or establish [their] own form of government." Felix S. Cohen, *Handbook of Federal Indian Law* 247 (1982). Indeed, "[t]his power is the first element of sovereignty." *Id.* Tribes accordingly allocate authority to their elected officials in the manner that they view as most conducive to the effective functioning of their political communities. "Tribal government ... may reflect the tribe's determination as to what form best fits its needs based on practical, cultural, historical, or religious considerations." *Id.*; *see also Holmes v. St. Croix*

14. *Id.* at 92–93; *see* Art. IV, Sec. 2, 1937 Constitution of the Saginaw Chippewa Indian Tribe of Michigan.

15. *Id.*; *see* Art. III, 1937 Constitution of the Saginaw Chippewa Indian Tribe of Michigan.

16. *Id.*

Casino, 26 Indian L. Rep. 6089, 6092 (St. Croix App. Ct. 1999) ("The first element of sovereignty … is the power of the tribe to determine and define its own form of government. *Such powers include the right to define the power and duties of its officials.*") (emphasis added); *Coin v. Mowa*, 25 Indian L. Rep. 6208, 6210 (Hopi App. Ct. 1997) ("In the federal scheme, the Tribe retains any power not abrogated by the federal government. *The Tribe exercises its retained sovereignty by allocating this power as it sees fit.*") (citation omitted and emphasis added).

Tribal constitutions frequently serve as the vehicle that Tribes use to define the allocation of power to their governing institutions, *see Terry-Carpenter v. Las Vegas Paiute Tribal Council*, 29 Indian L. Rep 6041, 6043 (Las Vegas Paiute Ct. App. 2002), and, as this Court stressed in *Chamberlain*, in constitutional systems it is often the solemn responsibility of the tribal courts to ensure that the Tribe's governing bodies do not exceed the bounds of their authority. *Chamberlain*, 27 Indian L. Rep. at 6089 ("'Among the most important functions of courts are constitutional interpretation and the closely connected power of determining whether law and acts of the legislature comport with the provisions of the Constitution. Courts were created to serve these purposes.'") (quoting *Moran v. Council of the Confederated Salish & Kootenai Tribes*, 22 Indian L. Rep. 6149, 6155 (C.S. & K.T. Ct. App. 1995)).

A. Structure of the Saginaw Chippewa Tribal Constitution of 1986

A central element in this process of establishing a constitutional government is the allocation of power between the Tribal Government and the 'people.'[17] In determining what is the *constitutional* range of the Tribe's power to disenroll individuals who currently are legally recognized as *Tribal* members, it is helpful to review the overall structural design of the 1986 Constitution. The essential historical types of constitutions in Indian country are the 'plenary' model, in which all power is expressly granted to the Tribal Council, or the enumerated or 'limited' powers model, in which the Tribal Council is provided a limited set of *enumerated* powers with a reservation of all such non-enumerated powers to 'the people.' An example of the former is the Grand Traverse Band of Ottawa and Chippewa Indians Constitution at Art. IV:

> The Tribal Council … shall be vested with all of the sovereign governmental executive and legislative powers of the Tribe not inconsistent with any provision(s) of the Constitution or federal law. *Such*

17. Depending on the tribe, power may be reserved to the community, the clan, the *tiyospaye* (extended family) or more generally 'the people.'

> *powers shall include, but not be limited to, the following* … (emphasis added).

An example of the latter is the Turtle Mt. Band of Chippewa Indians Constitution at Art. X:

> Any right [or] power heretofore vested in the [Band], but not expressly referred to in the Constitution, shall remain in the Band, and may be exercised by the [Band] or by the Tribal Council through the adoption of appropriate constitutional amendment if that be the wishes of the people.[18]

Needless to say the Constitution of the United States is also an enumerated powers constitution. *See, e.g.*, Amendment Ten reserving powers to both the states and 'the people.'

The 1986 Saginaw Chippewa Constitution is clearly an enumerated powers Constitution at Art. VI (Powers of the Tribal Council) Sec. 2:

> The Tribal Council may exercise such further powers as may in the future be *delegated to it by members of the Tribe* (emphasis added).

Since Sec. 1 of Art. VI enumerates the powers of the Tribal Council, there is no doubt that Sec. 2 is a direct limitation of Tribal Council authority to those powers specifically identified in Sec. 1.

B. Express Constitutional Power to Disenroll

Sec. 1(m) of Art. VI of the Constitution expressly addresses issues of membership by recognizing Tribal Council authority:

> To enact resolutions or ordinances not inconsistent with Art. III of this Constitution governing adoptions and abandonment of membership.

This language does not reflect any extensive or generalized power to disenroll. At best, it is reasonable to interpret the language as including Tribal Council authority to *enact* ordinances relevant to disenrollment in the context of "adoption" or "abandonment of membership." Apparently no such ordinances have ever been adopted and therefore Art. VI Sec. 1(m) is not relevant to the case at hand.

---

18. *See also* Art. IV (Powers of the Rosebud Sioux Tribal Council) of the Rosebud Sioux Tribal Constitution (1935) in which Section 1 refers to the "enumerated powers" of the Tribal Council and Sec. 3 to "reserved powers." Section 3 states in its entirety: "Any rights, and powers heretofore vested in the Rosebud Sioux Tribe but not expressly referred to in this Constitution shall not be abridged by this article, but may be exercised by *the People* of the Rosebud Sioux Tribe through the adoption of appropriate by-law and constitutional amendments." (emphasis added).

Art. III of the Constitution deals directly with membership. Sec. I deals with the qualifications for enrollment. (In fact, Sec. 1, and more particularly Sec. 1(c), is the Constitutional core of the *Bryant* case). Sec. 1 provides no authority to the Tribal Council to legislate in the area of enrollment except as to "adoption." Sec. 1 contains no express powers of disenrollment.

Secs. 2 and 3 deal expressly with disenrollment and basically track the language of Art. VI(1)(m) about "abandonment" and "adoption." Sec. 2 mandates disenrollment if a tribal member becomes "an enrolled member of any other federally recognized tribe." Sec. 3 involves the potential disenrollment of an "adopted member" of the Tribe "by reason of marriage" wherein said marriage is dissolved by either annulment or divorce and said individual neither maintains Reservation residence nor remarries another tribal member within twelve months. An "adopted" tribal member is also subject to potential disenrollment by "re-establishing tribal relations with the tribe from which they are descendants by blood." Disenrollment under Sec. 2 is mandatory (*i.e.* "shall"). Disenrollment under Sec. 3 is discretionary (*i.e.* "may").

In sum, the only *express* constitutional authority to disenroll is limited to certain situations involving "adopted" tribal members and tribal members who "abandon" Saginaw Chippewa Tribal membership by enrolling in another federal recognized tribe.

C. Implied Constitutional Power to Disenroll

Both sides presumably do not dispute any of the above, which merely establishes the background and context for examining the pivotal issue whether there are any *implied* powers of disenrollment and if so, what they are. The fact that the Constitution is an enumerated powers constitution with limited express powers of disenrollment does *not* automatically foreclose the possibility of some limited—presumably very limited—implied powers of disenrollment.

Before examining such possibilities, it is necessary to address the Tribe's observation that this Court has made an "unwarranted assumption … that all persons listed on the tribal rolls had, in fact, been admitted to membership after first proving that they in fact and in law actually met the Tribe's constitutional membership criteria." (Appellee's Brief at 15). This Court's "assumption" is indeed warranted and required by both legal and cultural norms of integrity. If someone has achieved a legal status (even if erroneously), they are entitled to that status until the government *proves* adequately to the contrary. The Tribe would have us *assume* the "guilt" rather than the "innocence" of Appellants. Such an approach would necessarily taint and even erode this Court's bedrock commitment to due process and cultural respect.

No constitutional text is completely transparent or self-disclosing and no constitution is beyond the necessity of interpretation. In fact, that is the request of the parties in this litigation, that the Court engage in constitutional adjudication. In this regard, the Tribe makes rather extensive claims that it has wide-ranging implied powers to disenroll that flow from Art. VI Secs. (e), (j), (n) and (o).

The core of the Tribe's argument is that the interplay of Art. VI Secs. (e), (j), (n) and (o) particularly the "general welfare" clauses of Secs (j) and (o) along with the "economic affairs" clause of Sec. (e) provide the Tribal Council with authority "essentially unrestricted as to *subject matter* so long as the Council's legislation can be fairly said to promote the Tribe's "general welfare" or "economic affairs" ... so long as that legislation does not contravene any other explicit limitation on the Council's powers." (Appellee's Brief at 19). This claim is rather bold, if not extravagant, in that it seeks to convert an enumerated powers Constitution into a plenary powers Constitution with an overwhelming presumption in favor of *any and all* Tribal Council action that would put the burden on the non-Tribal Council party to show "explicit limitation on the Council's power." This goes too far and would necessarily unhinge Tribal Council authority from the history and text of the Constitution.

The "general welfare" clauses at Secs. (j) and (o) are primarily related to matters of "tribal property ... natural resources ... to cultivate Indian arts, crafts" (Sec. j) and "regulating the conduct of trade and the use and disposition of property." (Sec. o) Neither of these enumerations, whether using the statutory interpretation maxims of *ejusdem generis* or *noscitur a sociis*[19] or ordinary common sense, appear related to issues of membership and more particularly to issues of disenrollment, and therefore they do not support any wide-ranging Tribal Council power to disenroll.

---

19. These Latin phrases, staples of statutory interpretation, may be translated as follows: *ejusdem generis* means of the same kind or class and refers to the textual principle that "[w]here general words follow specific words in a [textual] enumeration, the general words are construed to embrace only objects similar in nature to those objects enumerated by the preceding specific words." 2A Sutherland, *Statutes and Statutory Construction* § 47.17 (6th Ed., Norman Singer, ed.). *Noscitur a sociis* literally means that something is known from its associates or more colloquially a word is known by the company it keeps. *See, e.g.*, Gustafson v. Alloyd Co., Inc., 513 U.S. 561, 575–76. These principles of statutory construction add up to the commonsensical notion that where the framers of a document group together a number of items in a particular textual enumeration, they do not do so randomly, but because they think of the items as related to one another and intend them to be read as such. *See, e.g.*, Jarecki v. G.D. Searle & Co., 367 U.S. 303, 307 (1961).

The Appellants' argument goes too far in the other direction. They claim that a limited powers Constitution—such as the one at bar—contains no implied powers whatsoever and the power to disenroll is limited to the express power to disenroll relative to "adoption" and "abandonment" as set out at Art. III Secs 2 and 3 and Art. VI Sec. 1(m). For the Appellants, these limited express grounds for disenrollment negate any implied grounds for disenrollment.

The logic of this assertion is that the overall structure of the Constitution constrains any attempt to go beyond the express language of disenrollment. This argument is credible, but it is not compelling. The express grounds for disenrollment are really designed to cover a specific kind of disenrollment—disenrollment that comes into play *after* legitimate enrollment through the occurrence of a *condition subsequent* such as the divorce of an "adopted" tribal member or "abandonment" of membership by obtaining membership in another federally recognized tribe.

The Constitution is silent on the ability of the Tribal Council to disenroll someone who did *not* meet—at the front end—the basic conditions for enrollment set out in Art. III Sec. 1. To interpret this constitutional silence as an absolute bar to *potential* disenrollment of such individuals would create a constitutional anomaly that would, for example, put 'fraud' in the membership context beyond the pale of the constitutional text. Such a reading would seem a clear failure of constitutional justice.

A survey of other tribal constitutions is informative and consistent in this regard. No tribal constitution cited by the parties or otherwise known by the Court contains any express provision to disenroll on such basic grounds like 'fraud' and 'mistake.' This does *not* lead to the conclusion that such power does *not* exist in any Tribe, but rather that it is so basic and ingrained in the understanding of what is necessary to become a (legitimate) tribal member that there is a very, very limited *implied* power to disenroll on grounds of fraud and mistake that inheres in the right to enroll itself. To put it another way, there is a very, very limited, but necessary, constitutional corollary relative to disenrollment that is an ineluctable part of the constitutional mandate of enrollment itself. Without such implied constitutional power, the Tribe would be powerless to deal with fraud and mistake in the enrollment process. Such an interpretation of the constitutional text would improperly exalt form over substance.

No, the Tribe may not disenroll people for whatever 'good' reasons it might identify. No, the Constitution does not (and cannot) condone any constitutional failure of justice that would potentially endorse (constitutional) fraud and mistake in obtaining membership. Beyond such quite limited constitutional authority to disenroll on grounds of fraud or mistake, there are *no* other *implied* grounds for disenrollment.[20]

This Court has an unflagging duty to interpret the Constitution. That is, in fact, its highest calling. This duty and calling are never taken lightly and never confused with a mere review of policy. Tribal membership involves not only constitutional status, but also serves as the ultimate indication of cultural belonging. With this in mind, we urge the parties, as we did in the *Chamberlain* case, to place themselves in the heart of Native American jurisprudence by "healing, restoring balance and harmony, accomplishing reconciliation, and making social relations whole again." 27 Indian L. Rep. 6085, 6097 (2000).

IV. Conclusion

For all of the above stated reasons, the decision of Community Court is reversed. The *implied* Constitutional power to disenroll is limited to matters of fraud and mistake.[21] Further, the guarantee of due process requires that exercise of such implied power must be set out in an appropriate ordinance that defines these substantive grounds for disenrollment and further complies with the procedural guarantees set out in Ordinance 14.

IT IS SO ORDERED.

FOR THE COURT:

____

Frank Pommersheim, Associate Justice

Dated: January 5, 2005

Notes on *Snowden v. Saginaw Chippewa Indian Tribe of Michigan* (2005)

In *Snowden*, the Court focused on a Tribal constitutional question regarding the *scope* of the Tribal Council's authority in matters of disenrollment, which in turn, raised a question as to the *structure* (plenary v. enumerated) of the Tribe's constitution. It is important to note that these structures and lim-

20. It is critical to remember that this case does *not* involve the review of any specific lower court decision to disenroll. The precise grounds for such potential disenrollment have *never* been established, much less applied. Identifying that relevant standard is what this case is about. Any actual case of disenrollment will be subject to the stringent due process and burden of proof standards of Ordinance 14 and subject to (potential) review by this Court.

21. The Constitution, of course, may be amended to make any further adjustments or changes. *See* Art. VII, Saginaw Chippewa Tribal Constitution.

its—given their *constitutional* nature—are not subject to legislative change by the Tribal Council. The only possible change would be through a Tribal constitutional amendment. The Saginaw Chippewa Tribe's Constitution expressly provides for this possibility in Art. VII:

> This Constitution and By-Laws may be amended by a majority vote of the qualified voters in each of the three voting districts at an election called for by the Secretary of the Interior: Provided that, at least thirty (30) percent of those entitled to vote in each district shall vote in such election; but no amendment shall be effective until it shall have been approved by the Secretary of the Interior.
>
> It shall be the duty of the Secretary of the Interior to call an election on any proposed amendment upon receipt of a petition signed by one-third of the resident qualified voters in each of the three voting districts.

It is also worth noting that both parties to this litigation wanted the Tribal Court of Appeals to answer this seminal constitutional question of first impression. That is why both parties waived the right to an *individual* case by case determination by the Tribal court. They wanted an answer to the larger question. There was nowhere else to turn.

In addition to the substantive question, there was the *procedural* question of *who* could and would be empowered (under Tribal law) to make these decisions and what would be the right, if any, of appeal? Previous efforts by the Tribe met with procedural challenges as being fundamentally unfair and lacking in due process. A revised Ordinance 14 has largely met these challenges.

Enrollment and disenrollment are core elements of tribal sovereignty and cultural integrity. These issues literally define tribal identity and citizenship. When such matters are contested, the burden of fair and just resolution most often falls on tribal courts. Not merely to make the decision, but for the decision to be thoughtful, persuasive, and respectful. Tribal court decisions are likely to be followed in letter and spirit only if they can carry this burden.

A. Disenrollment

The extent of the tribal court's ability to evaluate disenrollment decisions for the Grand Traverse Band was discussed by the court in *Cholewka v. Grand Traverse Band Tribal Council*, 8 Am. Tribal Law 174 (Grand Traverse Band Tribal Ct. 2009). The court expressly noted the right to judicial review of any Tribal Council decision to disenroll (or deny enrollment) through Art. II Section 4 of the Tribe's constitution which states: "Any person whose application for membership has been denied, who has been disenrolled by the Tribal Council, or whose membership has been deemed to be automatically forfeited shall have a right of appeal to the Tribal Judiciary." *Id.* at 176.

Similarly, in *Delgado v. Puyallup Tribal Council*, No. 95-3604 (Puyallup Tribal Ct. 1996), when a member was out of the country and was not given notice of her disenrollment proceedings, the Puyallup Tribal Court held that "disenrollment of a member of the Puyallup Tribe of Indians without notice to the member and an opportunity to be heard is a denial of due process and is unconstitutional." *See also Deverney v. Grand Traverse Band of Ottawa and Chippewa Indians*, 2000 WL 35749822 (Grand Traverse Band Tribal App. Ct. 2000) (holding that revocation of membership in the Grand Traverse Band Tribe was not void *ab initio* but only when it was judicially determined that the plaintiff was enrolled in another tribe).

In *Muscogee Nation Citizenship Board v. Todd*, 7 Okla. Tribal Ct. Rep. 9 (Muscogee Nation Sup. Ct. 2000), MATTHEW L.M. FLETCHER, AMERICAN INDIAN TRIBAL LAW 262–63 (2011), the Muscogee Nation Supreme Court affirmed the trial court's decision to remand the case to the Muscogee (Creek) Nation Citizenship Board and ordered the Board to comply with the due process guarantees of mandated disenrollment procedures.

The case of *In re the Membership Revocation of Meza*, 7 NICS App. 111 (Sauk-Suiattle Tribal Ct. App. 2006) provides an alternative perspective. In this case, the Court upheld the disenrollment of several Tribal members and rejected due process arguments even when the Tribal Council rescinded previous resolutions to include plaintiffs in the Tribe and also lost evidence used in passing the rescinded resolutions.

B. The Cherokee Freedmen: History, Race, and Disenrollment

Perhaps the most well-known disenrollment struggle is that of the descendants of Cherokee Freedmen. This ongoing and lengthy legal saga presents a complicated question about the potential boundaries of tribal sovereignty for disenrollment decisions and their intersection with cultural and racial identity. After the Civil War, tribes that held slaves, including the Cherokee, signed treaties with the federal government agreeing to recognize as Tribal citizens former slaves that were held by tribal members. ROBERT T. ANDERSON ET AL., EDS., AMERICAN INDIAN LAW: CASES AND COMMENTARY 6 (2d ed. West 2010 (Autumn 2014 Update)). Although there was a great deal of interracial mixing, for the purposes of the Dawes Allotment Act, those who physically appeared Indian were placed on a "by blood" roll and those who physically appeared African-American were placed on "Freedmen" rolls, but both rolls were eligible for land allotments. *Id.* In 1983, the Cherokee Nation Code was amended by the Cherokee Tribal Council to specify that membership was to be based only upon the Blood Rolls. Circe Strum, *Race, Sovereignty, and Civil Rights: Understanding the Cherokee Freedmen Controversy*, 29 CULTURAL ANTHROPOLOGY 3, 575–77 (2014). As a result, the descendants of Freedmen, who were listed on a separate roll, were excluded from membership. *Id.*

Since the change, descendants of Freedmen have argued not only the violation of the 1866 treaty, but also a violation of the Cherokee Nation's constitution. *Id.* In 2004, Lucy Allen filed a lawsuit in Cherokee tribal court. *Id.* at 578. Allen is a decedent of both African-American and Indian ancestors, and although her ancestors were previously recorded as Indian on earlier pre-Dawes rolls, they were recorded as Freedmen on the Dawes Rolls. *Id.* Despite being Indian by ancestral racial background, Allen was denied tribal membership because of the wording of the blood roll requirement. *Id.* In 2006, the highest court of the Cherokee Nation agreed with Allen's argument that both the 1866 Treaty and Cherokee Constitution were violated. *Allen v. Tribal Council*, 6 Am. Tribal Law 18 (Cherokee National Judicial App. Tribunal 2006). The Court found that the code provision was inconsistent with Article III of the 1975 Cherokee Nation Constitution. *Id.* 30–31. The Court reasoned that in 1975, when the Tribe adopted its Constitution, it extended membership to anyone listed on the Dawes Commission Rolls as citizens of the Cherokee Nation; the Tribe did not racially qualify enrollment. *Id.* Thus, the Court held that the plain language of the Constitution did not require a blood quantum for citizenship and that without a constitutional amendment, the Tribal Council did not have the authority to restrict membership further than the Tribe's Constitution. *Id.*

In 2007, the Cherokee Nation voted on a constitutional provision to include the blood rolls only, and as a result, excluded the Freedmen from citizenship. ANDERSON, *supra* at 7. The new constitutional amendment was upheld in *Cherokee Nation Registrar v. Nash*, Case No. SC-2011-02 (Cherokee Nation Sup. Ct. 2011) by the Cherokee Nation Supreme Court which reversed a district court decision in favor of the plaintiff on the grounds that it was the Court's duty to interpret the Constitution, not to evaluate the merits of the substantive text. ANDERSON, *supra* at 8. The Court also ruled that the 1866 Treaty did not mandate Tribal citizenship or membership for Freedmen, but only that they be treated fairly.

The Cherokee Nation then excluded the Freedmen from voting in the 2011 election and as a result of this exclusion, HUD withheld 33 million dollars from the Tribe until the resolution of federal litigation. *Id.* Looking for a declaration that the Nation was within the bounds of tribal sovereignty and the

Freedmen were not entitled to Tribal membership, the Cherokee Nation filed suit against several Freedmen and the United States in *Cherokee Nation v. Nash* (D.D.C.), which is still ongoing. *Id.* The ultimate resolution of the Cherokee Freedmen membership issues will likely have significant reverberations as to the boundaries of tribal sovereignty in the context of enrollment, disenrollment, cultural belonging, and political disenfranchisement.

For a nuanced discussion of race and national identity as it pertains to the Cherokee Freedmen *see, e.g.*, S. Alan Ray, *A Race or Nation? Cherokee National Identity and the Status of Freedmen's Descendants*, 12 MICH. J. RACE & L. 387 (2007) (analyzing the concepts of "law and biology" to determine whether these two traditional models offer a solution for determining tribal identity for the purposes of enrollment. The author advocates for a sustained dialogue amongst all stakeholders as the "wisest use of sovereignty"); *see also* Circe Strum, *Race, Sovereignty, and Civil Rights: Understanding the Cherokee Freedmen Controversy*, 29 CULTURAL ANTHROPOLOGY 3, 575–98 (2014) (providing a historical background to the controversy, as well as discussing the dispute through a lens that examines race, civil rights, national identity, and their intersection with tribal sovereignty). For an alternative vantage point for viewing civil rights violations in tribal disenrollment actions *see* Greg Rubio, *Reclaiming Indian Civil Rights: The Application of International Human Rights Law to Tribal Disenrollment Actions*, 11 OR. REV. INT'L L. 1 (2009) (wherein the author questions whether tribal courts are the appropriate forums for remedying civil rights violations in terms of enrollment and disenrollment and offers the alternative of approaching these issues through an international human rights focus).

For a discussion of disenrollment—its history, its causes, and its consequences *see, e.g.*, Angela R. Riley, *Tribal Sovereignty in a Post-9/11 World*, 82 N.D. L. REV. 953, 959–60 (2006); Angela R. Riley, *Good (Native) Governance*, 107 COLUM. L. REV. 1049 (2007). For further and more detailed discussion about how tribal membership criteria has changed over time *see* Kristy Gover, *Genealogy as Continuity: Explaining the Growing Tribal Preference for Descent Rules in Membership Governance in the United States*, 33 AM. INDIAN L. REV. 243 (2009) (explaining the shift from parental enrollment and residency rules to blood quantum and descent rules. Notably, Gover draws her information from 322 different tribal constitutions. The author notes that tribal membership requirements tend to diverge between tribes depending on the age of their constitution. Tribes amending older constitutions tend to add blood quantum rules to their original enrollment provisions and tribes that are adopting constitutions for the first time opt more often for lineal descent rules). *See also* Paul Spruhan, *A Legal History of Blood Quantum in Federal Indian Law to 1935*,

51 S.D. L. Rev. 1 (2006) (tracing the history of the policy of blood quantum and specifically the federal government's use of blood quantum in Indian policy. The author argues that blood quantum was not actually entrenched in federal Indian policy until the passage of the Indian Reorganization Act, which delineates a shift from the use of political definitions to biological definitions).

C. Enrollment

The enrollment decisions of tribal courts are varied, nuanced, and often depend on the particular way that citizenship is defined by the tribal nation, and whether it be by constitution, ordinance, or statute. For example, in *Cooke v. Yurok Tribe*, 7 NICS App. 78 (Yurok Ct. App. 2005) an appeal from trial court's grant of summary judgment in favor of the Tribe, the constitutional provision in question provided: "No person who is a lineal descendant of a *present or former* member of another Tribe and who is without a parent enrolled with the Yurok Tribe shall qualify for membership in the Yurok Tribe." *Id.* at 80. The Court concluded that Cooke's argument that there was a distinction between his mother being a "deceased" member of the Hoopa Tribe rather than a "former" member was not persuasive in light of the language of the Yurok Constitution. *Id.* at 81. The Court also reaffirmed the fundamental right of a sovereign nation to determine citizenship under *Santa Clara Pueblo. Id.*

Chapoose v. Ute Indian Tribe of the Uintah-Ouray Reservation, 13 I.L.R. 6023 (Ute Tribal Ct. 1986) addressed the constitutionality of a Tribal ordinance adopted by the Ute Tribal Business Committee, as well as whether the Court had jurisdiction to review the Ute Tribal Business Committee's actions in light of the Tribal ordinance that "revoke[d] the Tribal court's jurisdiction 'to enforce or in any way be involved in those matters concerning enrollment into the Ute Tribe.'" The Court had issued final orders regarding the membership of at least nineteen different plaintiffs, including the plaintiffs here, and the Business Committee had withdrawn the Court's jurisdiction by ordinance and refused to enforce the Court's orders. *Id.* at 6024. The Court held that it had jurisdiction to review the Business Committee's actions to ensure compliance with the Ute Constitution and the Indian Civil Rights Act, and that giving jurisdiction to enforce Tribal enrollment law solely to the Business Committee violated due process under ICRA. *Id.* at 6025–27. The Court also sanctioned the defense attorney for failure to appear and held the Business Committee defendants in contempt of court for failing to comply with the Court's final orders. *Id.* at 6027–28.

In *Whitewater v. Ho-Chunk Nation Office of Tribal Enrollment*, 3 Am. Tribal Law 359, 380–81 (Ho-Chunk Nation Sup. Ct. 2001), the Court held that a section of a membership act was unconstitutional and that the plaintiff's application was also improperly delayed:

> The basis for this case is a long-standing enrollment dispute. The plaintiffs had been trying for twenty-two (22) years to become enrolled members of the Wisconsin Winnebago Tribe of Wisconsin prior to the adoption of the new CONSTITUTION in 1994. With the adoption of the new CONSTITUTION, the plaintiffs became eligible for enrollment and submitted applications for enrollment. The enrollment process endured by the plaintiffs was improperly delayed by Enrollment placing their applications in a "pending" status without any authority to do so. The plaintiffs were also treated unequally compared to the fifty-eight (58) other applicants who did not depend on Nebraska Winnebago blood quantum to qualify for membership. The plaintiffs were also unconstitutionally required to re-submit their applications after the enactment of the MEMBERSHIP ACT. The Court orders that Enrollment remedy the plaintiffs by awarding a retroactive enrollment date of March 31, 1995. The plaintiffs have been awarded the per capita distributions [individual payments from the Tribe's casino revenue] that they were deprived of by the improper and unlawful actions of Enrollment and the Legislature. *Id.*

In *Hoffman v. Colville Confederated Tribes*, 24 I.L.R. 6163, 6163–64 (Colville Tribal Ct. App. 1997), the plaintiff, and his children and grandchildren, filed a petition for a Blood Degree Correction pursuant to the Confederated Tribes of the Colville Reservation Constitution and Tribal Code. Hoffman and his family sought to prove they had a higher blood quantum than what was recorded on the 1937 rolls so they would be allowed tribal membership. *Id.* at 6163–68. The Appellate Court affirmed the trial court's decision that Hoffman did not meet his burden of proof by the requisite clear and convincing evidence standard. *Id.* at 6166–72.

A constitutional amendment to narrow membership requirements for the Confederated Tribes of Grand Ronde has been interpreted in a series of decisions made by the tribal court. In *Ballini v. Confederated Tribes of Grand Ronde*, 4 Am. Tribal Law 107, 110–11 (Grand Ronde Tribal Ct. 2003), the question before the Court was whether it was proper for the Enrollment Committee to retroactively apply the new constitutional amendment to applications that were submitted prior to September 14, 1999, but were not evaluated until after the new amendment had been passed. The court held that the Enrollment Committee did not retroactively apply the new amendment, and thus did not act in an arbitrary or capricious manner. *Id.* at 121. As the court stated:

> At bottom, when the applicants filed for enrollment they did so knowing that a significant change in the enrollment criteria either may have been on the horizon or may already have been approved by the voters. With that knowledge, the applicants simply could not have been certain their applications would be evaluated under the pre-amendment law. It would not have been reasonable for any one of them to believe such certainty existed. The applicants, therefore, can claim neither a settled expectation that the prior law would apply to their applications nor any unfairness in the Enrollment Committee's reliance on the new law. At most, they are the victims of the timing of their enrollment applications, over which they had ultimate control. *Id.*

Analogous to *Ballini*, the plaintiff in *Loges v. Confederated Tribes of Grand Ronde*, 4 Am. Tribal Law 171, 174 (Grand Ronde Tribal Ct. 2003), sought to have the membership standards applied that were in place before the 1999 amendment because that was when the blood quantum of several of her ancestors was increased. Those standards would not have required her to have at least one parent who was an enrolled tribal member at her birth, but would have only required that she was descended from a member. *Id.* The court ruled against Loges, explaining that she simply applied for membership too late (in 2001) after the rules had changed. *Id.* at 174–75. The court also ruled against a plaintiff who appealed his membership denial for the same reasons in *Creed v. Confederated Tribes of Grand Ronde*, C-00-06-004, 3 Am. Tribal Law 151, 155 (Grand Ronde Tribal Ct. 2001). The court summarized its difficult role thusly:

> That the Court has not accepted the arguments and pleas of Petitioner in this case does not mean that the Court is not moved by Petitioner's often poignant complaints that families have been split, with some in the Tribe and some not, and that individuals have been cut off from a Tribe and a heritage that is meaningful and significant to them. But it is the Tribe's responsibility to define its membership, not the Court's. If those pleas are to have any effect, they must be made to the Tribal leadership and to the Tribal members who have the authority to shape the membership and the future of the Tribe. The Court has neither that responsibility nor the authority. The Court can only enforce the law, as it has done in this opinion and in these cases. *Id.*

Tribal constitutional due process and equal protection arguments were made by the plaintiffs in *Young v. Confederated Tribes of Grand Ronde*, 3 Am. Tribal Law 90, 92–93 (Grand Ronde Tribal Ct. 2001) and *Holder v. Confederated Tribes of Grand Ronde*, 3 Am. Tribal Law 74, 76–77 (Grand Ronde Tribal Ct. 2004). In both cases, the plaintiffs argued that the new tribal membership requirements were unconstitutional because other family members with the same blood quantum, were members of the Tribe. Plaintiffs further argued that application of the new amendment was arbitrary and capricious as it was creating a situation where family members with the same blood quantum were not allowed membership. The court found, that although the amendment created an unfortunate situation for the family, with some family members being official tribal members and others being denied membership, it was not in violation of due process or equal protection. It was not a complaint upon which the court could grant relief.

In *Loy v. Confederated Tribes of Grand Ronde,* 4 Am. Tribal Law 132, 135 (Grand Ronde Tribal Ct. 2003), the court held that the Tribal Council had overstepped its constitutional authority when it enacted an ordinance that limited applications for enrollment by implementing a one-year waiting period for those who had relinquished membership in another tribe. The Court reasoned that the Constitution allowed the Tribal Council to "'enact an ordinance establishing procedures for processing membership matters, including but not limited to application procedures.' Grand Ronde Constitution, Art. V, § 3." *Id.* at 134. The court stated:

> The Tribal Council did not, and does not, have the authority to create by ordinance membership requirements inconsistent with those expressly defined in the Constitution. The Tribal Council could no more add the one-year waiting period to the membership requirements than it could change the Indian blood quantum the Constitution requires. *Id.* at 135.

Thus, in Loy's case, the new constitutional amendment should not have been applied to her application as:

> [H]er enrollment application should have been considered no later than June 1, 1999, at a regularly scheduled meeting of the Committee, under the 1984 constitutional membership requirements. The Committee therefore violated her Tribal constitutional rights when, in rejecting her enrollment application, it applied the enrollment criteria adopted by constitutional amendment in 1999. *Id.*

For a discussion of sovereign immunity and the tribal court's ability to determine membership, *see Paul v. Southern Ute Indian Tribe*, 24 I.L.R. 6038 (S.W. Intertr. Ct. App. 1997) where the Court ruled that the Tribal Council had exclusive jurisdiction to determine membership, and sovereign immunity barred the Court from exercising jurisdiction over an appeal from the council denying membership applications. *See also Teasley v. Kootenai Tribe of Idaho*

25 I.L.R. 6148 (Kootenai Tr. Ct. 1998) (further discussing enrollment, jurisdiction, and sovereign immunity where sovereign immunity was upheld); *but see Terry-Carpenter v. Las Vegas Paiute Tribal Council*, 29 I.L.R. 6041 (Las Vegas Paiute Ct. App. 2002) (finding a waiver of sovereign immunity in enrollment disputes).

D. Attempts to Seek Federal and State Court Resolution and Bureau and Indian Affairs Intervention

Although the decisions of tribal courts are overwhelmingly followed, legal challenges to these decisions are not hard to find. This is especially true when a tribe does not have a tribal court in which to challenge tribal council or administrative agency decisions, relegating enrollment and disenrollment losers to seek resolution in state or federal court. Such approaches have been largely unsuccessful as beyond the scope of federal review, banned by tribal sovereign immunity, and even for the failure to exhaust tribal court remedies. The following cases are representative examples of these approaches and their ultimate failure.

The most well-known of these cases is *Santa Clara Pueblo v. Martinez*, 436 U.S. 49, 55 (1978), in which the Supreme Court reversed a ruling by the Tenth Circuit which had ruled in favor of the plaintiff in an enrollment dispute with the Santa Clara Pueblo Tribe. In this case, the plaintiff and her daughter brought an action for declaratory and injunctive relief against the Tribe in federal court under the equal protection clause of the Indian Civil Rights Act of 1968. *Id.* at 51–53. Plaintiff challenged a Santa Clara Pueblo Tribal statute which allowed the children of male Tribal members who married outside the Tribe to obtain Pueblo membership, but did not allow the same for the children of female tribal members who married outside the Tribe. *Id.* The Supreme Court held that the civil suit was barred because of the Santa Clara Pueblo's sovereign immunity, reasoning that Congress deliberately provided habeas corpus as the only form of relief under ICRA in deference to tribal sovereignty in the spirit of serving goals of tribal self-determination. *Id.* at 52–72. For further discussion of gender discrimination in the enrollment/disenrollment context *see* David H. Getches et al., eds., Cases and Materials on Federal Indian Law 389–91 (6th ed. 2011).

Santa Clara Pueblo was followed in *Smith v. Babbitt*, 100 F.3d 556 (8th Cir. 1996). This case ruled that despite the petitioner's allegations of violations of federal statutes and liability on the part of the Secretary of Interior, the complaint was ultimately an attempt to move a membership dispute from tribal court to federal court and the federal court did not have jurisdiction.

Other circuit courts have also refused to intervene in disenrollment disputes on jurisdictional grounds. The Ninth Circuit in *Jeffredo v. Macarro*, 599 F.3d 913, 915 (9th Cir. 2010), held that the court lacked jurisdiction to review the disenrollment decision of the Pechanga Band of the Luiseño Mission. Although the appellants sought habeas relief under the Indian Civil Rights Act, arguing that disenrollment is equivalent to unlawful detention, the court ultimately held that they were not detained or in custody, and thus were outside of the scope of the court's jurisdiction. *Id.*

Additionally, the Fifth Circuit in *Apodaca v. Silvas*, 19 F.3d 1015, 1017 (5th Cir. 1994), succinctly stated the reasons that it refused to intervene through the Restoration Act and provide a private civil remedy for the plaintiffs who were disenrolled from the Yeleta del Sur Pueblo Tribe for failing to meet membership requirements:

> [T]here is no evidence that Congress created a federal civil remedy, especially because Congress probably would have used explicit language in doing so given the presence of *Santa Clara Pueblo* on the books ... [A]ny such private remedy would be inconsistent with a statute seeking to protect Indian sovereignty. And [], the cause of action is one that has traditionally been relegated to tribal law because, as mentioned in *Santa Clara Pueblo,* the right to determine tribal membership is crucial to the existence of the tribe as an independent political community. *Id.*

These same issues can also be found in a host of other cases: *see, e.g., Johnson v. Eastern Band Cherokee Nation,* 718 F. Supp. 6 (N.D.N.Y 1989) (where plaintiff was denied enrollment in the Eastern Band Cherokee Indian Nation and the district court dismissed due to lack of jurisdiction); *Alvarado v. Table Mountain Rancheria*, 509 F.3d 1008, 1016, 1020 (9th Cir. 2007), (where the Ninth Circuit upheld a district court's decision to dismiss due to lack of subject matter jurisdiction and sovereign immunity). In *Lamere v. Superior Court,* 31 Cal.Rptr.3d 880 (Cal. Ct. App. 2005), a California state court dismissed for lack of subject matter jurisdiction in a disenrollment dispute of the Temecula Band of Luiseno Mission Indians of the Pechanga Indian Reservation.

Along with attempts for federal and state court adjudication, there have also been attempts to have the Bureau of Indian Affairs step in and adjudicate such disputes. These attempts have had partial, but limited success. A group of forty-three individuals who applied for and were denied membership in the Eastern Shoshone Tribe formed a group called the Ordinance 59 Association and sought relief in federal court. *Ordinance 59 Ass'n v. U.S. Department of Interior Secretary*, 163 F.3d 1150, 1151–52 (10th Cir. 1998). Before their lawsuit, however, they also sought relief from the BIA who refused to intervene in the dispute. *Id.*

at 1153. Plaintiffs' counsel wrote to the Superintendent of the BIA on the Wind River Reservation and requested information on obtaining BIA recognition of enrolled tribal member status. The Superintendent responded that the BIA had no statutory, regulatory, or tribal authority to intervene on behalf of the individuals seeking enrollment. *Id.* However, the plaintiffs submitted applications to the BIA for enrollment anyway. *Id.* The BIA Area Director replied that "the Eastern Shoshone Tribe has complete authority over the enrollment procedures and the Tribe can enroll anyone meeting their criteria." He did agree, however, to forward the applications to the Superintendent. *Id.* The Superintendent denied all authority to intervene, stating, "I will again reiterate, we are not the forum to address this issue. I would suggest you contact the Tribal court or the Tribal Council." *Id.* When relief was denied, they sought injunctive and declaratory relief against the Tribe and the BIA and its officials for failing to enroll the plaintiffs. *Id.* Ultimately the Tenth Circuit affirmed the district court's dismissal for lack of subject matter jurisdiction. *Id.*

The BIA's decision to review and to render a decision on the Cahto Tribe of Laytonville Rancheria's action to disenroll several members was reviewed by the Ninth Circuit in *Cahto Tribe of Laytonville Rancheria v. Dutschke*, 715 F.3d 1225, 1230–31 (9th Cir. 2013). The court held that "[T]he Ordinance provides appeal rights only for rejected applications for enrollment. The Tribe thus did not grant the authority to the BIA to review appeals from disenrollment. While mindful of the obstacles faced by these disenrolled individuals ... we nevertheless encourage them to reapply and to seek review by the BIA." Similarly, the plaintiffs in *Williams v. Gover*, 490 F.3d 785, 791 (9th Cir. 2007) sued in federal court when they were excluded from full membership in a Tribe that was terminated and later reinstated. The Plaintiffs sued the BIA and its officials for what the plaintiffs contended was their role in members being squeezed out of the Tribe. *Id.* at 788–89. The court affirmed the decision of the district court to dismiss on summary judgment grounds when it stated, "Under *Santa Clara Pueblo*, Mooretown Rancheria had the power to squeeze the plaintiffs out, because it has the power to define its own membership. It did not need the BIA's permission and did not ask for it, and the BIA never purported to tell the Tribe how to define its membership." *Id.* at 790.

When the Seminole Nation of Oklahoma attempted to exclude its Freedmen through a constitutional amendment, the BIA intervened and refused to recognize the new amendment (some tribal constitutions require BIA approval of tribal constitutional amendments pursuant to 25 U.S.C. §476) and the Tribe appealed to federal court. *Seminole Nation of Oklahoma v. Norton*, 223 F. Supp. 2d 122, 147 (D.D.C. 2002). The court held that the actions of the BIA were appropriate. The court stated that, "where the Nation will not protect the Constitutional rights of its minority members, the BIA has the responsibility and indeed, the duty, to intervene and attempt to protect those rights through appropriate remedies." *Id.* at 147.

The plaintiffs in *Chapoose v. Clark*, 607 F. Supp. 1027, 1037 (D. Utah 1985) *aff'd.* (*Chapoose v. Hodel*, 831 F.2d 931 (10th Cir. 1987)) filed suit in federal court when the Secretary of Interior denied their applications for membership in the Ute Indian Tribe. The position of the Secretary of Interior was that only those Indians who are 'full-bloods' can be members of the tribe. Also, according to the Secretary, " 'full-bloods' are only those who 'possess [ ] one-half degree of Ute Indian blood and a total of Indian blood in excess of one-half.' 25 U.S.C. §677a(b). None of the plaintiffs meet this blood-quantum requirement." *Id.* at 1028. The Ute Tribal Court had already found that the plaintiffs were entitled to membership per the Tribe's constitution and "had ordered the Ute Business Committee to seek the Secretary's approval of an ordinance enrolling the plaintiffs in the Tribe." *Id.* at 1028. However, "[b]ecause the plaintiffs do not meet the blood-quantum requirement the Secretary believes to be mandated by §677a(b), the Secretary refused to approve the Ute Tribal Business Committee ordinance which would have enrolled them in the tribe. The Secretary's action means that the plaintiffs are not considered to be members of the tribe...." *Id.* at 1028. In a decision that was later upheld by the Tenth Circuit, the court held that:

> The intent of Congress in enacting the 1954 Act is clear. Congress intended the Ute Tribe to retain control over its membership. Even if this intention was not clear from the 1954 Act and its legislative history, the special canons of construction applicable in this type of case lead unambiguously to the same result. Because the Secretary's contrary interpretation of the Act is plainly erroneous, it cannot stand.
>
> As discussed in the previous memorandum decisions of this court, the Secretary has the authority and the responsibility to approve or disapprove tribal enrollment ordinances. Although this court holds that 25 U.S.C. §677d does not preclude the Secretary from approving the enrollment ordinance at issue here, the Secretary must still consider other factors and determine whether to approve or disapprove the ordinance. This court trusts that the Secretary will act as quickly as possible on this matter, giving great weight to the importance of allowing the Tribe to control its own membership whenever possible. *Id.* at 1037.

The consistent failure to get the BIA and federal courts to intervene in matters of tribal enrollment and disenrollment vividly demonstrates, yet again, the significance and high profile of tribal courts. Such a responsibility is likely to increase in the future, as the press of economics (*e.g.*, per capita payments from Indian gaming), race (*e.g.*, Cherokee and Seminole Freedman cases), and culture (*e.g.*, identity in a changing Native world) continues to take hold in tribal communities.

Political Processes—Elections

Chamberlain v. Peters

(Saginaw Chippewa Tribal Court of Appeals) (1999)

IN THE APPELLATE COURT OF THE
SAGINAW CHIPPEWA
INDIAN TRIBE OF MICHIGAN

Kevin Chamberlain, et al.,	)	Case No. App. Ct. 99-CI-771
Petitioners,	)	
v.	)	OPINION AND ORDER
Philip Peters, Sr., et al.,	)	
Respondents.	)	

Appearances: Dwight R. Carpenter, for Petitioners, and
John E. Jacobson and Henry M. Buffalo, Jr., for Respondents.

Before: Carey N. Vicenti, Chief Justice, Cheryl Demmert Fairbanks, Associate Justice and Frank R. Pommersheim, Associate Justice.

C. Vicenti, C.J., C. Fairbanks, A.J., and F. Pommersheim, A.J., jointly, for a unanimous Court.

This matter comes before this Court upon a petition submitted by Kevin Chamberlain and other members of his Council[1] (the Chamberlain Council) seeking extraordinary relief against Chief Philip Peters, Sr. and the members of his Council (the Peters Council) and invoking this Court's original jurisdiction[2] pursuant to the jurisdictional provisions of Resolution 99-024, Section 1.513.2 (b). By an Order entered September 25, 1999, this Court accepted jurisdiction over the subject matter and the parties to the case. Oral argument was heard on October 16, 1999. Briefs in this matter were submitted on October 1, 1999,

1. Shelly Foster, Benjamin Hinmon, Alvin Chamberlain, William Snowden and Valerie Sprague.

2. When the Appellate Court is called upon to take 'original jurisdiction' in an action, the Court is thereby required to conduct a fact-finding mission in addition to its customary role of hearing legal argument. There are no rules regarding this fact-finding mission when it is to be done by the Appellate Court. Peculiar to this case, as well, has been the need to proceed as expeditiously as possible in order to bring this matter to finality and repose.

and November 2, 1999. In short, this case asks whether the Secretary of the Interior of the United States of America, through the Assistant Secretary for Indian Affairs Kevin B. Gover, possesses the authority under federal or tribal law to determine the proper and valid elected leadership of this Tribe. This Court hereby holds in favor of the Petitioners as to their essential claim, but denies any extraordinary relief as unwarranted due to the Petitioners' own illegal actions and the Constitutional stability and repose that now exists on the Isabella Reservation. The Court is ever mindful of the far reaching implications of this case and therefore proceeds with due respect and caution.

I. Factual Summary

The facts of this case[3] reflect the typical convoluted saga experienced by many of the Indian tribes that were overrun by American expansion in the 18th and 19th centuries. In order to recover from the presence of an invading force, this Tribe was coerced to yield its lands, urged to reorganize governmentally, required to reassess its tribal identity through determining its foundation for membership, and, then compelled to revise its organic laws to accord with a transcendent vision of future tribal governance and society. Such things do not, and did not, in this case, proceed without conflict and confrontation.

A. Historical Background

The Saginaw Chippewa Indian Tribe originated as a collection of affiliated bands of Saginaw, Swan Creek, and Black River Chippewa, all of whom occupied the region around Mt. Pleasant, Michigan, the current seat of Tribal government. Through successive treaties entered between the Tribe and the United States in the years 1805, 1807, and 1817, the Tribe ceded large parcels of land in Michigan and Ohio to the United States government for its use and disposal.

In 1937, the Saginaw Bands reorganized pursuant to the provisions of the Indian Reorganization Act of 1934 as the "Saginaw Chippewa Indian Tribe of Michigan" through a newly adopted Constitution. The newly organized Council then promptly passed Ordinance 1 on October 3, 1938. This ordinance set the base membership of the Tribe and otherwise created procedures for the enrollment and adoption of persons into membership of the Tribe. Soon thereafter, Superintendent Peru Farber of the Michigan Agency of the Bureau of Indian Affairs (BIA) prepared a roll of names that contained the additional names

---

3. For ease of understanding much of the text that follows, extensive factual information has been culled from a 'Chronology of Events' that this Court required the parties to submit into the record.

of other persons who were not included in the initial roll of membership (the Farber roll), but who qualified, in his estimation, by the terms of the law for membership in the Tribe. This roll was not adopted by the Tribe at the time, and it did not receive an in-depth review for decades.

From 1973 to 1979 the Tribe litigated its claims to the ceded lands described above before the Indian Claims Commission (and the Court of Claims) until a judgment for monetary compensation was entered, thus requiring the federal government to pay $4.3 million to the Tribe. On the heels of this judgment, the Council repealed Ordinance 1, then issued a series of resolutions beginning on February 1, 1982 (TM-01-82, TM-02-82 and TM-03-82, hereinafter the 'TM Resolutions') that purportedly expanded the original roll set out in Ordinance 1. Some of these new names appeared on the previously mentioned Farber roll. Others were eligible by virtue of the terms of Article III of the 1937 Constitution. This process was completed on December 10, 1982, a date that figures prominently in this case.

On a parallel course, the U.S. Congress, after a failed attempt, finally worked out a bill to compensate the Saginaw Chippewa Tribe for the lands it lost. Public Law 99-346, 100 Stat. 674 (1986), authorized the release of the monies previously adjudged by the Court of Claims to be owed to the Tribe. A portion of that law required the Tribe to make changes to its Constitution as a condition precedent to the distribution of the money to the Tribe's membership. Sec.3 (b)(3). As requested, the Tribe obliged with the adoption of a new Constitution on November 4, 1986. Most notable in that Constitution was the language of Article III, Section 1 (a) which provides that membership extends to "[a]ll persons whose names appeared on any of the following rolls: (1) November 10, 1883; (2) November 13, 1885; (3) November 7, 1891; or (4) *December 10, 1982*." (emphasis added.)

In November of 1995, Kevin Chamberlain and nine others (the Chamberlain Council), some of whom are signatory to the present petition, were elected to represent District 1 by the base voter rolls represented in the 1986 Constitution which included those persons also named in the TM Resolutions. Part of the platform of this Council included a promise to reform membership problems and a commitment to effectuate constitutional reforms. During these years, though, scant progress was made toward these intended reforms. Instead, the Council proved itself more successful in constructing the expanded Soaring Eagle Casino, the economic cornerstone of the Tribe. After two years had passed, it was time for new elections to take place, as required by the Saginaw Chippewa Tribal Constitution.

B. The Elections

On October 16, 1997, a primary election was held for District 1. The field of candidates was reduced to twenty as the law required. The following month, on November 4, the General Election was held. Only four of the sitting members of the Chamberlain Council were re-elected. The election results were challenged, and, as was the procedure of the time, the Council examined the results. The Council ruled the election was invalid. This declaration led to a curative General Election. This election, held on January 27, 1998, had virtually the same results. The Chamberlain Council, again, declared the election to be invalid. This occurred as their terms of office expired and their mandate of reform came to an end.

From this point, and precisely beginning on February 18, 1998, a series of tribal court challenges advanced toward what appeared to be a cure to the problem of membership and the proper legal succession to office. In fulfillment of the court's directions to complete both its membership examination and the election process, the Chamberlain Council tried unsuccessfully to secure the services of genealogist Betty Bell. It then successfully secured the services of James Mills. Mr. Mills produced his recommendations, citing what he perceived to be shortcomings in various categories of documents that should be produced in order to bring finality to questions of membership in the Tribe. Acting upon these recommendations, the Chamberlain Council issued notices in October of 1998 to more than 140 persons, who previously had been considered members of the Tribe, telling them that they had been 'temporarily suspended' from membership unless they could produce documentation which would satisfy Mr. Mills and the Enrollment Advisory Board (EAB). The subsequent cascade of documentation, involving some 500 files, led Mr. Mills and the EAB to conclude that only six individuals truly appeared to have been questionably enrolled. After notification, two of these voluntarily relinquished membership in the Tribe. This, arguably, set the stage for a valid election.[4]

---

4. There can be no doubt that the summary 'temporary suspension' from tribal membership of more than 140 individuals (approximately 10% of the electorate) without advance notice and an opportunity to be heard clearly violated notions of tribal fairness and due process under the Indian Civil Rights Act of 1968, 25 U.S.C. §1302(8). This is especially troubling since it prevented such individuals from voting and running for office, which are surely core elements of tribal citizenship and membership. All of this was exacerbated by the fact that the Tribal enrollment of the suspended individuals was determined in accordance with Article III, Sec. 1 of the Saginaw Chippewa Indian Tribal Constitution.

If tribal membership requirements as set out in the Tribal Constitution are somehow defective or flawed, they may only be changed with due tribal deliberation and constitu-

On November 24, 1998, a second primary election was held for District 1. Surprisingly, the persons who had been temporarily suspended from membership were disallowed from either voting or running for office in this election. The election took place leading to the selection of twenty finalists. Of these twenty, only one person was a member of the Chamberlain Council. The suspended members, all except for the questionable remaining four, were then inexplicably restored to membership. Before a general election could be held, acting upon protests submitted by several members of the Tribe, the Chamberlain Council acted on December 15, 1998 to again nullify the election process. But, also in that month, the Council enacted law that established an Appellate Court to hear appeals from the Community Court.[5] It is this resolution that created this Court and the original jurisdiction contemplated in this case.

The day following the Council's nullification, the Community Court issued notices that a hearing would be convened to determine whether the Chamberlain Council should be held in contempt of court for its apparent failure to hold a curative election. On December 29, 1998, Judge Bruce Havens convened the Community Court. After a disruptive proceeding, the Chief Judge prepared his ruling. He determined that "the Tribal Council Defendants have shown a consistent pattern of disregard for the Constitutional and Ordinance mandates [of the Tribe] and thus are acting outside of the scope of employment with the Tribe thereby subjecting themselves to individual liability for their conduct." Members of the Chamberlain Council found themselves under prosecution for criminal contempt before Associate Judge Ronald Douglas, after Judge Havens summarily recused himself, and subsequently resigned.

The second year of the Chamberlain Council's 'holdover' term began with a dismissal of the contempt charges. The Tribe proceeded to its third round of elections. The third primary election was held on January 19, 1999. This time the Chamberlain Council again invalidated the election in a ruling entered on February 25, 1999, stating that the TM Resolutions unconstitutionally increased the membership rolls. These two events are the most significant developments relevant to this case: first, it is from the January 19, 1999 primary election that the Peters Council comes; and second, it is the

tional reform in accordance with the Tribal Constitution itself. While such constitutional reform (whether good or bad) may have been contemplated by the Chamberlain Council, it was never effectuated during its time in office.

5. Resolution 99-024 (enacted on December 24, 1998). Chief Justice Vicenti was sworn into office later in the month on December 30, 1998. Justices Fairbanks and Pommersheim were sworn in early in 1999 on March 20, 1999.

unconstitutionality of the TM Resolutions that the Chamberlain Council relies upon for its continued maintenance of control beyond the end of its term of office.

Obviously incensed by this last turn of events, a group of members of the Tribe began to organize an alternative election outside of any existing governmental backing and purportedly authorized by Ordinance 4. They announced their intentions. The Chamberlain Council countered this initiative by enacting a law of sedition making the 'simulation of governmental processes' a crime and punishable by imprisonment. On March 9, 1999, the alternative election proceeded, nonetheless, and resulted in a voter participation of approximately 37% of the voters in District 1. Several persons were then issued criminal citations, subsequently dismissed, pursuant to the sedition law.

It is important to note that the elections and court cases were not the only tracks of activity. From late in 1998 until the March 1999 alternative election, both the supporters of the alternative election—which included the current Peters Council—and the Chamberlain Council were actively engaged in the pursuit of the political backing of the Assistant Secretary of the Interior Kevin B. Gover. As part of this strategy, while Assistant Secretary Gover postponed official action in this controversy, the Chamberlain Council initiated an alleged media critique of Gover's B.I.A. Administration.

On March 11, 1999, the Chamberlain Council passed a law redistricting District 1, the Isabella District, such that the District expanded beyond the boundaries of the reservation to include lands which had previously encompassed Saginaw lands as they appeared before those lands were ceded to the federal government.

On March 16, 1999, the victors in the March 9 alternative election took the oath of office but there was no officially recognized transfer of governmental power. In the Community Court, on the same day, Judge Bruce S. Hinmon dismissed challenges to the Chamberlain Council's rulings that invalidated the November 1998 Primary and the December 1999 General Elections. Judge Hinmon based his decision on the sovereign immunity and political question doctrines.

Meanwhile, Assistant Secretary Gover finally weighed in on the controversy. By a letter dated June 9, 1999, he urged the Chamberlain Council to hold an election within the next forty-five days. The letter implied that his office considered the January 19, 1999, primary election to have been valid—in spite of the Chamberlain Council's and the Court's rulings to the contrary. He further challenged that his Administration would be forced, in the absence of such election, to "deal with the representatives of the two off-reservation districts and the ten persons from the Isabella District who received the highest number of votes in January 1999 as representatives of the Tribe."

The Chamberlain Council, aware of Gover's threatened course, nonetheless, scheduled a fourth round of elections beginning with a primary set for some time in September 1999, outside of the forty-five day window established by Assistant Secretary Gover in his letter of June 9, 1999. As a result, on August 10, 1999, Assistant Secretary Gover adhered to his word and issued a letter stating:

> I am instructing the Area Director to proceed with the instructions I gave him on June 9. He is to deal with the representatives of the two off-reservation districts and the eleven persons from the Isabella District who received the highest votes in January 1999 as representatives of the Tribe on an interim basis.

Assistant Secretary Gover, letter of August 10, 1999.[6]

It is not entirely clear what had happened at this juncture. Copies of the Assistant Secretary's letter were provided to Tribal and BIA law enforcement, as well as the Federal Bureau of Investigation and the United States Marshall Service. Many of the Tribal law enforcement personnel were employed directly by the B.I.A. and also held supervisory positions. There is some suggestion in the record that Attorney Michael Phelan, who served in the capacity of legal counsel to the Tribe during the Chamberlain Administration had advised the police that they should give effect to the Secretary's letter. The Peters Council was sworn into office by a notary public. Conflict and confrontation ensued in the following month. It is from these series of events that this petition emerged.

The Peters Council then went directly to produce its version of curative elections. In order to accomplish this, the Peters Council enacted laws that restored the electorate—the body of eligible voters—to the *status quo* as it existed before the Chamberlain Council took office. In addition, it set up an election challenge process which involved neither the Council nor the Courts. Primary elections were held on October 2, 1999, by which twenty-four finalist candidates were selected. Immediately following this election, a petition was submitted to this Court in an attempt to receive a ruling of invalidation.[7] This Court denied the request. A general election took place on November 2, 1999, in which twelve persons were selected to take office. Five minutes before the close of business on December 6, 1999, another petition was submitted, this

---

6. A copy of this letter appears in its entirety as an appendix to this opinion and order.

7. *Helen Black, et al. v. Philip Peters, Sr., et al.*, Case No. App. Ct.1005 (filed November 2, 1999).

time by Kevin Chamberlain and Benjamin Hinmon,[8] asking this Court to issue a temporary restraining order calling for a halt to the administration of the oaths of office on December 6, 1999, to the prevailing candidates in the November election. This Court has stayed its hand pending its ruling in this case, fully aware that the two are inextricably intertwined.[9]

A final note to this factual summary is in order regarding the participation of the federal government, or lack thereof, in these proceedings. This Court convened two sessions, the first, as a pre-trial conference, and the second, as oral argument regarding the issues presented here. In anticipation of these hearings, and, at least, in the latter hearing, at the urging of both parties, we *sua sponte* invited the participation of the federal government in these proceedings and have received a mere letter of declination.[10]

II. Issues Presented

Through the two proceedings conducted by this Court in its original jurisdiction we have gathered the foregoing facts, limited, however, by the nature of proceedings of this sort. Although there are a myriad of subsidiary issues raised by the parties, we find the following to be most salient and ripe for consideration:

A. Whether the Chamberlain Council possessed an unfettered right to continue to hold over in office despite the expiration of its constitutionally defined term of office;

B. Whether the Assistant Secretary of the Interior for Indian Affairs possessed the lawful authority to replace the Chamberlain Council;

C. Whether the Peters Council possessed lawful authority to sit as the Interim Council for the Tribe;

D. Whether the answers to these questions affect the legality of the Council recently elected; and

E. Whether the findings of this Court require the granting of extraordinary relief.

---

8. *Kevin Chamberlain and Ben A. Hinmon v. Chief Judge, Tribal Community Court*, Docket Number unassigned.

9. A final motion was submitted in this case on December 14, 1999, as we were in the midst of penning this opinion. Attorney Dwight R. Carpenter renewed, in this petition, his request for an award of attorney's fees. Because this request requires additional facts, we reserve ruling on this matter to a later date.

10. We received indirect notification from the B.I.A. that it was prohibited by 28 CFR 0.20(c) from participating in a tribal court proceedings in an *amicus curiae* capacity without the approval of the Solicitor General.

III. Discussion

A. Validity of the Actions of the 'Holdover'[11] Chamberlain Council

We begin our discussion with the question of whether the Chamberlain Council possessed an unfettered right to continue to hold over in office despite the expiration of its constitutionally defined term of office. The answer to that question lies in its constituent elements. What authority did the Chamberlain Council have to continue in office beyond the end of its term? Did the Constitution mention the prospects of a holdover? If not, is there something within the theory and structure of the Constitution that provides for such a 'holdover'? What, therefore, were the limits of its authority, if any? And if there were limits, how do we treat such unconstitutional actions?

It takes only a minimal review to recognize that the Constitution, adopted in 1986, and the laws of the Tribe,[12] have not a single provision regarding the transition of power from one Council to the next. It does not follow that the Council in office at the time that a transition should occur is, therefore, left with open authority to reshape the government of the Tribe. Various other provisions of the Constitution provide either direct or implied limitations against Tribal Council action, irrespective of whether it is legally or illegally constituted. The most notable of such provisions, in this case, concern Article III, regarding membership,[13] Article VI, Section 1(m),[14] and Article VII.[15] In addition, the Tribe is presumptively bound by the mandates of the Indian Civil Rights Act of 1968, 25 U.S.C. § 1302(8), in particular, its references to 'due process of law' and 'equal protection of the laws.'

We recognize that at the heart of the Chamberlain Council's justification for its continued validity beyond the end of the term of office is its assertion that the membership mandate had to be fulfilled *before* any valid elections could take place. In its estimation, it was, thus, essential to change the membership of the Tribe. This was effectuated by the dual initiatives to investigate the validity of membership claims and to amend the Constitution to reflect its

11. This term was used first by Assistant Secretary Gover in his letter of August 10, 1999, in paragraph 4.

12. Even if such laws existed, such laws would be subject to scrutiny to determine whether they would comport with specific portions of the Constitution through a judicial process.

13. This Article sets the parameters for membership in the Tribe.

14. This Article allows the Council to pass laws "not inconsistent with Article III."

15. This Article provides a process for amendment of the Constitution to accommodate such laws that might be contrary to other terms within the Constitution.

vision of an ideal profile for membership. Both are problematic on legal and theoretical grounds.

Read together, Article III—which sets a base membership roll based upon the particular rolls taken on November 10, 1883, November 13, 1885, November 7, 1891, and December 10, 1982,[16]—and Article VI, Section 1(m)—which denies the Council any authority to pass laws affecting membership—signal a clear barrier to such Council actions that would affect the status of membership. Even the attempt to force individuals by law *ex post facto*[17] to produce proof of membership is highly suspect. *See supra* note 4. From a practical perspective, however, we concede that some laws that touch upon the issue of membership are allowable, though, tempered by the 'due process' and equal protection' clauses of the ICRA. Due process and notions of fundamental fairness suggest that the status of membership cannot be assessed without ample procedures, and especially so after a person has been admitted to membership in the Tribe.

The status of nominal membership is not the sole concern raised by the Chamberlain Council's actions. Membership consists of a bundle of rights and privileges, including, but not limited to the right to be secure in one's identity as a member, the right to receive tribal benefits on an equal footing with other members, and the right to participate in the political process. The fact that over 140 persons were denied that right strips the Chamberlain Council of any cover of innocence and righteousness.

The theory and structure of the Constitution also serve to erode the Chamberlain Council's dual initiatives and its continued occupancy of office. Article IV, Section 8 provides that the Council "*shall* be elected every two years." (emphasis added). This modest statement forms the foundation for the government of the Tribe. It is mandatory and not discretionary. The election *must* take place. The performance of the election is a duty incumbent upon the Council, and the failure to hold an election can be deemed a neglect of that duty thus serving as a basis for removal from office. *See* Article IV, Section 14(a).

The 'two year' limitation, moreover, places a very finite limitation upon the elected Council. A candidate knows before running for office that his or her term

---

16. Constitution of the Saginaw Chippewa Indian Tribe of Michigan, Article III, 1 (a)(1–4).

17. Consider that every person who was subject to produce proof of their membership had been confirmed to be a member of the Tribe and should have been able to feel a sense of security in that status. This expectation was shattered by the Chamberlain Council's actions.

may last only two years and not beyond. And, in order to gain the public trust, a candidate voices certain public concerns that either do or do not succeed in gaining the public validation through the voting process. *See generally* Article IV. In this case, the Chamberlain Council ran on a particular platform that did indeed gain the public trust. But there is a clear Constitutional implication that such a platform must be fulfilled or completed within the given two years.

The holdover actions of the Chamberlain Council were clearly in violation of the Saginaw Chippewa Indian Tribal Constitution. The Tribal Constitution makes no provision for a holdover tribal council and implicitly rejects such a possibility. Act IV, Section 8 of the Constitution states: "The Tribal Council shall be elected every two years in the month of November." This Constitutional provision clearly does not envision any holdover possibility.[18] In fact, it constitutionally guarantees members the right to elect a tribal council every two years.

The Chamberlain Council argument that its holdover actions were constitutionally authorized rests more directly, as counsel conceded at the hearing on October 16, 1999, on language in election Ordinance No. 4 (at that time) that stated:

> Any voter may protest an election for the district in which he/she voted. The written notice of protest must be made to the Tribal Council within seven (7) days after the election. The notice must set out the grounds of the protest. The Tribal Council shall schedule a hearing on the protest within ten days. The Tribal Council decision will be *final.* (emphasis added).

While this election ordinance did grant substantial authority to the Tribal Council to decide election protests, it cannot be said that it granted authority in excess of constitutional limits. To do so would render the constitutional requirement of tribal elections every two years in November as guaranteed in Art. IV, Sec. 8, a mere nullity. To state the obvious, no tribal ordinance may render constitutional provisions inoperative.

The 'logic' of the Chamberlain Council argument is fatally flawed at its core. It presumes an ongoing right to set aside tribal elections without reference to the Tribal constitution or potential review by a tribal court. This is profoundly undemocratic and contrary to any notion of the balance of governmental powers. The mandate for reform that originally carried the Chamberlain Council

---

18. While a holdover possibility might potentially exist in some unforeseen, extraordinary circumstances, the constitution certainly does not envision a tribal council maintaining itself in office by setting aside election results.

to elected office eventually became a justification for what looked more and more like despotism. Lofty motives do not excuse unconstitutional and illegal actions.

The jurisprudential implications of such matters have been noted by other tribal courts. For example, the Confederated Salish and Kootenai Tribal Court of Appeals observed:

> Interpretation and application of the law to determine the legality of a particular act is the 'heart of the judicial function'. [Citing *Menominee Indian Tribe ex rel. The Menominee Indian Tribal Legislature v. Menominee Indian Tribal Court*, 20 IND. L. REP., 6066, 6068 (Men. Tr. S. Ct. 1993)]. Among the most important functions of courts are constitutional interpretation and the closely connected power of determining whether law and acts of the legislature comport with the provisions of the Constitution. Courts were created to serve these purposes.

Moran v. Council of the Confederated Salish and Kootenai Tribes, 22 IND. L. REP, 6149, 7155 (C.S. & K.T. Ct. App. 1995). *See also* the classic federal precedent of *Marbury v. Madison*, 5 U.S. (1 Cranch.) 137 (1803).

The Chamberlain Council had two years to complete its pledge of resolving membership, election, and Constitutional issues before its term of office expired in November 1997. *See* Saginaw Chippewa Indian Tribe of Michigan Constitution and Bylaws, as amended, Article IV, Sec. 8. During its tenure, it should be noted that its primary focus was on economic development and it did achieve major success in establishing a sound economic base for the Tribe. However, the alleged necessary governmental reforms were not extensively dealt with until late in its term or until its official term of office had expired. At the end of those first two years the Chamberlain Council could only be considered a 'holdover' Council.

Arguably, the political mandate that elected it to office had to be accounted for *at that time* to the voting public, leaving the question to the existing membership whether membership and constitutional reforms should be continued under the same government. The Chamberlain Council's political platform *at that time* could have been the very same assertions made before Assistant Secretary Gover and before this Court throughout these proceedings, that it had identified issues of membership which required a curative constitutional amendment, and, that it would be its electoral platform to so amend the Constitution.

Nonetheless, continuing its quest to fulfill its expired political mandate, this 'holdover' council finally began to act on the political reforms it had promised, which involved a series of meetings with the federal government. Nearly one year after its term expired, on December 23, 1998, Chief Chamberlain and several representatives of the Tribe met with the B.I.A. requesting Assistant Secretary Gover's assistance in expediting an election on a proposed Constitutional amendment that would address the Tribe's enrollment and membership problems.

As a 'holdover' body, the Chamberlain Council did have a duty at the expiration of its term to ensure a Constitutionally elected government and a proper and orderly transition of that body. This 'holdover' Chamberlain Council failed in its efforts to conduct a valid election and consequently has not since been able to effectuate an orderly transfer of government within the internal mechanisms of the Tribe's government. Both the Chamberlain Council and the Peters Council thereafter sought to rely on a political resolution of the Chamberlain created problem from the B.I.A.'s Assistant Secretary of Interior, Kevin Gover. Both of these requests to the Assistant Secretary totally ignored the internal tribal law and institutions of the Saginaw Chippewa Indian Tribe. In sum, both the 'holdover' and 'interim' councils were in error. *See* discussion *infra* pp. 19–33 (pp. 148–50 here). Moreover, this appeal to the United States government exemplifies both the negative impact that historical federal policy has had upon Indian tribes, and the all-too-often tribal populist reliance on the well-established paternalistic posture of the B.I.A.[19] This reliance on the federal government rather than upon the basic right and responsibility of self-government is counter to the established principles of tribal sovereignty and, as we shall see below, yielded a major intrusion into the internal governmental functions of this Tribe.

The previous discussion brings into question, though, the validity of the actions of the Chamberlain Council taken from the end of its two-year term to the installation of the Peters Council—the 'holdover' period. As stated above, the Tribal Constitution does not have any provision for an interim governing body or a 'holdover' Council. Thus, the Chamberlain Council, after its term expired, apparently acted outside the scope of Tribal constitutional authority. Such actions outside the scope of constitutional authority place the overall tribal government in a very tenuous position. There are a myriad of potential circumstances where a Council may be legally required to hold over. If, for instance, a major snowstorm had caused power shortages, road closures, and a resultant failure of the election process, a Council may be required to hold over to ensure that such elections eventually take place. Such

---

19. *See* FELIX S. COHEN'S HANDBOOK OF FEDERAL INDIAN LAW 42 (1982). This treatise provides a detailed history of federal Indian policy and its impact on tribal governments.

events may require the expenditure of funds and, perhaps, an adjustment of the internal laws. But, it is clear that such 'holdover' authority converts the mandate of such leadership away from initial platform concerns toward the primary duty to hold such elections. One cannot, in retrospect, say that any holdover or interim actions during such an emergency are manifestly illegal—*that* would require a case-by-case analysis. And under such analysis, the most suspect of actions must be those which accrue to the benefit of those holding office, or, are contrary to the Constitution, the laws of the Tribe, and applicable federal law.

Clearly, to provide the necessary continued stability and regularity in government, the actions of the 'holdover' council must be deemed presumptively valid unless it can be established by clear and convincing evidence[20] that those actions were contrary to the Tribal Constitution or applicable federal law, or, provided an undue benefit to those persons holding such 'holdover' office. The most relevant areas that have surfaced as issues of concern include the adoption of an amended election code. *See* Saginaw Chippewa Indian Tribe of Michigan, Tribal Council Resolutions #99-101 & #99-104.

Even though the Chamberlain Council, in good faith, began these broad constitutional reforms, the timing for these actions was constitutionally erroneous. Its term had expired. In addition, to begin constitutional reforms during the 'holdover' period is questionable as it is well-settled law that tribal officials are limited to the authority conferred upon them by their tribal constitutions or statutes. Thus, the timing of the Chamberlain Council's actions is not only contestable, but the adoption of such ordinances containing provisions relating to a currently contested election is questionable.

Finally, according to the Constitution, the Tribal Council is vested with the authority to make provisions for all elections, "by *proper* ordinance." *See* SCITM Constitution, Article IV, Section 7. (emphasis added). Where a 'holdover' or 'interim' government attempts to change the Constitutional democratic processes from those that existed at the time of its own election, we can only conclude that such changes are *improper* and violative of Article IV, Section 7. These changes occurred on July 15 and 16, 1999. *See* SCITM Tribal Council Resolutions #99-101 & 104.

20. We have chosen this particular standard after recognizing that the relationship of a member to his or her tribe is significantly similar to the relationship of a person to his or her family. The rules of a family leader must be accorded considerable weight under the presumption that such rules are to the ultimate benefit of the family, and, likewise for political leadership.

The timing of these actions brings to question the intent of the Chamberlain Council to cure any defect in the election process and conduct a legitimate tribal election. Once its terms had expired, it was foreclosed from changing the laws of the Tribe that pertain to political succession. The Chamberlain Council was bound by the laws that installed it into office. Its primary duty was to ensure compliance with the pre-existing tribal law and to effect an orderly transition of government. To initiate any laws outside their constitutional authority, exceeded their legal and political mandate.

B. Validity of the Recognition of the "Peters Council" by Assistant Secretary Gover

1. Introduction and Background

Although the essential facts are set out above, *supra* pp. 2–10 (pp. 135–41 here), these additional facts are particularly relevant in this section dealing with Assistant Gover's recognition of the "Peters Council." In the aftermath of the several failed elections discussed in Part I of this opinion, during the period from December 1998 through August 1999, there were extensive contacts by both the Chamberlain Council and the Peters Council with Mr. Gover. During this period, representatives of the Chamberlain Council met with Mr. Gover at least four times and with high level assistants of Mr. Gover on at least two other occasions. The Peters Council met with Mr. Gover at least twice. Despite its obvious importance, Mr. Gover never effectuated a face-to-face meeting of the Chamberlain Council, the Peters Council, and himself. Even more startling, no administrative appeal[21] in this matter was ever filed, much less pursued, by the Peters Council.

All of these meetings—not surprisingly—dealt with the mutually agreed upon necessity to conduct a tribal council election that was legitimate and without flaw. The critical items of disagreement appeared to be over the timing of the election, which would include both a primary and general election, and whether this was possible without a prior election involving constitutional reform relating to membership, redistricting, and changing the size of the tribal council. Although agreement between the parties and Assistant Secretary Gover appeared imminent at times, it never materialized.

During this period, Assistant Secretary Gover wrote at least four letters to the Chamberlain Council. In a June 9, 1999 letter, Mr. Gover wrote, "I strongly urge you to conduct an election within the next forty-five days to select ten individuals to serve as Tribal Council members for the Isabella District from

21. *See, e.g.*, 25 C.F.R. Part 2 (1999) setting forth the administrative procedure for challenging actions (or, as in this case, alleged inactions) of the Bureau of Indian Affairs.

among the twenty persons from the Isabella District who were the successful candidates at the latest primary election in January 1999." Mr. Gover further indicated that if this did not happen, he "would direct the local B.I.A. Superintendent and Area Director to deal with the representatives for the two off-reservation districts and the ten persons from the Isabella District who received the highest number of votes in [the] January 1999 [primary] as representatives of the Tribe."

Pursuant to a subsequent letter from the Chamberlain Council, Mr. Gover wrote again on July 6, 1999 indicating his perception of a "prolonged and (sic) undeterminable limbo thereby frustrating the clear will of the people" yet he also indicated a willingness "to consider any other reasonable alternatives to resolving the current frustration of the voters." Three days later, Mr. Chamberlain met personally with Mr. Gover. In a written communication, Assistant Secretary Gover subsequently extended the election deadline until August 6, 1999. A final round of separate meetings of members of the Chamberlain Council and the Peters Council with Mr. Gover ensued. Following these meetings, Mr. Gover's legal representative requested the submission of any final arguments and/or documents by the Chamberlain Council and the Peters Council to be made by August 6, 1999.

On August 10, 1999, Mr. Gover made his decision in a letter directed to both the parties. As noted above, *supra* p. 9 (pp. 139–40 here), and in the appendix, he recognized the *eleven* top vote getters in the January 1999 primary as the representatives of the Isabella District. Since two vote-getters tied for the tenth highest spot, he directed that those two individuals "share the vote for that seat on the Council." Assistant Secretary Gover further indicated that this recognition was on an "interim basis" and he looked "forward to a time when *normal* government-to-government relations with the tribe can be re-established." (emphasis added)[22]

As will become more clear in the discussion of relevant statutory and case law, *infra* pp. 22–33 (pp. 150–59 here), Mr. Gover's letter is remarkable in at least three respects. First, it provides absolutely *no* legal authority for Mr. Gover's decision. No part of the United States or Saginaw Chippewa Tribe's constitution, no federal or tribal statute, no federal or tribal regulation, and no case law—federal or tribal—are cited, much less discussed. It necessarily

22. Mr. Gover's letter also contains a somewhat bizarre disclaimer that "the holdover [i.e., Chamberlain] Council's public relations activities [concerning an 'unflattering newspaper article about me'] have not caused me to feel any bias against them. I have decided this matter strictly on the merits." *See* full text at Appendix.

follows, of course, that there is no reference to the procedural posture of the case as being an administrative appeal or otherwise authorized by law. Second, Mr. Gover's decision clearly *violates* the Constitution of the Saginaw Chippewa Tribe of Michigan in recognizing eleven instead of ten representatives from the Isabella District.[23] Third, it breaks entirely new (and Tribally unconstitutional) ground in recognizing individuals who have not won any general election but only are top vote getters in a primary election.[24]

2. Federal Substantive and Procedural Law

a. Substantive Law

Given the remarkable sweep of the Assistant Secretary's (alleged) power to "recognize" one set of elected tribal officials over another, one would expect express congressional authorization and delegation of such authority to the Bureau of Indian Affairs. Yet this is not so. As attorneys for the Peters Council—the clear beneficiaries of Assistant Secretary Gover's actions—admitted, "there is no statute or regulation which states in so many words that the Secretary must decide which persons to recognize as the lawfully elected leadership of the Tribe." (Respondent's Supplemental Brief at 3). This candid statement bears further scrutiny.

It is—in this Court's opinion—a necessary and unavoidable conclusion as well. While it is true that the United States Constitution recognizes Congress' power to regulate "commerce with Indian tribes" (Art. I. Sec. 8 cl. 3), *see, e.g., White Mountain Apache Tribe v. Bracker*, 448 U.S. 136, 142–43 (1980) and while Congress has delegated much of that authority to the executive branch at 25 U.S.C. § 9[25] with corresponding subdelegations to the Secretary of Interior and to the Commission of Indian Affairs at 25 USC §§ 1, 1(a),[26] and 2(a), such delegations are properly contingent on "carrying into effect the various provisions of any *act* relating to Indian Affairs." 25 USC § 9 (1994) (emphasis

---

23. *See* Art. IV, Sec. 2(1), Saginaw Chippewa Tribe of Michigan Constitution. In addition, the Tribal Constitution makes no provision to "share the vote for that seat on the Council."

24. *See* Art. IV, Sec. 1, Saginaw Chippewa Tribe of Michigan Constitution.

25. 25 U.S.C. § 9 provides: "The President may prescribe such regulations as he may think fit for carrying into effect the various provisions of any act relating to Indian affairs, and for the settlement of the accounts of Indian affairs."

26. 25 USC § 1a provides:

> For the purpose of facilitating and simplifying the administration of the laws governing Indian affairs, the Secretary of the Interior is authorized to delegate, from time to time, and to the extent and under such regulations as he deems proper, his powers and duties under said laws to the Commissioner of Indian Affairs, insofar as such powers and duties relate to action in individual cases arising under

added). Of course, there is no act of Congress that purports to confer authority on the Secretary of Interior to decide tribal elections.[27] Therefore such an argument quickly runs out of steam and comes up empty.

In conventional administrative law parlance, it appears that the Assistant Secretary's actions are clearly *ultra vires* and therefore of no force and effect. For example, federal executive officials are limited to the authority conferred on them by the Constitution or statute. *See, e.g., Citizens to Preserve Overton Park, Inc. v. Volpe*, 401 U.S. 402 (1971). This may even be more true in Indian law. *See, e.g., Morton v. Ruiz*, 415 U.S. 199 (1974).

The Assistant Secretary's actions in this matter are further remarkable in their complete failure to heed the essential precepts of the pivotal cases of *National Farmers Union Insurance Cos. v. Crow Tribe of Indians*, 471 U.S. 845 (1985) and *Iowa Mutual Insurance v. LaPlante*, 480 U.S. 9 (1987) to exhaust tribal court remedies—including tribal appellate remedies—before invoking

---

> general regulations promulgated by the Secretary of the Interior pursuant to law. Subject to the supervision and direction of the Secretary, the Commissioner is authorized to delegate, in like manner, any powers and duties so delegated to him by the Secretary, or vested in him by law, to the assistant commissioners, or the officer in charge of any branch, division, office, or agency of the Bureau of Indian Affairs, insofar as such powers and duties relate to action in individual cases arising under general regulations promulgated by the Secretary of the Interior or the Commissioner of Indian Affairs pursuant to law. Such delegated powers shall be exercised subject to appeal to the Secretary, under regulations to be prescribed by him, or, as from time to time determined by him, to the Under Secretary or to an Assistant Secretary of the Department of the Interior, or to the Commissioner of Indian Affairs. The Secretary or the Commissioner, as the case may be, may at any time revoke the whole or any part of a delegation made pursuant to this section, but no such revocation shall be given retroactive effect. Nothing in this section shall be deemed to abrogate or curtail any authority to make delegations conferred by any other provision of law, nor shall anything in this section be deemed to convey authority to delegate any power to issue regulations.

27. If such an act of Congress existed, it would arguably extend beyond any reasonable definition of "Indian commerce" and could only be 'justified' by the plenary power doctrine articulated in Lone Wolf v. Hitchcock, 187 U.S. 553 (1903). While this doctrine and the few ensuing limitations set out Delaware Tribal Business Committee v. Weeks, 430 U.S. 73 (1977) and United States v. Sioux Nation of Indians, 448 U.S. 371 (1980) are well established in federal Indian Law, this Court regards the plenary power doctrine as essentially extra-constitutional and illegitimate especially when it is used as a sword against tribal sovereignty instead of shield to protect tribes from state encroachment. *See, e.g.*, FRANK POMMERSHEIM, BRAID OF FEATHERS 46–50 (1995); Philip Frickey, *Marshalling Past and Present: Colonialism, Constitutionalism, and Interpretation of Federal Indian Law*, 107 HARV. L. REV. 381, 395 (1993).

federal court jurisdiction to challenge tribal authority. Perhaps the Assistant Secretary considered his unilateral actions as *sui generis* and beyond such precedential constraint. In fact, this failure of the Assistant Secretary, in part, was the basis for the Chamberlain Council's action brought against the Assistant Secretary in the federal courts. *See* further discussion *infra* pp. 30–33 (pp. 156–59 here).

b. Procedural Law

Despite the existence of a well-recognized administrative process set out at 25 C.F.R. Part 2 (1999) to bring claims against the Bureau of Indians for what it did or failed to do,[28] the process was not used by the Peters Council in this matter. Instead, it, as well as the Chamberlain Council, engaged the Assistant Secretary Gover directly and repeatedly in this matter. Counsel for both parties could not provide any legal authority for this process. Certainly, this was not a legal or administrative law proceeding in any sense of that term in that it never involved a face to face meeting of the parties, resulted in no record or findings of fact and conclusions of law, and it was completely without the existence of administrative due process and regularity. To be blunt, it was basically a bold political attempt by both sides to have the Assistant Secretary weigh-in in their favor in this not unimportant election dispute. Each side seemed to think that the Assistant Secretary, regardless of the law, held the necessary political power in his hands. And, curiously enough, this was not a completely unfounded assumption for at least two reasons. First, there exists both the unique element of the trust relationship in Indian law, and second, there was plenty of case law of various stripes involving B.I.A. 'resolution' of tribal election disputes. However, as the following analysis demonstrates neither of these two possibilities permits the naked use of Secretarial power as it was used in this case.

3. Trust Relationship between the Federal Government and Indian Tribes

While the absence of positive law on point is usually dispositive in most areas of law, it is not necessarily so in Indian law. One reason is the existence of the trust relationship. The trust relationship, which is rooted in the early, seminal cases of *Cherokee Nation v. Georgia*, 30 U.S. 1 (1831) and *Worcester v.*

---

28. *See, e.g.*, the case law discussion *infra* pp. 30–33 (pp. 156–59 here) in which *all* the tribal (election) cases mentioned are rooted in proper administrative appeals in accordance with 25 C.F.R. Part 2. The Assistant Secretary engaged in a course of conduct without a single precedent supporting his (procedural) actions and dozens of cases to the contrary. This is quite astounding.

Georgia, 31 U.S. 6 (1832), articulates a special affirmative duty of the federal government "trustee" to act in such a way as to protect and advance the status of the tribal "beneficiary." This is most often seen in matters of land and natural resources, but also exists in matters of the delivery of governmental services. For example, this is the entire undergirding for the provision of such essential governmental services as police and social services by the B.I.A. on many reservations. In addition, it is the basis for encouraging many tribes to provide these services *directly* though the popular '638 contracts' authorized by the Indian Self-Determination and Education Act of 1975, 25 U.S.C. §§450a–450n (1998).

Many (federal) courts have routinely—but without any compelling or persuasive analysis—assumed that one of the elements or duties of the trust relationship includes umpiring tribal election disputes. *See, e.g., Milam v. United States Dep't. of Interior*, 10 Ind. L. Reporter 3013 (D. DC 1982); *Goodface v. Grassrope*, 708 F.2d 338 (8th Cir 1983), *Ransom v. Babbitt*, 1999 WL 825126 (D. DC 1999). Yet these cases and others fail adequately to distinguish between (1) the federal trustee's responsibility to itself as a disburser of federal money to tribes (and others) and (2) its responsibility (if any) to guarantee to the beneficiary tribe the 'right' of any particular group of elected tribal officials to take office or remain in office.

The former situation was the one most often alluded to by attorneys for the Peters Council in their citation to such statutes as the Indian Self-Determination and Education Act of 1975 and the Indian Gaming Regulatory Act, 25 U.S.C. §§2701–2721 (1998) which make reference to the Secretary's responsibility to deal with "the recognized governing body of any Indian tribe."[29] Yet these seem rather unremarkable provisions subject to the common sense interpretation that the federal government should not disburse public money to any government—such as a tribal government—that is *not* the proper or legitimate governing body from some appropriate federal perspective. This is to protect the public fisc. Within the limits of notice and basic fairness, surely the federal

29. This contention by the Peters Council appears to be belied by the fact that the Assistant Secretary's letter of "recognition" was presented to the local B.I.A. police for its presumed enforcement which seems to go beyond matters of funding into matters of power. It is further true that there is not a single reported case in which a tribe was successful in resisting the decision of the B.I.A. in an election dispute without recourse to a federal appeal. B.I.A. decisions resolving tribal election disputes—at least in the federal arena—are not merely advisory opinions about federal funding but enforceable decisions likely backed by invocation of the Supremacy Clause. This, of course, is not necessarily the view subscribed to by this Court. *See* further discussion *infra* pp. 30–33 (pp. 156–59 here).

government—with applicable regulations—can make such funding decisions (as it already does) concerning money that goes to states, counties, and municipalities across this land. You either meet the requirements to qualify for federal funding or you don't. Yet it is much more difficult to extend this obvious federal governmental responsibility to the right and duty (again without any statutory or regulatory authorization) to legally decide who is the "recognized" governing body of the tribe. That responsibility, it seems, belongs to the Tribe alone as a quintessential element of tribal sovereignty and the right of self-government. To let the Federal Government decide can only be viewed as a remarkable intrusion into tribal sovereignty.[30]

The second view of the trust relationship contends that it includes an affirmative responsibility on the part of the Federal Government to protect the right of tribal members to select a government of their choice. *See, e.g.*, *Ransom v. Babbitt*, discussed *infra* pp. 31–33 (pp. 157–59 here). Yet this is equally problematic in that such an assertion, as noted above, invades the province of tribal sovereignty and the heart of self-government. While such a view of the trust relationship situates itself on high ground as the democratic 'enforcer' of the Tribal right to elect its own government, it is only legitimate upon the exhaustion of tribal remedies that have proved to be futile, non-functioning, or non-existent, and it is only plausible within an administrative process governed by appropriate regulations rather than invoking the raw power politics of the Assistant Secretary's office. A trust relationship that is grounded in dependence and subservience is inherently at odds with any notion of sovereignty and meaningful self-government. That is why the safeguards mentioned above are not extravagances or mere window dressing, but are absolutely necessary to safeguard tribal self-determination.

In essence, if the trust relationship is to be of any mutual benefit to both the federal government and the contending tribal parties, it must be in the context of supporting tribal institutions—particularly tribal courts—as the primary arbiters of election disputes with the B.I.A. as a forum of last, not first, resort. Such a supportive, respectful attitude on the part of the Assistant Secretary's office was not much in evidence in the case at hand. The Assistant Secretary's

30. Yet this Court is not unmindful of those instances—duly reported in the cases—in which tribal institutions for whatever reasons sometimes prove incapable of resolving election disputes and political turmoil and even violence ensue. Such cases—but not the case at bar—do need the prophylactic availability of B.I.A. administrative forums to resolve such disputes in the context of interpreting (tribal) law. However, naked pleas (whatever their intentions) to the Assistant Secretary do not invoke the rule of law but rather rely on power politics and an all too available dangerous residue of colonialism within the B.I.A.

office appeared to assume from beginning to end (without the benefit of any inquiry, hearings, or findings) that the Saginaw Chippewa Indian Tribal Appellate Court was somehow incapable of resolving the election dispute.[31]

The record before this Court reveals the uncontroverted fact that—despite the adverse ruling of the Tribal trial court against the Peters Council—*no* appeal was ever filed with the Tribal Appellate Court. As counsel for the Peters Council admitted, he was aware that a newly established Tribal Appellate Court had been formed but when several of his telephone inquiries to the then appellate clerk about the necessary procedures to be followed were not returned, he abandoned the idea of filing any appeal as essentially fruitless. While counsel's candor is refreshing, it is not persuasive. And while his frustration at the time is quite understandable, it does not excuse his failure to appeal. The newly formed Tribal Appellate Court was created pursuant to a tribal ordinance that outlined its basic procedures.[32] Obviously, the failure, however rude, of a court clerk to return a party's telephone inquiries cannot excuse the party's failure to comply with tribal law.

In addition, even after the initial failure to timely appeal, subsequent inquiry to the new clerk would have confirmed that indeed the Appellate Court was up and running and was already considering its first case. *See, e.g., Saginaw Chippewa Tribe of Michigan v. Cunningham*, No. 98-CI-220. Such a set of circumstances should have set the stage for the Peters Council to file for a extraordinary writ invoking the original jurisdiction of this Court. At oral argument in this case, John Jacobson, counsel for the Peters' Council, wistfully admitted as much when he observed that had he been better informed his client would be the petitioner instead of the respondent in the case at bar and perhaps, just perhaps, there would have been no need to call on the Office of the Assistant Secretary.

For want of such effort, the integrity of Saginaw Chippewa Tribal institutions—particularly its Tribal Appellate Court—were severely and needlessly impugned. The Assistant Secretary made no inquiry—formally or informally—of the Court. His office sought no declaratory or extraordinary relief in any official proceeding nor did it seek the simplest verification about whether any action had been or could be brought to adjudicate the election dispute. He simply

31. *Durfee v. Chamberlain*, though decided by Judge Hinmon to be nonjusticiable on grounds of sovereign immunity and political question doctrines, could have been appealed to this Court.

32. *See, e.g.*, Tribal Council Resolution 99-024 (1998), Saginaw Chippewa Indian Tribe of Michigan.

assumed the worst and proceeded accordingly. This is the trustee not as helpful partner, but as arrogant superior. Nor does this Court intend to cast the Chamberlain Council as innocent and without fault. As Part III (A) of this opinion fully indicates, *supra* pp. 11–19 (pp. 142–48 here), the Chamberlain Council did act illegally and outside the scope of the Tribal Constitution in its several holdover actions, but it did, nevertheless, create a Tribal Appellate Court fully empowered in either a direct appeal or in an original action seeking an extraordinary writ to resolve the election dispute that is finally before us.[33]

In sum, while the trust relationship remains an important component of the government-to-government relationship between the federal government and Indian tribes, it does *not* authorize the Assistant Secretary to act with unbridled discretion in resolving tribal election disputes. At best—upon exhaustion of tribal remedies—the B.I.A. must provide adequate opportunity for administrative hearings and appeals in which the dispositive law will always be tribal—not federal—law.

4. Case Law

All the relevant case law[34] in the area of B.I.A. and federal court resolution of tribal court election disputes affirms two broad propositions. First is the necessity of exhausting and deferring to tribal remedies and second, that the governing law for resolving such disputes is tribal—not federal—law. For example, the Tenth Circuit has held that, where an independent tribal forum has exercised jurisdiction, the Secretary is without authority to rule on an election dispute, *Wheeler v. United State Department of Interior*, 811 F.2d 549 (10th Cir. 1987). *See also Wheeler v. Swimmer* 835 F.2d 259, 262 (10th Cir. 1987) (holding the right to conduct an election without federal interference is essential to the exercise of the right of self-government).

---

33. It is worth noting in this regard that although the Respondent Peters Council explicitly waived its sovereign immunity in this matter (*see* Respondents' Opening Brief at pp 1–2), this Court does not concede that it had any sovereign immunity to waive. It would seem, for example, that the explicit authorization of the extraordinary relief made possible in cases such as this through the Tribal Council's express lawmaking in Resolution 99-024, necessarily contemplates a waiver of tribal sovereign immunity for purposes of awarding any non-monetary, remedial relief. Given the 'waiver' in this case, specific consideration of the extent of the Tribal Council's sovereign immunity in such matters is left for another day.

34. In addition to the cases discussed in the text, *see, e.g.*, *Displaced Elem. Lineage Emancipated Members Alliance v. Sacramento Area Director*, 34 IBIA 74, (3/10/99); *Duncan v. Portland Area Director*, 33 IBIA 220 (4/1/99); *Wadena v. Acting Minneapolis Area Director*, 30 IBIA 130 (12/11/96).

Respondents rely most heavily on two cases to support the actions of the Assistant Secretary in this matter. They are *Goodface v. Goodrope*, 708 F.2d 338 (8th Cir. 1983) and the very recently decided case of *Ransom v. Babbitt*, 69 F. Supp. 2d 141 (DDC 1999). In *Goodface*, the Eighth Circuit held that the Secretary of Interior could not decide to not decide which elected faction to recognize in a dispute on the Lower Brule Sioux Reservation in South Dakota. Yet the case expressly stated that such action by the B.I.A. was "interim" only and "should continue only so long as the dispute remains unresolved by a Tribal Court." In the case at bar, the actions of the Assistant Secretary foreclosed—or attempted to foreclose—use of tribal court appellate or original jurisdictional authority to resolve the matter at hand. Yes, the Secretary must do something when his authority is invoked in an election dispute but only when tribal remedies have been exhausted and have proved ineffective. In this case, tribal court remedies, regardless of what the Assistant Secretary thought, had not been exhausted and of course could not have been deemed ineffective.[35]

The Eighth Circuit found it was an abuse of discretion to recognize "both Tribal councils only on a *de facto* basis." Specifically:

> We recognize that the district court faced a practical problem. The BIA's action effectively recognized a two-headed administration with no real power to govern. Although it was necessary to remedy the situation by ordering the BIA to recognize one governing body, the district court overstepped the boundaries of its jurisdiction in interpreting the tribal constitution and bylaws and addressing the merits of the election dispute. *Goodface*, 708 F.2d at 338.

In addition, the situation on the Lower Brule Reservation involved "interim recognition" of a group of individuals who appeared to have won a *general* election as opposed to merely surviving a primary election.[36] This case is therefore not at all similar to *Goodface.*

The Respondents also rely heavily on the recent case of *Ransom v. Babbitt*, 69 F. Supp. 2d 141 (D.DC 1999). In *Ransom*, a federal district court held that a determination of the B.I.A. to recognize the new "Constitutional Government" of the St. Regis Mohawk Tribe in New York State as opposed to the old "Three Chief System" of government was "arbitrary, capricious, and contrary

35. *See, e.g.*, National Farmers Union Ins. Cos. v. Crow Tribe of Indians, 471 U.S. 845 (1985) and Iowa Mutual Ins. v. LaPlante, 480 U.S. 9 (1987).

36. Respondents also elide the crucial fact that the posture of *Goodface* is that of an administrative appeal of a B.I.A. decision rather than any *sua sponte* decision of the Assistant Secretary.

to law." The basis of this decision was the Court's view that the B.I.A. acted erroneously in deferring to a tribal (trial) court decisions in the matter and ignoring a subsequent tribal referendum that rejected the tribal court's decision concerning the very close tribal election to adopt the new form of constitutional government in the first instance.

The Court found that it was necessary for the B.I.A. to insure that Tribal Court decisions were "reasonable" *Ransom*, 69 F. Supp. 2d at 151 and that it had failed to do so in this instance by ignoring information that the tribal court had become "non-functional," and by refusing to accept a tribal referendum that expressly rejected the tribal court's difficult and controversial decision about the results of the original constitutional election.

While *Ransom* is indeed a difficult case involving an extremely close, hotly contested election that changed the *structure* of tribal government and about which reasonable people might differ, it seems to us that the federal district court in adopting a "reasonableness" standard of review clearly went beyond the "arbitrary, capricious, and abuse of discretion" standard set out in the Administrative Procedures Act (APA).[37] In addition, the reasonableness standard does not seem to us to provide adequate recognition of tribal sovereignty and self-determination.

In any event, *Ransom* is not analogous to the case at bar. *Ransom* proceeds from an extensive set of administrative appeals (hence the necessity of applying the APA "arbitrary, capricious, and abuse of discretion" standard) which included on the record evidence about the then "non-functioning" tribal court, the results of a specific referendum about the validity of the tribal court decision,[38] and clear evidence of a B.I.A. tilt in favor of the constitution reform government.[39] The precedential value of *Ransom* is further qualified by the fact that it did not exist at the time Assistant Secretary Gover made his decision and may well be subject to appeal itself. Yet *Ransom* is instructive in a positive way—not as legal precedent—but as a model of the benefit of extensive ad-

37. *See, e.g.*, federal Administrative Procedure Act, 5 U.S.C. §706(2)(A) (1998). Federal courts are empowered to "hold unlawful and set aside agency action, findings, and conclusions found to be arbitrary, capricious, and an abuse of discretion, or otherwise not in accordance with law." United States v. Garno, 974 F. Supp. 628, 633 (E.D. Mich. 1997).

38. While the District Court found this quite probative, this Court is much more cautious about endorsing precedent that appears to subject the validity of specific tribal court decisions to review in the "court of popular opinion." This is not something that we routinely see in the federal and state context. Why is it somehow appropriate in the tribal court context?

39. *See Ransom*, 69 F. Supp. 2d at 149–50.

ministrative proceedings in developing a meaningful record to bring before a federal court. Needless to say, no such administrative proceeding occurred in this case.

In sum, the relevant case law identifies three essential steps that must be taken to resolve any tribal election dispute. They are:

1. The necessity of exhausting tribal court remedies, including tribal appellate remedies;
2. Then (and only then), if necessary, taking appropriate B.I.A. administrative appeals in accordance with 25 C.F.R. Part 2 in which the dispositive law is tribal—not federal—law; and
3. Finally, subsequent federal judicial review, if any, of the B.I.A. administrative determination shall be based on the APA "arbitrary, capricious, and abuse of discretion" standard.

None of these ingredients are present in the case at bar and therefore the Assistant Secretary's action is "arbitrary, capricious, and an abuse of discretion," and wholly contrary to law.

5. Government-to-Government Relationship

In a larger, more public policy and diplomatic focus, the actions of the Assistant Secretary did nothing to advance the government-to-government relationship between the Federal Government and the Saginaw Chippewa Tribe of Michigan. In fact the Assistant Secretary's actions were directly contrary to the current federal policy of supporting tribal sovereignty and advancing tribal self-government. This government-to-government policy has been endorsed by all recent Presidents of the United States including Mr. Gover's current boss, President William Jefferson Clinton. The Assistant Secretary's extreme course of conduct in this matter ripped and tore at the fabric of tribal sovereignty. Examples are manifest. He showed no respect for the integrity of tribal institutions, particularly this Tribal Appellate Court. Neither he nor any of his staff made any inquiry—official or unofficial—directly to this Court about its operational status or likely jurisdictional purview in this matter.

This initial unwillingness to inquire has mutated into a current unwillingness to participate as *amicus curiae* in the present proceeding.[40] This Court in

---

40. On September 23, 1999, this Court issued an order that *inter alia* invited the Federal Government acting through the Secretary of Interior and the Assistant Secretary to submit an *amicus curiae* friend of the court brief in this matter. This offer was declined by Assistant Solicitor Scott Keep on the grounds that it was "currently engaged in related litigation in the United States District Court for the Eastern District of Michigan." This seems

its subsequent order of October 18, 1999 again requested an *amicus curiae* brief from the Assistant Secretary's office. This time there was no direct response to this Court by the Secretary, except through a footnote in its supplemental brief submitted in the federal proceeding. The footnote stated that authority to submit an *amicus curiae* brief requires approval of the Solicitor General of the United States, 28 C.F.R. 0.20(c),[41] but as a "practical matter" it had no problem with either of the tribal parties providing this Court with a copy of its brief. Mr. John Jacobson, counsel for the Peters Council, kindly provided a copy of the Federal Government's Supplemental Memorandum to this Court. It is only six pages in length and is remarkably unilluminating and is much less thoroughly researched than the brief submitted to the Court by the Peters Council. It is hard to fathom how these evasive, if not actually disrespectful, actions are in line with the government-to-government relationship. As noted elsewhere in this opinion, *supra* pp. 11–19 (pp. 142–48 here), this does not mean that the Chamberlain holdover Council was without fault. Indeed it was guilty of wrongdoing, but its wrongdoing cannot excuse the wrongdoing of the Assistant Secretary. In law, as in life, two wrongs do not make a right.

In addition, the actions of the Assistant Secretary have resulted in extensive negative publicity for the tribe,[42] have resulted in tribal attorneys' fees in the

---

somewhat of a *non sequitur* since the Secretary was already "defending" its actions in the federal case, it would take no extra effort to provide those same explanations to this Court. Assistant Solicitor's Keep's letter to this Court of September 30, 1999, goes on to note "[A]s to the merits of the Assistant Secretary's August 10 decision, I believe that decision is adequately explained in the Assistant Secretary's letter of that date and his earlier one of June 9." Of course, this cannot be so since neither of those letters contain any legal authority or justification whatsoever.

The U.S. Supreme Court recognizes the ability of tribal courts as a general matter to decide questions of federal law. Specifically, "[u]nder normal circumstances, tribal courts, like state courts, can and do decide questions of federal law, and there is no reason to think questions of federal preemption are any different." El Paso Natural Gas Co. v. Neztsosie, 526 U.S. 473, 485 n.7 (1999).

41. Of course, we are troubled by the fact that the U.S. Supreme Court has urged parties to exhaust tribal remedies through the use of the tribal courts, *see* discussion *infra* at pp. 40–41 (pp. 164–66 here), yet the Executive branch of the U.S. government has chosen to support a different policy through this cumbersome regulation which, to this Court's knowledge, finds no basis in statute.

42. *See, e.g.*, *Indian Country Today*: David Melmer, "Membership Problems Void Four Elections" at C1 (June 28, 1999); "Saginaw Chippewa in Turmoil," at A1 (August 23, 1999); "Saginaw Offices Seized," at A1 (September 27, 1999); *see also* Elizabeth Amon, "What's U.S. Tribal Role? Feds Replace Tribal Council with Rival But Face Court Challenge," *National*

excess of one hundred thousand dollars[43] and have potentially created a very bad precedent relative to condoning extensive Secretarial discretion in deciding internal tribal matters. All of this for want of simple inquiry to this Court about its operational existence and reasonable reliance on its integrity to make a thoughtful, expeditious, and reliable decision.[44]

C. Validity of the Actions of the 'Interim'[45] Peters Council

As demonstrated above, *supra* pp. 19–33 (pp. 148–59 here), the Assistant Secretary acted illegally in recognizing the Peters Council as the 'interim' government of the Saginaw Chippewa Indian Tribe of Michigan. Therefore it is necessary to analyze the validity and status of the actions taken by the Peters Council during its interim phase. Concern for stability and government regularity creates a necessary presumption in favor of the legality of interim governmental actions. Such a presumption is nevertheless rebuttable in a given circumstance by clear and convincing evidence that such actions violated tribal or federal law.[46]

The problem in this case is not the fact that the Peters Council was 'interim' in nature,[47] but rather that its recognition by the Assistant Secretary as such was erroneous and illegal as a matter of both tribal and federal law. This in no way, however, makes the holdover actions of the Chamberlain Council legal. *See* discussion *supra* pp. 17–19 (pp. 146–48 here). Unfortunately, these actions—taken together—have created the stressful and anomalous situation of

Law Journal, at A1 (November 8, 1999). Similar articles appeared in newspapers around the country ranging from *The Grand Rapids Press* to *The Washington Post*.

43. *See, e.g.*, billing submitted by the Law Firm of Jacobson, Buffalo, Schoeseler, and Magnuson, Ltd. to the Saginaw Chippewa Tribe.

44. In this regard, it is fair to note (again) that the Peters Council itself is not without fault. It has never explained adequately to this Court why it failed to initiate any administrative appeal challenging the conduct of the Chamberlain Council and the necessity for B.I.A. corrective action, but instead called on the Assistant Secretary for direct assistance.

45. Again, we rely upon the term used by Assistant Secretary Gover in his letter of August 10, 1999. p.2.

46. *See* discussion *supra* pp. 17–19 (pp. 146–48 here). We consider this equally applicable both to the Peters and Chamberlain Councils.

47. Any number of tribal election cases correctly note the authority of the B.I.A. *under proper circumstances* (which are not present here) to recognize one tribal group over another in contested elections. *See* discussion supra at pp. 30–33 (pp. 156–59 here). *See also* such cases as Goodface v. Goodrope, 708 F.2d 338 (8th Cir. 1983); Ransom v. Babbitt, 69 F. Supp. 2d 141 (D. D. C. 1999).

pitting an illegal 'holdover' Tribal Council against an illegal 'interim' Tribal Council.

While it is not the duty of the Court to scrutinize every action taken by the Peters Council during its interim phase, there are two necessary areas of inquiry and they are the areas of membership reform and changes in the electoral process. These are legitimate questions for investigation as they—in one form or another—constitute the core elements of the differences between the Chamberlain and Peters Councils.

As to membership, the Peters Council enacted no new legislation, took no action to remove anyone currently enrolled, and otherwise proceeded in accordance with the 'base enrollees' list as adopted in the Saginaw Chippewa Indian Tribal Constitution of 1986. Therefore, the eligible pool of candidates and voters has remained identical under the Peters interim regime as existed prior to its recognition.

In regards to the Tribal election procedure, the interim Peters Council was active. In fact, it substantially amended Ordinance No. 4, the Tribal Election Ordinance. Specifically, it amended Sections 7, 20, and 27 of Ordinance 4 relative to voting requirements, election protest, and violation of election laws. Most significantly, the new Section 20 repealed this Court's original jurisdiction to hear election challenges and established the new position of Election Appeals Judge. In addition, the decision of the Election Appeals Judge was deemed "final" without "consent to the jurisdiction of the tribal court over decisions of the Election Appeals Judge." This enactment gives the Court significant pause. While it may be entirely legitimate to repeal this Court's original jurisdiction in election challenges, it is significantly less likely that repeal of all judicial appeals in election matters comports with essential notions of tribal fairness and due process under the Indian Civil Rights Act of 1968, 25 U.S.C. § 1302(8). This issue is not currently before the Court and therefore is properly left for another day.

In sum, the Peters Council committed major legal error by its failure to exhaust tribal (appellate) remedies, and then, if necessary, to file a B.I.A. administrative appeal in accordance with 25 C.F.R. Part 2. This failure did not cause the Tribal election crisis, which was sparked by the Chamberlain Council's illegal holdover actions, but it did exacerbate the resulting problems. As this opinion amply demonstrates elsewhere, it didn't have to be this way. And hopefully, it will not be so in the future.

This case demonstrates the potential for genuine crisis when there is a failure of confidence in, and respect for, tribal law and tribal institutions. In this instance, it generated the painful paradox of an illegal 'holdover' government in contention with an illegal 'interim' government aided and abetted by the illegal actions of the Assistant Secretary's Office. This is not to say that any side intended to create harm or crisis, but only that it did happen. No one welcomes painful experience but it can provide the benefit of learning, perhaps even wisdom, if it is carefully examined. If it is merely ignored or trivialized, it invites tragedy. This Court has taken the road of close examination in an attempt to render justice with compassion and without recrimination; an examination that might lead to a new beginning of cultural conciliation and democratic respect.

IV. A New Beginning

Implicit throughout this opinion is the Court's perception that there needs to be a new beginning between the contending Tribal parties as well as between the Saginaw Chippewa Indian Tribe of Michigan and the Federal Government. Hopefully, this process has begun and will continue. Let us examine what has already happened and what might yet happen. With regard to the relationship between the Peters and Chamberlain Councils, several very positive steps appear to have already taken place. They include the respect each party accorded each other and this Court throughout these proceedings. The Court commends both sides in this regard. This very advance was made all the more likely by the judicial and cultural atmosphere created by the Court. Specifically, for example, the Court invited both parties to come forward and shake the hands of the members of the Court of Appeals as a gesture of respect and good will. In addition, the Court invited each side—through a designated representative—to offer a prayer or blessing at the beginning of the hearing (Chamberlain Council) and at the close of the hearing (Peters Council). These events appeared to create an atmosphere of high purpose and dignity. Each party noted its gratitude for the existence of the Tribal Appellate Court and its commitment to accept and to abide by the Court's decision in this matter.

Each member of the Court also spoke briefly on the record to the parties. These comments served to provide a thumbnail sketch of the Justices' background for the parties, but more importantly each Justice spoke earnestly of the honor to serve on the first ever Saginaw Chippewa Tribal Appellate Court.[48] In addition, each Justice emphasized the historical, cultural, and legal impor-

48. None of the three justices are members of the Saginaw Chippewa Indian Tribe. Two of the Court's members are tribal members elsewhere and all three are longtime scholars, teachers, and/or practitioners of Indian law.

tance of the case before it and his or her sincerest hope that its resolution would be the beginning of a new tribal jurisprudence of respect, cultural sensitivity, and legal integrity.[49] Without tempering the cogency or force of their arguments, the demeanor of the parties and their counsel indicated a willingness to acknowledge and to accept the responsibilities of such a momentous occasion. Nor did such willingness apparently end with the hearing. Since the hearing on October 16, 1999, the Tribe has concluded a primary and general election without major incident or protest.[50] These developments are indeed remarkable and hopefully presage a new era of intra-tribal cooperation in strengthening democratic processes and institutions of the Saginaw Chippewa Indian Tribe.

Unfortunately, the relationship of the Federal Government to the Saginaw Chippewa Indian Tribe of Michigan appears to be on less settled, less harmonious ground. There continues to be vigorous—if not hostile—litigation involving all three parties in federal court. As described above, *supra* pp. 33–35 (pp. 158–61 here), the Federal Government has been less than cooperative in assisting this Court. Perhaps the Federal Government, acting through the B.I.A., simply moves more slowly, more deliberately before it can change its posture so that it can reconfigure the balance in the trust relationship away from a vertical, neo-colonialist paradigm to a more horizontal, collaborative model. Of course, there can be no doubt about the necessity of such approach to give genuine substance to the meaning of government-to-government relationship in the modern era. And while there is some evidence of this progressive movement in other efforts of the B.I.A., it is not present in current federal interaction with the Saginaw Chippewa Indian Tribe. This needs to change and this Court is committed to playing any positive role available to it in this area of concern.

---

49. *See, e.g.*, the Hearing Transcript October 16, 1999, at 119, Chief Justice Vicenti; "We don't want to make any illusions about it, ... that we endorse Native belief and Native tradition, at the outset ... we want to foster what we consider to be the central principles of respect, generosity, of co-operation, and of self sacrifice for the good of the whole. And we recognize that that has its ... correlatives in the four directions of the wind, the four colors you have on your flag in front of you [the Tribal flag], ... and [the] four sacred substances of sage, cedar, sweetgrass and tobacco;" Justice Fairbanks, at 120–21, "And so I see us as helping restore ... this Tribe and ... bringing some unity to this Tribe;" and Justice Pommersheim, at 119, "We hope, as people have said, that people will pull together, because the future and the importance of future generations is what is the key. And that will help—hopefully to guide our own deliberations in this matter."

50. *See also* discussion *supra* pp. 37 (pp. 161–63 here) as to whether this fact obviates the necessity of granting the "extraordinary writ" sought in this action.

This case is a test case on many different levels. The 1986 Constitution makes no provisions for the circumstance where there is a breakdown in the transitional process between successive Councils within the representative democracy prescribed by the current Constitutional order. There are no prior documented and applicable cases that may guide the current Appellate Court either within the past cases of this Tribe or of any other Court. The situation described here finds its most apt analogy in events that occur in newly independent third world countries and therefore there is a resulting necessity to forge a new and appropriate jurisprudence—a point of 'jurisgenesis.'[51]

We have determined in the course of examining the facts and law applicable to this case that the Chamberlain Council wrongly held over, pursuing a course of action that was ineluctably contrary to the Constitution of the Tribe. Nonetheless, the Council wisely created an appellate process, and, when time came to query the validity of the Assistant Secretary's actions, properly invoked the Court's original jurisdiction. We can commend the Assistant Secretary for finding in principle, at least, that the Chamberlain Council was motivated by an erroneous perception of the Tribal membership laws. But we conclude here that the Assistant Secretary then violated both tribal and federal law in recognizing the Peters Council—a reckless misuse of the power and authority of that office that created anomalous and trying circumstances for all involved that may never be corrected even in a Court's most brilliant and creative moments. We cannot overlook the Assistant Secretary's failure to turn to the tribal judiciary, to give vivid endorsement to the policy of deference to tribal institutions as set forth in *National Farmers Union Insurance Cos. v. Crow Tribe of Indians*,[52] *Iowa Mutual Insurance Co. v. LaPlante*,[53] and Executive Order 13084 (May 14, 1998) notwithstanding the existence of 28 C.F.R. 0.20(c).[54] Our examination of the facts herein also allows us to commend the Peters Council for the solid adherence to an interest in ensuring the proper and lawful transition of government. But, it too, compromised the integrity of the Tribe's sovereignty by seeking the

---

51. Robert Cover, *Forward: Nomos and Narrative*, 97 HARV. L. REV. 4, 11 (1983) ("That the creation of legal meaning—'jurisgenesis'—takes place always through an essentially cultural medium.").

52. 471 U.S. 845 (1985).

53. 480 U.S. 9 (1987).

54. As we have repeatedly noted above, the Appellate Court was fully constituted and functional very early in 1999. The Assistant Secretary did not make inquiry into its existence, but had he done so, and, had he conformed his priorities to the deference noted here, he would have had ample time to consult the Department of Justice and, with its approval, petitioned this Court to issue a declaratory judgment, well before he was faced with the need to consider the issuance of the fateful August 10 letter.

approval of the Assistant Secretary to accede to its leadership, as if his approval meant anything under the circumstances and existing tribal law.

In the American system of jurisprudence, litigation is conducted on an adversarial basis. There are clear winners and clear losers. Traditional notions of Native American jurisprudence are concerned with healing, restoring balance and harmony, accomplishing reconciliation, and making social relations whole again—no winners or losers—rather, there are survivors who must be nourished back to health. Although the Petitioners do prevail in their claims regarding the Assistant Secretary's authority, we cannot conclude that they should be restored to leadership as a continuation of an unlawful holdover Council—to do so would not be mindful of the Tribal members' need for healing and transcendence. Neither can we uniformly endorse the enactments of the Peters Council except to the extent that they restored the political processes that elected the Chamberlain Council and this current Council to office. We must, accordingly, deny the relief requested in the Chamberlain petitions.[55]

In part, our closing comments here are an admission, as is more often the case, that the parties are each at fault and each to be acclaimed. We would only urge that each accept responsibility for the errors each has committed and each accept the responsibility to work cooperatively in the future. Traditions of generosity, respect, integrity, and cooperation compel each party to do what good grace and a proper way of life would dictate, well beyond what a Court may order. The rest remains to a higher source.

V. Conclusion

In sum, for all the reasons discussed above, the Court finds that Assistant Secretary Gover did violate both tribal and federal law in his August 10, 1999, 'recognition' of the 'interim' Peters Council. Therefore, the 'interim' Peters Council was not lawfully holding office. However, this Court also finds that the Chamberlain Council violated the Saginaw Chippewa Indian Tribal Constitution in its 'holdover' actions by setting aside the results of at least three elections after the expiration of its constitutional term of office and therefore it is not entitled to any relief in this matter. The actions of both the 'holdover' Chamberlain Council and the 'interim' Peters Council—except as to matters

55. This holding is applicable to both the present case, and the request for a temporary restraining order as filed on December 5, 1999, in *Chamberlain and Hinmon v. Chief Judge, Tribal Community Court*, Ct. App. Docket Number unassigned. Their request for the temporary restraining order is also denied.

relative to perpetuating their occupancy of office—are nevertheless presumptively valid unless a party with proper standing can demonstrate by clear and convincing evidence that such action violated tribal or federal law, or, conferred an undue benefit of those persons then seated in office.

The Court also concludes that at this time the Tribal Council officials who were sworn in on December 6, 1999, pursuant to their victory in the November 2, 1999 general election, properly and lawfully hold office in accordance with the laws and Constitution of the Saginaw Chippewa Indian Tribe of Michigan.

Finally, the Court, again, commends both parties to this action for the dignity and respect with which they approached this Court and we urge that its judgment be received with the same dignity and respect.

IT IS SO ORDERED.

This 5th day of January, 1999.

____

Carey N. Vicenti, Chief Justice

____

Cheryl D. Fairbanks, Associate Justice

____

Frank R. Pommersheim, Associate Justice

Appendix

United States Department of the Interior

OFFICE OF THE SECRETARY
Washington, D.C. 20240

AUG 10 1999

Honorable Kevin Chamberlain
The Saginaw Chippewa Indian Tribe
7070 East Broadway
Mt. Pleasant, Michigan 48858

Dear Chief Chamberlain:

On June 9, I wrote you and expressed my concern over the Tribe's failure to complete the constitutionally mandated election of representatives for the Isabella District. I urged you and your Council to call and conduct an election within the next 45 days to select 10 individuals to serve as Tribal Council members for the Isabella District from among the twenty persons from the Isabella District who were the successful candidates at the latest primary election in January 1999. I indicated further that if the Tribe failed to resolve this matter through an election of Tribal Council members for the Isabella District, I had instructed the Area Director and Superintendent to the deal with the representatives for the two off-reservation districts and the ten persons from the Isabella District who received the highest number of votes in January 1999 as representatives of the Tribe.

Based on our meetings and documents you submitted, I extended my original 45-day deadline to permit you a further opportunity to persuade me that the Tribal Council had taken or was taking the steps necessary to restore constitutionally elected government to the Tribe. I have reviewed the actions of the Tribal Council in adopting a new election code and an amended enrollment ordinance. I have considered the comments of those opposed to the Tribal Council's actions, and I have considered the Tribal Council's response to those comments.

I appreciate the efforts of the Tribal Council to explore broad, governmental reforms. However, the reforms the Tribal Council has initiated through the election code and amended enrollment ordinance contain provisions which amount to substantive changes in the Tribal Constitution, changes which can only be legally effected through amendments to the Constitution. They are fundamental changes which are beyond the Council's authority to accomplish by ordinance. They can not resolve the current disputes without a constitutional amendment to put them in place by the majority vote of the tribal members.

Thus, the critical fact is that the holdover Council, scheduled to leave office after the November 1997 election, has failed in four efforts to conduct elections and effect a lawful transition of power. I note that most of the holdover Council members have not been successful candidates in these four elections.

The Area Director is still reviewing the petitions requesting an election to consider the adoption of a new constitution. An amendment of the Tribal Constitution, whether it is the amendment currently before the Area Director or another one or several other smaller amendments, may be

Appendix (continued)

2

one way for the tribal members to resolve the current disputes. However, any resolution based on an amendment of the Tribal Constitution is necessarily some time off.

In the meantime, I believe that the Federal government needs certainty in dealing with representatives of the Tribe for purposes of carrying on the day-to-day, government-to-government relationship of the Federal government with the Tribe. Accordingly, I am instructing the Area Director to proceed with the instructions I gave him on June 9. He is to the deal with the representatives for the two off-reservation districts and the eleven persons from the Isabella District who received the highest number of votes in January 1999 as representatives of the Tribe on an interim basis. While this interim council is an incomplete reflection of the democratic will of the people, it is the clearest and most recent expression of the sentiments of the tribal membership.

I realize that the Isabella District is entitled to only 10 representatives under the Tribal Constitution and that two individuals were tied for the tenth highest number of votes in the January 1999 primary. I see no reason why the two individuals can not share the vote for that seat on the Council. If they agree, they can cast one vote for the agreed upon position. If they disagree on a matter, their votes will simply cancel each other out.

Finally, I note for the record that I am aware of information suggesting that the holdover Council, or its agents, caused or contributed to the publication of an unflattering newspaper article about me. I have conferred with the Ethics Office for the Department and been advised that, notwithstanding my knowledge of this information, I may properly be the deciding official on this matter. The holdover Council's public relations activities have not caused me to feel any bias against them. I have decided this matter strictly on the merits.

I continue to look forward to a time when normal, government-to-government relations with the Tribe can be reestablished.

Sincerely,

Kevin Gover
Assistant Secretary - Indian Affairs

cc: Alysia LaCoumte, Esq.
Richard A. Monette, Esq.
Brown & LaCounte LLP
2916 Market Place Drive
Suite 104
Madison, WI 53719

Appendix (continued)

3

Philip Baker-Shenk
Dorsey & Whitney, LLP
Suite 300 South
1001 Pennsylvania Avenue, N.W.
Washington, D.C. 20004

John Jacobson, Esq.
Jacobson, Buffalo, Schoessler & Magnuson, Ltd.
246 Iris Park Place
1885 University Avenue, West
Saint Paul, Minn. 55104

Larry Morrin
Director, Minneapolis Ares, Bureau of Indian Affairs

Anne Bolton
Superintendent, Michigan Agency, Bureau of Indian Affairs

Note that Chief Justice Vicenti authored the first half of this opinion from the beginning through the Discussion of Part III.A., *supra* pp. 134–48 and Associate Justice Pommersheim wrote the second half from Part III.B. through the Conclusion, *supra* pp. 148–67.

Notes on *Chamberlain v. Peters* (1999)

Despite the intense turmoil surrounding this case, which included political demonstrations and even threats of violence, the decision was accepted. A peaceful transition of power occurred; the reins of governance were passed without incident or rancor. As the opinion itself makes clear, the Court made extra efforts to show respect to the parties by providing a unique cultural opportunity in allowing a representative from each side to address the Court in the context of prayer and consilience. While one can never know for sure, I believe such efforts by the Court were instrumental in establishing a reciprocal respect for the decision itself.

Electoral struggles in Indian country are wide-ranging. Strategies for redress fall into three essential categories: (1) tribal court resolution as we saw in the *Chamberlain* case, (2) application to the Bureau of Indian Affairs for resolution, and (3) litigation in state or federal court.

There are hundreds of tribal court cases addressing electoral issues. The following cases are illustrative of only some of the breadth of issues that tribal courts address in this category. Beginning with perhaps the most basic question of all: do tribal courts have jurisdiction over these disputes? The answers to such jurisdictional questions are complex and varied when they are addressed by tribal courts. In *Campion v. Swanaset*, 4 NICS App. 159 (Nooksack Tribal Ct. App. 1996), the Nooksack Tribal Court of Appeals reversed the rulings of the trial court and clarified previous precedent holding that the tribal court lacked jurisdiction to review Election Committee decisions. *Id.* at 160–62. The appellate court found that it had jurisdiction under the Nooksack Constitution provision, which gave jurisdiction to the court in "all civil matters concerning members of the Nooksack Tribe." *Id.* at 161. Ultimately, the case was remanded to the trial court to see if the failure to notify tribal members of the changes to the election ordinance deprived tribal members of their voting rights. *Id.* at 159, 161–63. In the case of *In re Election of 2000*, 6 NICS App. 45 (Sauk-Suiattle Tribal App. Ct. App. 2001), the Sauk-Suiattle appellate court held that it lacked subject matter jurisdiction to hear election disputes because under the Tribe's Code, the trial court was the court of last resort. *Id.* at 46. Thus, the Court issued an order reinstating the decision of the trial court as the final decision on the matter. *Id.*

In *Two Crow v. Grand Traverse Band Election Board*, 2008 WL 6192001 (Grand Traverse Tribal Ct.), the Grand Traverse Band of Ottawa and Chippewa Indians Tribal court held that it did not have jurisdiction to review the decision of the Election Board prohibiting a candidate from running for office, who did not turn in her required background check consent form in a timely manner. The Tribal Constitution states that "[t]he Election Board shall be authorized to issue such rules and procedures as may be necessary to carry out tribal elections and to provide for ongoing voter registration." Given this language, the court held that "the Constitution gives sole authority to resolve 'election disputes' to the Defendant Election Board, except for allegations of impropriety by the Election Board." *Id.* at 2–3. *See also Darden v. Chitimacha Election Board*, 28 I.L.R. 6043 (Chitimacha Tribal Ct. App. 2001) (finding that the tribal court lacked subject matter jurisdiction and that the Chitimacha Tribal Code renders the Election Board's decisions final and not appealable); *Hornbuckle v. Cherokee Board of Elections*, 6 Cher. Rep. 4 (E. Band Cherokee Sup. Ct. 2007) (limiting the scope of review to cases in which the petitioner has demonstrated that the "alleged irregularities unfairly and improperly or illegally affected the actual outcome of the election").

Examples of how the standard of review is handled in these disputes are addressed in *Yellow Bird v. Three Affiliated Tribes Tribal Election Board*, 29 I.L.R. 6018, 6019 (Three Aff. Trib. Ft. Berthold Reservation Dist. Ct. 2001) (applying the common law rule that election disputes are reviewed under the "clearly erroneous" standard as to questions of fact and *de novo* as to questions of law), and *Byrd v. Cherokee Nation Election Commission*, 8 Okla. Trib. 172, 178 (Cherokee Nation Jud. App. Trib. 2003) (holding that the challenger has to show the outcome would have been affected beyond a reasonable doubt).

In *Begay v. Navajo Nation Election Administration*, 4 Am. Tribal Law 604 (Nav. Sup. Ct. 2002), the petitioner attempted to run for President of the Navajo Nation, but the Navajo Nation Election Administration ("NNEA") denied his application after determining that he did not meet the residency requirements. *Id.* at 605. Begay filed suit in tribal court claiming the NNEA applied the requirements of permanent residency and continual presence unequally when candidates were evaluated. *Id.* at 605–06. The Court, when addressing the due process concerns of the case, adopted the rule that if "any ambiguities exist in an election statute, the presumption lies in favor of the candidate," and that if a statute is open to different interpretations, it may not violate due process if applied in a "fair and consistent manner." *Id.* at 608.

The Court found from the facts that the NNEA denied Begay the same opportunity it gave to other candidates to argue that he satisfied the "continually present" requirement stating "[v]agueness of the election law and its loose and unequal application led to a denial of the Appellant's right to participate." *Id.* at 610. As the Court expressly noted: "If law is to mean anything, it must be consistent in the way people are treated. In this case, the candidacy definitions were unequally applied." *Id.* The Court found that the appropriate remedy according to the precedent of *Deswood v. Navajo Board of Election Supervisors*, 1 Navajo R. 306 (1978) was to place Begay on the ballot. *Id.* at 610.

Interestingly, in *In re Wagner*, 7 Am. Tribal Law 528 (Nav. Sup. Ct. 2007), the Navajo Supreme Court upheld a decision by the Office of Hearings and Appeals that banned simultaneous service on the tribal council and in the state legislature. The Court found the Election Code requirement to "maintain unswerving loyalty to the Navajo Nation" and the oath of office requirement to "support, obey, and defend the Navajo Nation and all the laws of the Navajo Nation" required "absolute loyalty" to the Navajo Nation making the prohibition proper.

In the case of *Little Axe v. Nuckolls*, 4 Okla. Trib. 54 (Ab. Shawnee Sup. Ct. 1994), the Absentee Shawnee Supreme Court addressed the authority of the Election Commission to void an entire election. Irregularities were reported by a candidate who lost, and the candidate requested that the Election Commission void the election. *Id.* at 62–63. The Court held that the Election Commission did not have this authority, as the Tribal Constitution and Election Ordinance did not grant the Commission this authority. *Id.* at 80–81. The Court, however, made it a point to note that the Election Commission did have the authority to conduct a recount. *Id.* at 80.

A petition requesting injunctive relief for a stay of an election for reasons regarding allegations of impropriety was addressed in *Crampton v. Election Board*, 8 Am. Tribal Law 295 (Little River Tribal Ct. 2009). Although the Petitioner failed to meet the burden of proving the necessary elements normally required for a stay to be issued, the court still held that the "impropriety here is so egregious ... that the impropriety cannot be ignored or excused. The Petitioner will be allowed to move to an evidentiary hearing to further explore this issue." *Id.* at 296. The court ultimately stayed the certification for the Tribal Council seat until after the evidentiary hearing. *Id.*

In *Chee v. Navajo Election Administration*, 9 Am. Tribal Law 369 (Nav. Sup. Ct. 2010), the Office of Hearings and Appeals invalidated the unofficial general election results for two chapters and ordered a special election based on issues concerning ballot shortages. The Court found, however, that the petitioners did not meet their burden of proving by clear and convincing evidence that the results would have been different. *Id.* at 374–76. The Court also addressed what constitutes an obstruction of a free and intelligent vote when it plainly stated:

> In its decision, the OHA suggested that a ballot shortage that causes voters to be turned away or otherwise be unable to vote constituted an "obstruction of a free and intelligent vote" pursuant to *Johnson*....

> We clarify that "free and intelligent vote" is not appropriately used in the context of ballot shortages or other circumstances impacting the physical exercise of the voting right.
>
> "Free and intelligent vote" is hereby clarified as follows: by "free," a voter votes pursuant to his or her conscience, unrestrained, unburdened and unforced by outside pressure. By "intelligent," a voter casts an informed vote with a good understanding of the matter voted on.
>
> *Id.* at 376–77.

Ultimately, the Court reversed the decision by the OHA to invalidate the election and declared the results valid. *Id.* at 377.

Cornelius v. Oneida Election Board, 2005 WL 6408993 (Oneida App. Ct.), is a short but interesting case in which the Oneida Tribal Appellate Court reprimanded the Oneida Election Board for its failure to follow proper procedure when a candidate challenged the decision to not rule on her candidacy. The candidate was told that her candidate packet was incomplete, but she was not allowed to appeal this decision because the Oneida Election Board did not rule whether she was eligible or ineligible as a candidate. *Id.* at 1–2. The Court sharply noted that "[i]t is within the scope and authority of the Oneida Election Board to deny a candidate's application. What the OEB cannot do is place a candidate in limbo." *Id.* at 2. The Court continued, "[t]he OEB letter states that Ms. Cornelius has no right to appeal the OEB final determination [on her packet] ... because she was not considered eligible or ineligible as a candidate. Ms. Cornelius has no opportunity for an appeal." *Id.* The Court expressly explained the correct procedure stating that "[t]he proper procedure would have been to determine Ms. Cornelius ineligible as a candidate, and state that she is ineligible because her candidate packet was incomplete. This would allow Ms. Cornelius an appeal opportunity. At the appeal, the OEB could rule on the merits." *Id.* Ultimately, the court remanded with express instructions to the OEB to follow the outlined procedure. *Id.*

In the case of the *Sac & Fox Tribe of Mississippi In Iowa Election Board v. Bureau of Indian Affairs*, 439 F.3d 832 (8th Cir. 2006), the federal court addressed a complex tribal election situation involving an attempted recall election and an intra-tribal dispute with two competing factions, one elected and one appointed, vying for official governing recognition. The court held that it lacked subject matter jurisdiction to adjudicate the claim as the relief requested necessarily required an interpretation of the Tribe's Constitution and resolution of an intra-tribal dispute. This case also exemplifies a successful attempt to have the BIA intervene. The BIA ultimately made a decision that the federal government would recognize the dissident faction.

There is a significant amount of academic scholarship concerning tribal elections. *See, e.g.*, Paul W. Shagen, *Safeguarding the Integrity of Tribal Elections Through Campaign Finance Regulation*, 8 Cardozo Pub. L. Pol'y & Ethics J. 103 (2009) (arguing that tribes should adopt comprehensive campaign finance regulatory schemes to protect the integrity of tribal elections and discussing how regulating nonmember donations could work under federal Indian law jurisprudence); Derek H. Ross, *Protecting the Democratic Process in Indian Country Through Election Monitoring: A Solution to Tribal Election Disputes*, 36 Am. Indian L. Rev. 423 (2012) (discussing tribal court approaches to election disputes, as well as other domestic and international models).

Political Processes—Reapportionment

Woods, et al. v. Cheyenne River Sioux Tribal Council, et al.

(Cheyenne River Sioux Tribal Court of Appeals) (2012)

CHEYENNE RIVER SIOUX TRIBAL COURT OF APPEALS
CHEYENNE RIVER SIOUX TRIBE
CHEYENNE RIVER INDIAN RESERVATION

****

BERNARD WOODS, ROBIN LEBEAU,	)	Case No. 10C126
LANNY LAPLANTE, STEVE MORAN	)	Case No. A-005-11
and TISHA MORAN,	)	
PLAINTIFFS /APPELLANTS,	)	
v.	)	MEMORANDUM OPINION
CHEYENNE RIVER SIOUX TRIBAL COUNCIL	)	AND ORDER
and Individual Members of the Tribal Council,	)	
excluding Plaintiff Robin LeBeau:	)	
Ardys Cook	)	
Maynard Dupris, deceased, open seat	)	
Bryce In The Woods	)	
Ted Knife	)	
Sharon Lee	)	
Ryman LeBeau	)	
De Anna LeBeau	)	
Dixie LeCompte	)	
Merrie Miller White Bull	)	
Frank Thompson	)	
Raymond Uses Knife	)	
Robert Walters	)	
Todd Ward	)	
Edward Widow	)	
DEFENDANTS/APPELLEES.	)	

****

Per Curiam (Chief Justice Frank Pommersheim and Associate Justices Taylor Bald Eagle and Robert Clinton)[1]

---

1. Please note that while Justice Clinton's resignation from the Court became effective on December 31, 2011, he fully participated in the Court's deliberations in this case, which were concluded *before* the effective date of his resignation.

I. Introduction

The plaintiffs, appellants on appeal, are all enrolled members of the Cheyenne River Sioux Tribe. In November 2010, they brought an action in Tribal Court against the Cheyenne River Sioux Tribal Council and its individual members (hereinafter referred to collectively as the Tribal Council) seeking declaratory and injunctive relief to the effect that the due process and equal protection guarantees of the Indian Civil Rights Act, 25 U.S.C. § 1302(8), as well as the decision in *Brown v. United States*, 486 F.2d 658 (8th Cir. 1973), mandated redistricting of the Tribe's election districts in accordance with the principles of 'one man, one vote' as established in the seminal case of *Baker v. Carr*, 369 U.S. 186 (1962).

The Tribal Council filed an answer and a motion to dismiss on the grounds that the Tribal Council had not waived its sovereign immunity and that the plaintiffs failed to state a claim upon which relief might be granted. The matter was heard before Special Judge B.J. Jones. Both parties were represented by counsel.[2]

The core of Judge Jones' order of dismissal (without prejudice) of May 10, 2011 was his finding that the power of redistricting the Tribal Council legislative districts was constitutionally defined in such a way that redistricting could only be accomplished through the process of a Tribal constitutional amendment[3] and that the Tribal Court lacked any (constitutional) authority to effectuate redistricting outside the process of constitutional amendment. Specifically, Judge Jones noted that:

> It is facile to suggest that the Defendants with a stroke of a pen may come into compliance with *Brown* by taking Council action to redistrict the Reservation. The Tribal Constitution is the supreme law of

2. On appeal, plaintiffs/appellants have proceeded *pro se* due to their inability to find counsel who would take the case without compensation.

3. Cheyenne River Sioux Tribe Constitution, Art. IX (1935) provides:

> SECTION 1. This constitution and the appended by-laws may be amended by a majority of the qualified voters of the tribe voting at an election called for that purpose by the Secretary of the Interior, provided that at least 30 per cent of those entitled to vote shall vote in such election; but no amendment shall become effective until it shall have been approved by the Secretary of the Interior.
>
> SECTION 2. It shall be the duty of the Secretary of the Interior, upon presentation of a petition signed by at least two hundred (200) legal voters of the Tribe, and upon request by the Council, to call an election on any proposed amendment.

> the Tribal land and must be adhered to and that Constitution provides a process for *amending* the Constitution that must be heeded.[4]

Given this interpretation of the Tribal Constitution text, along with his finding that the Tribal Council had begun to examine the issue of redistricting,[5] he did not rule on the merits of the due process and equal protection claims, but rather decided to "dismiss the action without prejudice to allow plaintiffs to refile should the process currently underway not be pursued or followed by the defendants."[6] Judge Jones' dismissal was ultimately ordered "for failure to state a claim upon which relief can be granted."[7]

A timely notice of appeal was subsequently filed and oral argument was heard before this Court on December 20, 2011.[8]

---

4. Slip Opinion at 2 (emphasis added). The mention of the *Brown* case refers to Brown v. United States, 486 F.2d 658 (8th Cir. 1973), *see infra* note 8.

5. *See* Tribal Council Resolution 422-2010-CR (December 27, 2010) which provides:

> Therefore Be It Resolved, that the Cheyenne River Sioux Tribal Council directs the Judiciary and Codification Committee to undertake the drafting of a Constitutional amendment for re-districting of the reservation pursuant to Article III, §3 of the CRST Constitution, viz., the Committee will draft and submit to the Tribal Council a draft constitutional amendment or amendments requisite to accomplish the task of re-districting; and
>
> Be It Further Resolved, that the Tribal Council further directs that the Judiciary and Codification Committee complete the task of drafting the said constitutional amendment or amendments in sufficient time that a Secretarial Election may be held thereon and concluded at least one year prior to the next Tribal Primary Election so that candidates may have adequate time to establish residency before the said election; and
>
> Be It Finally Resolved, that nothing in this Resolution diminishes, divests, alters, or otherwise affects any inherent, treaty, statutory, or other rights of the Cheyenne River Sioux Tribe over the property or activities described herein. The Cheyenne River Sioux Tribe expressly retains all rights and authority over the property and activities described herein, including but not limited to legislative, regulatory, adjudicatory, and taxing powers.

6. Slip Opinion at 3.

7. *Id.* at 3–4. Judge Jones made no ruling on the Tribe's sovereign immunity claim and the Tribe did not pursue it on appeal.

8. It is to be noted that on appeal the plaintiffs/appellants dropped their request for injunctive relief and only pursue their request for declaratory relief.

In addition, the plaintiffs/appellants withdrew that part of their argument that relied on the continued vitality or applicability of the case of Brown v. United States, 486 F.2d 658 (8th Cir. 1973) to the case at bar. Therefore this Court will not engage in extensive analysis of *Brown* except to note that the question of whether it was effectively overruled by Santa Clara Pueblo v. Martinez, 436 U.S. 49 (1978) is, of course, a question of *federal* law, as is the related question of whether the decision in *Brown* ordering redistricting of Cheyenne

II. Issues

This appeal raises four issues, namely:

(1) Whether appellants' appeal was timely filed;

(2) Whether Judge Jones' order is an appealable order;

(3) Whether the issue of redistricting is textually assigned by the Tribe's Constitution solely to the Tribal Council (or the people) and thus is a nonreviewable political question; and

(4) Whether Judge Jones erred in his constitutional interpretation of the Tribal Constitution requirements on redistricting.

Each issue will be discussed in turn.

III. Discussion

A. Timeliness of Appeal

Rule 84(c) of the Cheyenne River Sioux Tribe Rules of Civil Procedure provides that:

> Within 30 days from the entry of the order of judgment appealed from, the party taking the appeal must file with the trial court a written notice of appeal specifying the parties to the appeal, the order of judgment appealed from, a short statement of the reasons and grounds for the appeal.

Judge Jones' order is dated May 11, 2011 which is also presumed to be the date of the entry of judgment. The notice of appeal is dated (and noted as received) on June 9, 2011. Neither of these dates are contested. What is the relevant computation? May has 31 days and thus 20 days run in May (31–11=20) and 9 days run in June, which adds up to 29 days and thus the notice of appeal was timely filed within the 30 day period.[9]

B. Appealability of Judge Jones' Order

Appellees assert that a dismissal 'without prejudice' is not an appealable order because the plaintiffs/appellants may simply refile their complaint at a

---

River Sioux Tribal Council districts based on the due process and equal protection guarantees of the Indian Civil Rights Act of 1968, 25 U.S.C. § 1302(8), remains an enforceable judgment.

9. Oddly, the appellee Tribal Council did not perform any of the relevant computation, but simply requested the Court "to take judicial notice that this appeal is filed out of time." (Appellee's Brief at 6). Matters of timeliness are not subject to judicial notice because they do not involve a court's acceptance of "well-known and indisputable facts." Black's Law Dictionary 851 (7th ed. 1999).

later date in civil court. Appellees provide insufficient and incorrect authority for this proposition. The primary case cited by the appellees is inapposite. The case of *New York C. and St. L. R. Co. v. Landeman*, 181 F.2d 769 (8th Cir. 1950), involved a voluntary dismissal by the *plaintiffs* pursuant to Federal Rule of Civil Procedure 41(a)(2). In the case at bar, the dismissal was on the defendant Tribal Council's motion and vigorously opposed by the plaintiffs. The resulting dismissal for failure to state a claim upon which relief may be granted was quintessentially a dismissal on the merits and plaintiffs have an absolute right to appeal such a dismissal. *See* Rule 37(b) of the Cheyenne River Sioux Rules of Civil Procedure which provides:

> Right to Appeal. Any party who is aggrieved by any final order, commitment or judgment of the trial court may appeal in the manner prescribed by this Rule.

C. Re-districting Authority is Textually Committed to the Tribal Council in the Tribal Constitution as a Non-Reviewable Political Question

In this case of first impression, appellee Tribal Council offers a very incomplete and truncated argument as to why this Court should not act in this matter. The nub of this argument appears to be that because the Tribal Constitution assigns "sole authority" for redistricting to the Tribal Council, this Court has no authority in this matter. While appellee identifies no authority—tribal, state, or federal—for its assertion, presumably appellee Tribal Council is referring to the 'political question' doctrine. Noted scholar Erwin Chemerinsky describes the doctrine in this manner:

> The Supreme Court has held that certain allegations of unconstitutional government conduct should not be ruled on by the federal courts even though all of the jurisdictional and other justiciability requirements are met. The Court has said that constitutional interpretation in these areas should be left to the politically accountable branches of government, the president and Congress. In other words, the "political question doctrine" refers to subject matter that the Court deems to be inappropriate for judicial review. Although there is an allegation that the Constitution has been violated, the federal courts refuse to rule and instead dismiss the case, leaving the constitutional question to be resolved in the political process.[10]

Although scholars differ greatly as to the roots, utility, and applicability of the doctrine, there is uniform agreement that the doctrine does in fact exist.

---

10. ERWIN CHEMERINSKY, FEDERAL JURISDICTION 147 (5th ed. 2007).

For example, there is near overwhelming judicial agreement that the political question doctrine is appropriate in the context of challenges directed to the legality of particular wars.[11]

Conversely, however, there is also overwhelming agreement that the reapportionment questions are *not* political questions. This is true at the federal, tribal, and state level. The premier Supreme Court case in this regard is *Baker v. Carr*, 369 U.S. 186 (1962);[12] which held that legislative districts that did not reflect the 'one man, one vote' concept were in violation of the equal protection guarantee of the 14th Amendment.[13] The principles of *Baker v. Carr* have been upheld and followed in both state and tribal contexts. *See*, for example, *In the Matter of the Certification of a Question of Law from the United States District Court, District of South Dakota, Western Division*, 615 N.W.2d 590 (SD 2000), holding that South Dakota courts have the authority to review South Dakota legislative reapportionment plans required by the South Dakota State Constitution. More importantly, in the tribal context, *see Yazzie v. Navajo Tribal Board of Election Supervisors*, 1 Nav. R. 213 (1978), holding that the courts of the Navajo Nation have the authority to review Tribal Council reapportionment plans in light of both the equal protection guarantee of the Indian Civil Rights Act of 1968, 25 U.S.C. § 1302(8), and Navajo tradition and custom.[14]

In light of these persuasive authorities from all three—federal, tribal, and state—sovereigns (and *no* contrary authority cited by the appellee), the Court *holds* that questions of reapportionment pursuant to the Cheyenne River Sioux

---

11. For example, more than seventy lawsuits were bought challenging American military involvement in Vietnam and Southeast Asia. Reasoning by the courts varied widely, yet in no case was the involvement held unconstitutional. The striking fact is that most of the courts refused to reach the merits of the constitutional issue, finding instead that the suits raised a political question or were otherwise nonjusticiable. *See* Schoen, *A Strange Silence: Vietnam and the Supreme Court*, 33 Washburn L. J., 275 (1994).

12. This case also includes a classic statement describing the political question doctrine:

> Prominent on the surface of any case held to involve a political question is found a textually demonstrable commitment of the issue to a coordinate political department; or a lack of judicially discoverable and manageable standards for resolving it; or the impossibility of deciding without an initial policy determination of a kind clearly for nonjudicial discretion; or the impossibility of a court's undertaking independent resolution without expressing lack of the respect due coordinate branches of government; or an unusual need for unquestioning adherence to a political decision already made; or the potentiality of embarrassment from multifarious pronouncements by various departments on one question. *Id.* at 317 n.233.

13. *Baker v. Carr*, 369 U.S. 186, 237 (1962).

14. *See also Mudd v. Ho-Chunk Nation Legislature* (CV 03-01, HCN Tr. Ct. 2003) upholding judicial review of the Tribal Legislature's redistricting and reapportionment plan.

Tribe Constitution that are challenged pursuant to the Civil Rights Act of 1968, 25 U.S.C. §1302(8) and Lakota tradition and custom, *Bank of Hoven v. Long Family Land and Cattle Co.* (#003-002-7 (2004)) are not 'political questions' and are subject to judicial review.

D. The Trial Court's Interpretation of the Cheyenne River Sioux Tribe Constitution Provision on Redistricting is Erroneous as a Matter of Tribal Constitutional Law

The core of this issue centers on the meaning and interpretation of Art. III, Sec. 3 of the Tribal Constitution, which provides after the enumeration of the thirteen (13) 'agency precincts':[15]

> Provided: That the Cheyenne River Tribal Council shall have the power both to redistrict the reservation and its precincts, and to reassign the number of councilmen to be elected from each district in proportion to the number of qualified voters residing therein, or on a population basis.

Judge Jones' order, as noted above, interpreted any such redistricting or reassigning to require an *amendment* to the Tribal constitution in accordance with the provisions of Art. IX. Article IX provides:

> SECTION 1. This constitution and the appended by-laws may be amended by a majority of the qualified voters of the tribe voting at an election called for that purpose by the Secretary of the Interior, provided that at least 30 per cent of those entitled to vote shall vote in such election; but no amendment shall become effective until it shall have been approved by the Secretary of the Interior.
>
> SECTION 2. It shall be the duty of the Secretary of the Interior, upon presentation of a petition signed by at least two hundred (200) legal voters of the tribe, and upon request by the council, to call an election on any proposed amendment.

As to the amendment process itself, Judge Jones appears to misconstrue how it works. While his order never quotes the text of the amendment article, he writes as if the amendment process leading up to the Secretarial election is controlled solely by the Tribal Council. For example, Judge Jones states:

15. Note that the thirteen agency 'precincts' were consolidated into six 'districts' pursuant to Brown v. United States, 486 F.2d 658 (8th Cir. 1973) and Tribal Council Resolution #33-78-CR (March 10, 1978). This change did not affect the number of Tribal Council representatives, which remains at fifteen. This 1978 action further belies the notion that Tribal Council redistricting or reapportionment requires amending the Tribal Constitution.

> Because it will ultimately be up to the people in the form of a constitutional amendment to change the current constitutional districting of the reservation, the Defendants can only put that process into action, which they have now done.
>
> Because the Defendants have taken action to redistrict the reservation the Court finds that these Plaintiffs have failed to state a claim upon relief can be granted at this time. The Court cannot oversee the process, *which has been started by the Defendants*, because this is a constitutional provision that is left to the people to decide, not the Court.[16]

Such an interpretation puts the Constitutional cart before the horse. Section 2 of Article IX requires the Secretary of the Interior to "call an election on any proposed amendment upon presentation of a petition signed by at least two hundred (200) legal voters of the tribe (sic) *and* upon request of the council (sic)" (emphasis added). The word 'and' is crucial to understanding the meaning of the Constitutional text. The process for initiating a Secretarial election on a proposed amendment does not reside *solely* with the Tribal Council. The plain meaning of the text is that the process *begins* with a presentation of a petition signed by at least two hundred (200) legal voters of the Tribe. Then, presumably, the Tribal Council joins the petition and both items are submitted to the Secretary of the Interior.

Despite some inartfulness in the text of Sec. 2 of Art. IX, there is no doubt that the section envisions the petition of the 200 voters to precede or be simultaneous with the request of the Tribal Council for the Secretarial election. Section 2 does not under any circumstances give the Tribal Council the authority to call a secretarial election *without* the petition of the two hundred voters. This clearly—at least upon the record before this Court—was *not* done in this instance. Therefore much—if not all—of the proceedings before Judge Jones proceeded on a constitutionally incorrect understanding of the *process* of Tribal constitutional amendment.

More pertinent for purposes of this appeal is the *substantive* constitutional error contained in Judge Jones' decision below. Judge Jones' order assumes without explanation that the power of redistricting may only be effectuated by Constitutional amendment. This is manifestly incorrect as the most basic tex-

---

16. Slip Opinion at 3 (emphasis added). The process "which has been started by the Defendants" refers to Tribal Council Resolution, 422-2010-CR, adopted on December 27, 2010 directing the Tribe's Judiciary and Constitution Committee to start the process of "drafting a Constitutional amendment for redistricting pursuant to Article III, §3 of the Cheyenne River Sioux Tribal Constitution." *Id.* at 1.

tual plain meaning exegesis of Article III demonstrates. Article III in relevant part states:

> That the Cheyenne River Tribal Council *shall have the power* to both redistrict the reservation and its precincts and to reassign the number of councilmen to be elected from each district in proportion to the number of qualified voters residing therein, or on a population basis. (emphasis added)

This constitutional language unambiguously grants the Tribal Council the express *mandatory* power to redistrict.[17] 'Shall' is a mandatory not discretionary ('may') term. This reading and finding of mandatory authority in the Tribal Council was not contested by either party in their presentations—written and oral—to this Court. *See generally* CALEB NELSON, STATUTORY INTERPRETATION (West 2011).

In light of this interpretation by the Court, the issue then becomes what is the appropriate remedy to the current Constitutional impasse. The appellants urge that the Court become *directly* involved and "to control and to monitor the 2012 elections,"[18] while the appellee urges that the Court give the Tribal Council more time so that it can further discuss and prepare its redistricting plan. To put it bluntly, the appellants ask too much and the appellee offers too little. Certainly, this Court should not too readily decide "to control and to monitor" Tribal elections. To do so would strike at the core of the separation of powers doctrine and invade the power of the Tribal citizenry to chart its own path of legislative redistricting. However, to simply give the Tribal Council more time to discuss and to plan invites the likelihood of continued delay, now stretching over many years, on a core Constitutional issue.

With all of the above in mind, the Court orders the defendant/appellee Tribal Council to submit its final and specific plan for redistricting to Judge Jones within ninety days. This period of ninety (90) days provides the Tribal Council with sufficient time to develop and to adopt a final plan with full and informed input from all people and communities on the Reservation. In addition, though it may be changed by affirmative Tribal Council legislation, the Court determines that in light of federal constitutional practice and concern

---

17. Needless to say, Constitutional redistricting *may* be effectuated by Tribal Constitutional amendment, but it need not be and in no way does such a *possibility* excuse the Tribal Council's failure to carry out its mandatory constitutional duty.

18. In the alternative, appellants suggest that this Court "Request the Bureau of Indian Affairs to conduct the 2012 elections of the Cheyenne River Sioux Tribe." Appellants' Brief at 23.

for Lakota balance and reason that such Tribal redistricting shall take place at least once every ten years.

IV. Conclusion

For all of the above-stated reasons, the decision of Judge Jones is reversed and remanded with the order that the Cheyenne River Sioux Tribal Council submit its final and specific plan for redistricting to Judge Jones within ninety days of the Court's decision for his determination of its compliance with Art. III, Sec. 3 of the Tribal Constitution. That date is May 10, 2012

Ho Hec'etu Ye Lo

IT IS SO ORDERED.

FOR THE COURT:

____

Frank Pommersheim
Chief Justice

Dated February 7, 2012

Notes on *Woods v. Cheyenne River Sioux Tribal Council* (2012)

Tribal reapportionment cases most often arise from the alleged failure of the tribal council to comply with tribal constitutional provisions which require reapportionment. In the *Woods* case, the core issues were interpreting the meaning of the Tribal constitutional language on reapportionment and considering the applicability of the political question defense. The decision in this case was accepted by the Tribe and a subsequent reapportionment plan was adopted and implemented in the 2012 Tribal election. Legal wrangling continues concerning the need for new census data to more accurately assess population changes.

Other tribal court cases involving reapportionment have focused on both similar and dissimilar issues than those addressed in *Woods*. Other examples include *Lay v. Cherokee Nation*, 1 Am. Trib. Law 23, 25 (Cherokee Nation Judicial App. Tribunal 1998), where a Cherokee Nation constitutional amendment adopted in 1987 provided, in relevant part: "The Council shall establish representative districts which shall be within the historical boundaries of the Cherokee nation of Oklahoma. These districts shall be apportioned to afford a *reasonably equal* division of tribal membership among the districts." (emphasis added). Further, the Council passed an Act in 1989 that established nine legislative districts from which the fifteen council members would be selected to represent the general population. *Id.* 24–25. The same Act established a formula (based on membership population) for determining the apportionment of those fifteen seats. *Id.* In 1990, the Council determined the districting for the 1991 general election according to that formula. *Id.* at 25. However, despite access to new membership population information that showed the districts violated the "reasonably equal" provision of the Constitution, the Council voted in 1997 to freeze the districts until 2002. *Id.* at 25–28.

The Court found that absent a constitutionally valid government reason, the Council must reapportion the districts "whenever the population figures bear out the need to do so." *Id.* at 28. Thus, while the Court did not decide whether waiting twelve years to reapportion was reasonable, it did hold that as applied to these facts, the Council's decision to delay reapportionment to 2002 violated the "present right of every Cherokee voter to equal representation in [the Council] ... as guaranteed under the Cherokee Constitution." *Id.* at 27–29. As a result of this ruling, the court also ordered that the 1999 elections by the Election Commission follow a plan that changed the number of councilors in a few of the districts. *Id.* at 28.

The Court declined to modify or reverse the *Lay* case in *Terrell v. Cherokee Nation Election Commission*, 2 Am. Trib. Law 25 (Cherokee Nation Judicial App. Trib. 1999), despite concerns over separation of powers. The Court cited the closeness in time of the upcoming election and the need for the Tribal citizens to have confidence in the final orders of the appellate court. *Id.* at 26–27.

The Tribal Court of the Chickasaw Nation addressed reapportionment and constitutional requirements in the case of *In re Hensley*, 4 Okla. Trib. 524 (Chickasaw Trib. Ct. 1987). The Tribe's Constitution required the legislature to adopt a reapportionment plan within nine months of the first election of officers. *Id.* at 526. The Tribal Council decided that no significant change in the number of registered voters in the districts occurred since the reform process of 1983 began and therefore apportionment should remain the same. *Id.* The Court held "[s]uch action does not meet the constitutional requirement." *Id.* at 527. Furthermore, the Court ordered "that a plan for reapportionment shall be adopted by the Chickasaw Legislature according to the guidelines set out in Article VI, Section 5 of the Constitution, and presented to this Court ... [so] this Court can determine that the plan for reapportionment has been adopted in a manner as prescribed by the Constitution." *Id.* The reapportionment plan was later found by the Court to meet constitutional requirements in *In re Hensley*, 4 Okla. Trib. 532 (Chickasaw Trib. Ct. 1988).

In *Nelson v. Initiative Committee to Reduce Navajo Nation Council*, 8 Am. Tribal Law 407 (Nav.Sup.Ct. 2010), the Navajo Nation's Reduction in Council Initiative mandated a reapportionment plan that was consistent with the initiative. *Id.* at 419. The language of the initiative required a deadline for when the reapportionment plan was to be presented to Council, and if that deadline was not met, the President of the Nation was to develop a plan by another deadline. *Id.* As the Court noted, "Throughout this period, the Navajo Nation Council took no steps toward developing and approving a reapportionment plan, and in October, 2009, suspended the President from his duties by placing him on administrative leave before the October reapportionment plan deadline." *Id.* By the time the special election on December 15, 2009, neither reapportionment plan was complete or available. *Id.* The plaintiff argued that election results should be nullified, but the court did not find that argument compelling. *Id.* However, the Court noted that the failure for a plan to be implemented was not a matter of mere coincidence, instead finding that the failure to approve a plan was based on the "inaction by the NBOES [Navajo Board of Election Supervisors], and action and inaction by the Council which has challenged this Initiative, or assisted in challenges, at every step, even unlawfully removing the President from his duties at the very moment an alternative plan from the President was due." *Id.* Because of the purposeful delays that the Court found on the part of NBOES and the Council, the Court stated that:

> ... We affirm today that the Council may not use its power to frustrate the will of the People. The People's government must comply with the mandate issued by its People. The People do not want any more delays and uncertainty. In accordance with the new law, the President shall present a reapportionment plan that has been discussed at community meetings by June 11, 2010 and the NBOES shall approve the reapportionment plan by June 18, 2010. *Id.* at 420.

A Muscogee (Creek) District Court held in *Thomas v. Creek Nation Election Bd.*, 1 Okla. Trib. 124, 124–26 (Muscogee (Creek) D.Ct. 1987), that the plaintiff's request for reapportionment was justiciable and ordered "re-certification of the district citizens totals for purposes of determining the number of seats to be filled." *Id.* at 125. The Court further specified that the term 'District Citizen' as set out in the Constitution included absentee citizens who have declared a home district in accordance with Article IV, Sec. 9. *Id.* at 125–26.

A redistricting plan approved by the Ho-Chunk Nation resulted in some legislators no longer living in their districts. In *Robert A. Mudd v. Ho–Chunk Nation Legislature*, SU 03–02 (HCN S.Ct., Apr. 8, 2003), the Tribal Supreme Court stated:

> There appears to be nothing in the Ho–Chunk Nation Constitution, Ordinances, Resolutions or other law that prohibits a legislator from moving out of his or her district, if the legislator met the one year res-

> idency requirement at the time of the filing of the Declaration of Candidacy. Once a person has been elected to the HCN legislature that person has no limits on residency other than prudential ones of preserving his or her ties to their constituents. It is not however constitutionally mandated. The HCN Constitution mandates only that the legislator will have meetings in his or her district. *Id.* at 7–8.

See also Lowe v. Garvin, 2 Am. Tribal Law 308 (Ho-Chunk Nation Tr. Ct. 2000) (holding that plaintiffs were allowed to challenge the outcome of a redistricting election as they were still ordinary "election results" under the Constitution); *Abangan v. Ho-Chunk Nat. Election Bd.*, 4 Am. Tribal Law 314 (Ho-Chunk Nation Tr. Ct. 2002) (holding that although the notice that was given to the plaintiff and other tribal members was constitutionally defective, the plaintiff was not able to meet the burden of proving by clear and convincing evidence that the election results would have been different); *In re Two Initiative Petitions Filed by Shirley*, 7 Am. Tribal Law 628 (Nav. Sup. Ct. 2008) (holding that the Tribal Council did not have the unilateral right to amend a section of the Navajo Nation Code relating to the number of Tribal Council delegates. Only Navajo voters could amend this section); *Visintin v. Ho-Chunk Nation Nat. Election Bd.*, 7 Am. Tribal Law 280 (Ho-Chunk Nation Tr. Ct. 2002) (holding that unlike the election of candidates, a reapportionment plan did not require majority voter approval before being implemented).

Political Processes — Referendum

In the Matter of Tribal Council Ordinance 14

(Cheyenne River Sioux Tribal Court of Appeals) (2004)

CHEYENNE RIVER SIOUX TRIBAL COURT OF APPEALS
CHEYENNE RIVER SIOUX TRIBE
CHEYENNE RIVER SIOUX RESERVATION

****

	)	#04-001-A
IN THE MATTER OF TRIBAL COUNCIL	)	
ORDINANCE 14	)	MEMORANDUM OPINION
	)	AND ORDER
	)	

****

Per Curiam (Chief Justice Frank Pommersheim, Associate Justice Everett Dupris, and Associate Justice B.J. Jones)

I. Introduction

This is an original action filed by the Cheyenne River Sioux Tribe in the Cheyenne River Sioux Tribal Court of Appeals pursuant to Rule 76(b) of the Cheyenne River Sioux Tribe Rules of Civil Procedure.[1] The procedure that is set out in Rule 76(b) is expressly designed to permit the Tribal Council to file such an action whenever it "determines that it is necessary or appropriate to obtain a prompt judicial determination as to the validity of any ordinance or resolution adopted by the Tribal Council."[2] Commencement of *this* proceeding was expressly authorized by the Tribal Council through Resolution 27-04-CR that was passed on February 5, 2004, by a roll call vote of six yes, three no, one abstaining and five absent.

The complaint in this action was filed by the Tribe on March 4, 2004, and it sought a declaratory judgment that the amendments to Part VIII Section 6

---

1. Rule 76(b) states:

(b) Jurisdiction of the Tribal Court of Appeals

In addition to the existing jurisdiction of the Tribal Court of Appeals, the Tribal Court of Appeals shall have original jurisdiction over actions initiated by the Tribal Council to validate any ordinance or resolution adopted by the Tribal Council.

2. Rule 76(a).

of Ordinance 14 were "valid under the Constitution and any other applicable law." Complaint at 6.

Upon filing of the complaint in accordance with Rule 76(c), the Court must set a date and time for a hearing and that order along with a copy of the complaint and the subject ordinance or resolution, must be published in a local newspaper of general circulation once a week for three consecutive weeks. These same items must also be posted at the Tribal courthouse and Tribal administration building at least twenty-one days prior to the date of the hearing.[3]

Pursuant to Rule 76(e), any enrolled member of Cheyenne River Sioux Tribe may become a "responding party to the action by written motion or by answering the complaint at least three (3) business days before the time set for the hearing." Three individuals namely Ms. Bernice White Eagle, Ms. Bertha Charging Hawk, and Mr. Greg Ducheneaux filed written "answers" to the complaint in accordance with Rule 76(e).

Rule 76(f) requires a hearing be held to receive "evidence and argument" as to the validity of the subject ordinance. At the hearing, counsel for the Tribe shall present its case. Any "responding party" shall have the same opportunity with a final response reserved to counsel for the Tribe to "respond to any objections" to the subject ordinance. The hearing is otherwise governed by the Cheyenne River Sioux Tribe Rules of Civil Procedure.

The required hearing was held on September 13, 2004. Two of the three responders, namely Ms. Bernice White Eagle and Mr. Greg Ducheneaux, were present and offered "evidence and argument." In addition, without objection by counsel for the Tribe, five other individuals, who did not file written "answers," were given the opportunity to briefly present "evidence and argument." These individuals were identified as Ms. Candace Ducheneaux, Mr. Eagle Hunter, Mr. Bryce In The Woods, Mr. Bernard In The Woods, and Ms. Rochelle Ducheneaux.

Pursuant to Rule 76(f), this Court must "determine questions of law and fact" and within ten (10) business days of the hearing file a "written determination regarding the validity of the subject ordinance or resolution." This written determination must be published in a local paper of general circulation and posted at the Tribal courthouse and the Tribal administration building. In accordance with Rule 74(g), the determination of the Tribal Court of Appeals "shall be final."

---

3. Rule 76(d).

II. The Ordinance 14 Amendments

The subject ordinance of this proceeding are amendments to Ordinance 14 that specifically address the Tribal Constitutional provision that deals with Referendum.[4] These amendments to Ordinance 14 are rather extensive and are provided in full at Appendix A. Ordinance 14 is the Tribal Ordinance that deals with "Elections." Section 6 of Ordinance 14 deals specifically with the power of "referendum." Prior to the subject amendments enacted on February 5, 2004, there were no prior amendments to Ordinance 14 that dealt with the constitutional power of referendum. In other words, the constitutional authority regarding referendum was not subject to any Tribal legislative enactments since its adoption on December 7, 1935 until February 5, 2004.

III. Issues

Although the Ordinance 14 amendments relative to the power of referendum are somewhat complex and detailed, the core issues concerning their validity are whether they substantively impair the right of the people to petition for a referendum, or merely procedurally implement the constitutional right, and even if the amendments are merely procedural, whether they are constitutionally reasonable. Each issue will be examined in turn.

IV. Discussion

A. Whether the Ordinance 14 amendments substantively impair the constitutional right of referendum.

At the outset, the Court notes that the constitutional right of referendum in Art. VII neither expressly authorizes nor expressly prohibits Tribal Council legislative activity relative to the enumerated right. In the absence of such express language in the text of a constitution, the general rule of constitutional interpretation in that the legislative body may adopt procedural rules to reasonably implement the right, but such procedural rules may not substantively impair the right. If the rules do impair the substantive (constitutional) right, they must be struck down as unconstitutional.

---

4. Art. VII of Cheyenne River Sioux Tribe Constitution states:

ARTICLE VII—REFERENDUM

SECTION 1. Upon a petition of at least three hundred (300) qualified voters of the Cheyenne River Sioux Reservation a referendum may be demanded on any enacted or proposed ordinance or resolution of the Cheyenne River Sioux Tribal Council, and the vote of the majority of the qualified voters in such referendum shall be conclusive and binding on the tribal council.

The position of the Tribe, as thoughtfully expressed in its brief and at oral argument, is that the amendments to Ordinance 14 merely establish reasonable procedural rules for implementation of the right of referendum in order to provide uniformity and certainty in the (potential) exercise of this right. The Tribe cites a long line of state cases that all hold that such procedural rules relative to time limits for filing a referendum challenge are constitutional under the various state constitutions. In addition, counsel for the Tribe indicated there were no tribal court cases that dealt with this issue.

Counsel for the Tribe also correctly noted that state cases were not binding on this Court but in the absence of any relevant caselaw from this Court (or any other tribal court), it was argued that we might find such an unbroken line of cases as persuasive authority to uphold the Ordinance 14 amendments. While not an unreasonable claim, this Court does *not* find such argument constitutionally persuasive.

It is not constitutionally persuasive because the line of state cases all assume a constitutional predicate that does *not* exist on the Cheyenne River Sioux Reservation. That constitutional predicate involves the necessary due process element of notice.[5] In any state context, it is a constitutional given that actions of the state legislature are *daily* reported by press, radio, and television media. In addition, at the state level, actions of the legislature are promptly communicated to the public by the organized Democratic, Republican (and other) political parties. Lastly, at the state level, enacted legislation is routinely and immediately filed with a public official charged with that responsibility.

As testimony at the hearing indicated, little, if any, of such notice, is regularly available on the Cheyenne River Sioux Reservation. There is no daily press, radio, or television coverage of Tribal Council legislative activity. In fact, radio and television coverage is almost non-existent. There is no daily paper on the Reservation and the weekly *Eagle Butte News* has only sporadic and irregular coverage of Tribal Council activities. In addition, there are no organized political parties that function at the Tribal Council level and thus there is no potential for notice from such sources. Tribal Council ordinances and resolutions are filed with the Tribal Secretary, but testimony at the hearing indicated that

5. Due process is a core guarantee of the Indian Civil Rights Act of 1968, 25 USC § 1302(8) and Lakota tradition. *See, e.g., Bloomberg v. Dreamer*, Oglala Sioux Civ. Ap. 90-348 at 5–6 (1991). (Lakota tradition includes the due process concepts of notice and the opportunity to be heard.)

there were no timelines governing such filing. Nor are there rules in place describing the access of the Tribal membership to these enactments.

For all of the above reasons, this Court finds the amendments to Ordinance 14 unconstitutional because the amendments fail to provide adequate notice of Tribal Council legislative action as an essential ingredient of due process. This lack of notice substantively impairs the constitutional right of referendum. Notice is especially critical in the context of the Ordinance 14 amendments because the time frame for exercise of the constitutional power of referendum is only forty-five days from the enactment of the legislation and there is *no* notice requirement whatsoever.

The Court does not, however, find persuasive the argument presented by some of the Responders present at the hearing, who contended that the Tribal Council has no authority to enact procedural rules governing the referendum process if those rules in any way curtail the right of the people to seek a referendum. Although it is true that the Cheyenne River Sioux Tribe's Constitution vests the people with a right to petition for a referendum on any resolution or ordinance passed by the Council, and does not expressly grant to the Tribal Council the authority to regulate that referendum process, the Court notes that the Council does have the constitutional authority to impose reasonable regulations governing elections on the reservation. That grant of authority is broad enough to encompass the passage of reasonable regulations pertaining to the submission of referendum petitions and the processing of such petitions. Setting reasonable time frames for the exercise of the right does not impair the right provided those time frames are preceded by adequate notice both of the passage of an ordinance governing the referendum process,[6] and of the actions taken by Council, which could be subject to referendum.

There were many suggestions made by all participants (including the Tribe) at the hearing that taken together, and if passed by the Tribal Council, would overcome the constitutional shortfall. These elements of notice include express publication in the *Eagle Butte News*, posting of the ordinance or resolution at the tribal courthouse and tribal administration building, posting of the ordinance or resolution on the Tribe's website, and posting of the ordinance or

6. There were some excellent suggestions made at the hearing regarding the need for public hearings in the Districts when ordinances such as amendments to Ordinance 14 are enacted by the Council. Although the Court notes that such public hearings are not mandated under Tribal law, they would go a long way towards bolstering Tribal member confidence in the transparency and integrity of this political and constitutional process.

resolution in each of the six districts or "precincts" recognized in the Tribal Constitution.

B. Whether the Ordinance 14 Amendments that create a forty-five day time limit for the exercise of the constitutional right of referendum is constitutionally reasonable.

As indicated above, the Ordinance 14 amendments are unconstitutional because of the notice defect, but pursuant to the suggestions of all parties, including counsel for the Tribe, the Court agrees that it would be helpful for the Court to provide some constitutional guidance in this area. Given the extraordinary significance of the constitutional right of referendum to the "people" and the legitimate concern for the Tribe to provide certainty to its potential business partners, the Court finds that a proper constitutional time limit for exercising the right of referendum would be at least 120 days after completion of the notice requirements set forth in Part IV-A of this opinion. The Court also has concerns that any attempt to prevent Tribal members from correcting a petition (within the appropriate time limit) that is not certified for election may violate the constitutional right of referendum. As written, the amendments to Ordinance 14 appear to prohibit those proponents of a referendum petition from correcting any defect in the petition and resubmitting it for consideration by the Tribal Election Board. This should also be examined in the context of reevaluating the notice requirements.

The Court also acknowledges the thoughtfulness and respect provided by *all* parties who appeared before the Court in this important matter.

V. Conclusion

For all of the above reasons, the Court declares the subject amendments to Ordinance 14 to be unconstitutional.

It is so ordered.

Ho Hec'etu Ye Lo

FOR THE COURT:

____

Frank Pommersheim
Chief Justice

Dated September 24, 2004.

APPENDIX A
ORDINANCE 14
Part VIII

Section 6: REFERENDUM.

a) CONSTITUTION, ARTICLE VII, SECTION 1—REFERENDUM.

Upon a petition of at least three hundred (300) qualified voters of the Cheyenne Sioux Reservation a referendum may be demanded on any enacted or proposed ordinance or resolution of the Cheyenne River Sioux Tribal Council, and the vote of the majority of the qualified voters in such referendum shall be conclusive and binding on the Tribal Council.

b) PETITIONS.

APPLICATION. Upon request, the Tribal Secretary shall provide to any Tribal Member an application for referendum petition (see Form #24, Appendix). After the petition bearer completes the application for referendum petition and submission of the form to the Tribal Secretary's Office the Tribal Secretary shall provide to the petition bearer at no cost:

1. A certified copy of the ordinance or resolution to be referred.
2. A copy of the most recent certified voters list.
3. A sample petition form (see Form #25, Appendix).

TIME FRAME. Any petition for referendum election and all forms required by this Ordinance must be submitted to the Tribal Secretary's Office by the 45th calendar day following the date of enactment of the proposed Tribal Council resolution or ordinance which is the subject of the petition. If the 45th calendar day falls on a Saturday, a Sunday, or a holiday on which the Tribal Secretary's Office is not open, the period for submission of the petition and required forms shall be extended to the next day on which the Tribal Secretary's Office is open. This provision is mandatory and jurisdictional.

PETITION HEADING. When circulating a referendum petition(s), the petition heading shall contain identification of the enacted or proposed ordinance or resolution and specific reasons why the issue should be referred back to the qualified voters for their vote, to afford the voter the opportunity to review said reasons. After review of said petition the voter has the right to sign or not sign.

PETITION FORMAT. The format shall include:

- Heading stating reason(s) and identification of referred issue, including the official number of the ordinance or resolution referred.
- A statement in substantially the following form:

  "We, the undersigned eligible voters of the Cheyenne River Sioux Tribe, request a referendum on [name and official number of ordinance or resolution] enacted by the Tribal Council on [date of enactment]."
- Name column
- Signature column
- Address column
- District column
- Date column
- Valid mailing address and telephone number of petition bearer
- Notarized certification by petition bearer

If the petition fails to include the foregoing items, the Secretary shall immediately notify the petition bearer by certified mail, and if possible, by telephone, of the defects and of the invalidity of the petition. If all items in this paragraph are not completed with respect to any signature, that signature shall not be valid.

PETITION BEARER'S RESPONSIBILITIES:

- Only qualified voters, *i.e.*, enrolled members of the Tribe, eighteen years of age or older, who satisfy the residency and all other requirements for voting, may sign petitions and signatures of persons who are not qualified voters at the time at which they signed the petition shall not be counted when determining whether the required number of signatures. Whenever any signature is challenged by any person, including a member of the Election Board, the burden shall be on the petition bearer to prove that the signatory was a qualified voter at the time of signing by a preponderance of the evidence. The presence of the signatory's name on the most current voter's list shall be conclusive proof that the signatory is a qualified voter. If the signatory's name is not found on the most current voter's list, proof may be made by competent testimony by any person or affidavit by the signatory, which shall be considered against any competent evidence to the contrary. The Election Board shall determine by a preponderance of the evidence whether the signatory is a qualified voter. Decisions of the Election

Board concerning qualification to sign a petition shall be final and binding on all persons.

- Must obtain at least three hundred (300) or more signatures of qualified voters of the reservation.
- Must have copy of the enacted or proposed ordinance or resolution in their possession and be able to answer any questions a voter has prior to signing the petition.
- All petitions must have Petition Bearer's certification notarized by a notary public.
- Petitions and supporting documents are to be filed with the Tribal Secretary, once filed no additional petitions of the same heading will be accepted nor once filled will any petitions be returned to the petition bearer. Upon receipt of said petition the Tribal Secretary shall date stamp each individual page of the petition, shall retain the original and shall make and give one copy to the petition bearer.
- Shall be in attendance at the Tribal Election Board's meeting at which the referendum petition is addressed.

c) <u>CERTIFICATION BY ELECTION BOARD</u>.

On the business day following the receipt of a petition for a referendum, the Tribal Secretary shall notify, by personal service, the Chairman of the Election Board, who shall convene a meeting of the Election Board within five business days for the purpose of certifying that the filed referendum petition does contain three hundred (300) or more signatures of qualified voters of the Cheyenne River Reservation.

1) If the petition does meet the required three hundred (300) or more signatures, the Tribal Election Board shall schedule an election no less than 45 days after the receipt of the petition by the Secretary.
2) If the petition does not meet the 40% requirement, the Tribal Election Board shall invalidate said petition and notify the petition bearer(s) of their decision.

d) <u>HOLDING OF REFERENDUM ELECTION</u>.

Once the election is scheduled, all procedures set out in Ordinance 14 shall be followed. The Tribal Election Board may develop a short, objective explanatory statement of the referendum question and place such statement directly on the ballot or as a separate insert accompanying the ballot.

e) EFFECT OF DISAPPROVAL.

Any ordinance or resolution which shall be disapproved at a referendum election by a majority of eligible voters voting in such referendum shall be repealed upon the effective date of the result of the referendum election.

f) EFFECT OF APPROVAL.

Any ordinance or resolution which shall be submitted to referendum and which shall not be disapproved by a majority of eligible voters voting in such referendum shall not thereafter be subject to subsequent referendum.

Notes on *In the Matter of Tribal Council Ordinance 14* (2004)

It is important to note in regard to the *Ordinance 14* case that the Tribe invoked a unique provision of the Cheyenne River Sioux Tribal Law and Order Code to obtain an opinion from the Tribal Court of Appeals as to whether proposed amendments to Ordinance 14 were constitutional. Such an approach was presumably utilized to avoid unnecessary conflict down the road and functioned as a binding 'advisory' opinion.

Other tribal court cases involving referendums are less 'advisory' and more concerned with an actual controversy. For example, the Mashantucket Pequot Tribal Court addressed potential procedural and substantive defects in a referendum petition in the case of *Mashantucket Pequot Tribal Nation v. McKeon*, 5 Mash. Rep. 94 (Mash. Pequot Tribal Ct. 2008). The Tribe argued that the Tribal members' petition was invalid because it did not comply with certain requirements of the Interim Petition Process and Procedures (IPPP), which had not been formally codified or published and that the petition failed to properly frame a referendum subject. *Id.* at 96–97. The court held that the referendum petition could not be invalidated on the basis that it did not comply with the IPPP procedural requirements. *Id.* at 99–100. The court also held that since the referendum petition was seeking to have a meeting, rather than place a question on the ballot, it was constitutionally deficient in substance. *Id.* at 100–102.

In *Learned v. Cheyenne-Arapaho Election Bd.*, 2 Okla. Trib. 445 (Cheyenne-Arapaho Sup. Ct. 1992), a member of the Cheyenne-Arapaho Tribe's Business Committee was the subject of a recall petition. The requisite signatures were acquired, but the Business Committee refused to act on a resolution to allow the Election Board to conduct the recall. *Id.* Pursuant to the Tribe's Constitution, the Election Board requested that the BIA Superintendent of the Conco Agency direct the Election Board to hold the recall. *Id.* at 460. The Tribal Supreme Court held that the actions of the Business Committee were unconstitutional, that denial of injunctive relief for the removed Business Committee member was proper, and that the Business Committee did not have exclusive authority to validate petitions. The Election Board had the constitutional authority to establish rules and regulations for elections, including referendums, and established rules permitted Tribal members to present a petition for recall. *Id.* at 477–84.

The Little Traverse Tribal Court addressed a complex issue involving the failure of Tribal members to exhaust an administrative remedy in a referendum case. There was significant confusion among tribal members on where they should take their concerns, so the court did not dismiss the case for this reason. *Deckrow v. Little Traverse Bay Bands of Odawa Indians*, 1999 WL 35000425 (Little Traverse Trib. Ct.). The court ultimately held that it had the authority to review the matter because of its inherent jurisdiction. *Id.*

Addressing several issues regarding a proposed referendum, the Cherokee Judicial Appeals Tribunal held in *In re Referendum Petition for Referendum Vote on Legislative Act 28-99*, 7 Am. Tribal Law 12 (Cherokee Jud. App. Trib. 2001), that the passage of a similar act giving council members additional pay, while a referendum on a similar piece of legislation was pending, "violated the Constitutional right of Referendum reserved to the people, and is therefore, null and void." at 14. However, because the petition failed to include enough information that a person signing could understand the subject of the referendum, the Court also held:

> [W]e find ourselves having to reject an attempt at the exercise of the power of referendum because of a deficiency on the face of the petition. We do so with great reluctance. The Petitioners sought to exercise this power without the guidance mandated by the Constitution to be provided by the Council, resulting, at least in part, in the Council benefiting directly from their own inaction.

Id. at 15.

In *Pearce ex rel. Gen. Council v. Nuckolls*, ASSC-99-01, 1999 WL 33589156 (Ab. Shawnee Tribe Sup. Ct.), the General Council of the Absentee Shawnee Tribe had adopted a resolution establishing salaries for elected officials which were lower than those established by the Tribe's Executive Committee. *Id.* at 1. This resolution was subject to a referendum vote in the general election. *Id.* Addressing the constitutionality of this action, the court found that "[a]lthough the General Council does not have authority to establish salaries for elected officials of the Tribe, the Constitution expressly grants the General Council authority to 'refer issues or questions to the eligible voters for a referendum election....'" *Id.* at 3. The Court ultimately held "[although the] Court may, in the proper case, prohibit the use of referenda for issues which are not of major importance, are clearly violative of the Constitution, or which attempt to infringe upon the rights of tribal members ... [n]one of these factors are found to be present in this case." *Id.* Thus, the Court ultimately found that the adopted resolution was "properly referred by referendum to the eligible voters of the Tribe; and, was approved by the eligible voters and became binding upon the Executive Committee." *Id.*

Addressing the potential applicability of a referendum to an administrative decision, the Leech Lake Band of Ojibwe Tribal Court in *Sherman v. Enbridge Energy LLC*, 9 Am. Tribal Law 462 (Leech Lake Band of Ojibwe Tribal Ct. 2010), held that the Tribal constitutional right of referendum did not extend to a decision made by the Band's Reservation Business Committee to enter into a contract with an energy company to build a pipeline on the Reservation. The court noted that the Committee had legislative and executive power, but that the act in question qualified as an administrative decision. *Id.* 464–66. Before reaching its decision on the potential applicability of a referendum to the issue, the court looked to non-binding precedent from state court decisions on referendum law where referendums were not allowed for administrative decisions. *Id.* The court ultimately held that administrative decisions were not subject to referendum under the Tribe's constitution, and denied relief to the plaintiff:

> The action of the RBC being challenged in this case was clearly administrative in nature and not legislative. Although the Court certainly has understanding for the passion of the Plaintiffs in this case to fight against a project that they truly feel will undermine the long-term security of their home, their challenge must be brought in the political realm and not this Court. *Id.* 468.

In a case addressing referendum materials, *Metcalf v. Coquille Indian Tribe Election Board*, 9 Am. Tribal Law 25 (Coquille Indian Tribal Ct. 2009), the Coquille Indian Tribal Court held that

> Excluding the referendum petition from the Tribal mailing of Mr. Metcalf's candidacy materials was not "dependent on will or pleasure," "unrestrained" or "fancy." To the contrary, it was reasoned. It complied with Tribal constitutional provisions creating one procedure for referendum, Const. Art. IV §2, and another for election. Const. Art. V. Not all voters who would support a legislative referendum would nec-

essarily vote for Mr. Metcalf for Tribal Council, and vice versa. The October 2008 election was for the election of Tribal Council officers and not for referendum. It would have been folly *not* to have excluded the referendum materials from the Tribal election mailing. *Id.* at 26.

In *McLain v. Cherokee Nation Election Comm'n*, 1 Am. Tribal Law 38 (Cherokee Jud. App. Trib. 1998), the Cherokee Judicial Appeals Tribunal held that a referendum that amended the Tribe's constitution was unconstitutional because the Secretary of Interior, as required by the Cherokee Constitution, had not yet approved the amendment when the referendum vote occurred. This case can be compared with *Terrell v. Cherokee Nation Election Commission*, 3 Okla Trib. 23 (Cherokee Jud. App. Trib. 1997) where the court held that BIA approval appropriately occurred for a 1987 constitutional referendum as required by the Cherokee Constitution and thus was valid. *See also Cornsilk v. Byrd*, 6 Okla. Trib. 288 (Cherokee Jud. App. Trib. 1997) (acknowledging that Oklahoma referendum law is generally followed by the Cherokee Nation and holding that a referendum was an inappropriate vehicle for attempting to repeal a Tribal Council resolution and instead an initiative should have been used by those individuals opposed to the resolution).

In *In re Protest Against Initiative Petition*, SC 06-12, 2006 WL 6122524 (Cherokee Jud. App. Trib. 2006) the Cherokee Nation Judicial Appeals Tribunal reviewed an initiative petition for a constitutional amendment that would have changed citizenship requirements and effectively eliminate the Freedmen from the Tribe. The Court ultimately held that although there were some irregularities with the petition, there were enough valid signatures for a special election to proceed on the issue. *Id.* at 4. *See also In re Status of 1999 Constitution*, 9 Okla. Trib. 392 (Cherokee Sup.Ct. 2006) (holding that the requirement of BIA approval for constitutional changes was a self-imposed sovereignty limitation, but that the Tribe by virtue of its own inherent sovereign power had the ability to remove that limitation). For a discussion of the Cherokee Nation's ongoing legal struggle about the citizenship status of the Tribe's Freedmen *see supra* pp. 122–25.

In *Nelson v. Initiative Comm. to Reduce Navajo Nation Council*, 8 Am Tribal Law 407, 420 (Nav. Sup. Ct. 2010), the Navajo Nation Supreme Court declared a statute that would allow the Tribal Council to override a referendum by voters to be invalid. The Court candidly stated "The Council may not interfere with the People's choice." *Id.*

See also Hayward v. Mashantucket Pequot Tribal Council, 4 Mash. Rep. 136 (Mash. Pequot Tribal Ct. 2003) (holding that sovereign immunity barred plaintiffs' suit when Tribal Council members in their official capacity refused to act on a proposal to rescind approval of a project and that the alleged violation of "constitutional due process" rights was not a cognizable action for which plaintiffs could bring a claim); *Election Board v. Business Committee*, 8 Okla. Trib. 265 (Cheyenne-Arapaho Dist. Ct. 2003) (mandating the Business Committee to comply with constitutional requirements for assistance in a recall (or referendum) election and to appropriate necessary funds to the Election Committee); *Naganashe v. Little Traverse Bay Bands of Odawa Indians Election Board*, 1999 WL 34999581 (Little Traverse Trib. Ct.) (holding that Tribal member's failure bring her complaints to the Election Board for resolution before taking them to the tribal court warranted dismissal of her complaint about a referendum).

Criminal Law and Criminal Procedure—Ineffective Assistance of Counsel and *Miranda* Warnings

Rosebud Sioux Tribe v. Luxon

(Rosebud Sioux Tribe Supreme Court) (2009)

IN THE SUPREME COURT
OF THE
ROSEBUD SIOUX TRIBE

ROSEBUD SIOUX TRIBE, Plaintiff/Appellee, vs. WES LUXON, Defendant/Appellant.	MEMORANDUM OPINION AND ORDER

Per Curiam (Frank Pommersheim, Chief Justice and Associate Justices Leroy Greaves and Cheryl Three Stars Valandra)

I. Introduction

Wes Luxon, defendant/appellant, was arrested by Tribal law enforcement officers on the evening of November 17, 2008. He was charged with the offenses of Driving Under the Influence (Rosebud Sioux Law and Order Code §6-1-1(2) (Class B offense) and Possession of a Firearm While Intoxicated (Rosebud Sioux Law and Order Code §5-11-7 (Class B offense).[1]

After a series of continuances, Mr. Luxon, represented by a law-trained public defender, was tried at a bench trial before Judge Steve Emery. Judge Emery found the defendant guilty on both counts.[2] The defendant, represented on appeal by a capable lay advocate (who is a member in good standing of the Sicangu Oyate Bar Association), filed a timely Notice of Appeal. Oral argument was heard by this Court on September 11, 2009.

1. A third offense of Possession of a Firearm While Under the Influence of Marijuana was subsequently dismissed.

2. Judge Emery imposed a sentence of sixty days (with thirty days suspended) and a $500 fine on the DUI charges and sixty days (with forty-five days suspended) and a $500 fine on the DUI/Firearms charge sentence to run consecutively. Defendant was also to take a DUI class and write a letter of apology to the local newspaper.

II. Issues

This appeal raises two issues, namely whether there was ineffective assistance of counsel by the public defender at the trial level in this matter, and whether the new amendment to the Tribal Constitution found at Sec. 1(d) of Art. X (Bill of Rights) relative to *Miranda* warnings requires reversal of defendant's conviction.

Each issue will be discussed in turn.

III. Discussion

A. Ineffective Assistance of Counsel

This issue presents a matter of first impression and of significant importance before this Court. The initial question in this context is identifying the appropriate standard with which to determine whether defense counsel's representation was ineffective and if so, whether it was also prejudicial. The classic *federal constitutional* standard is articulated in *Strickland v. Washington*, 466 U.S. 668 (1984), but it does not automatically apply in this Tribal court context. That is so because the right to counsel in the tribal court context derives from the Tribal Constitution and federal statute, not the United States Constitution. The relevant Tribal constitutional provision is to be found at Art. X, Sec. 1(f), which guarantees the defendant the right "to have the assistance of counsel for his or her defense, including the right to have counsel subject to income guidelines." The analogous federal statutory provision is contained in the Indian Civil Rights Act, 25 U.S.C. § 1302(6), and provides a defendant with the right "at his own expense to have the assistance of counsel for his defense."

In light of the strong affirmative language in the Tribe's Constitution and the Tribe's concomitant commitment to enhanced constitutional governance, this Court adopts the standard articulated in *Strickland* as the proper measure to determine whether there has been ineffective assistance by counsel in a criminal case tried before the Rosebud Sioux Tribal Court. This well-known test consists of two parts:

> First, the defendant must show that counsel's performance was deficient. This requires showing that counsel made errors so serious that counsel was not functioning as the counsel guaranteed by the Sixth Amendment. Second, the defendant must show that the deficient performance prejudiced the defendant. This requires showing that counsel's errors were so serious as to deprive the defendant of a fair trial, a trial 'whose result is reliable.' 466 U.S. at 687.

A defendant's conviction may be set aside only if both parts of the test are satisfied.[3] *Id.*

1. Deficient Performance

Deficient performance of defense counsel is to be measured by an "objective standard of reasonableness." The reasonableness standard includes both an element of deference and flexibility relevant to the "prevailing norms of practice." Yet the reasonableness inquiry must center on the facts of the particular case, viewed as of the time of counsel's conduct. *Id.* at 690. A central component in this inquiry is defense counsel's duty to investigate so as to make "strategic choices."

The two primary grounds alleged to constitute deficient performance were the failure of defense counsel to file a pre-trial motion for a "probable cause and suppression" hearing and the failure to adequately cross-examine the law enforcement witnesses of the prosecution. Each ground will be examined separately.

a. Failure to Seek a Probable Cause and Suppression Hearing

The appellant consistently conjoins probable cause with suppression, but they are two quite different elements of criminal procedure. A probable cause hearing was determined to be constitutionally mandated (absent an arrest warrant) in the case of *Gerstein v. Pugh*, 420 U.S. 103 (1975). In the case at bar, the defendant was arrested without a warrant on November 17, 2008 and was released on a $500 cash bond on November 19, 2008. This two day period of incarceration normally would not trigger the requirement of an immediate probable cause hearing under the constitutional principle of due process articulated in the case of *County of Riverside v. McLaughlin*, 500 U.S. 44 (1991).

As noted above, such a constitutional principle does not apply against the tribes, *see Talton v. Mayes*, 163 U.S. 376 (1896), because the tribes are not subject to the strictures of the United States Constitution. Nevertheless, the tribes are subject to the Indian Civil Rights Act, including the due process provision

3. Since admission to practice before the Rosebud Sioux Tribal Court requires an individual—whether law-trained or not—to pass the Tribal bar examination, the *Strickland* standard will apply to all defense counsel, regardless of educational background. In addition, the *Strickland* standard shall apply in all cases when a defendant is sentenced to jail time, regardless of whether any of said jail time has been suspended, commuted, or otherwise served.

at 25 U.S.C. §1302(8), as well as its own constitutional provisions. The Rosebud Sioux Constitution contains a due process guarantee at Art. X, Sec. 1(f). This Court holds that the Tribal constitutional guarantee of due process requires a due process hearing within seventy-two hours if the defendant has not been released from custody. Such a due process hearing need not be adversarial and does not require that defendant have the right to call witnesses or cross-examine any witnesses of the prosecution. The requirement of a probable cause hearing, if otherwise timely, may be combined with the arraignment. In this case, the defendant was released on bond within forty-eight hours, promptly arraigned, and thus the issue is essentially moot.

As to the matter of suppression, this issue is more complicated. Certainly, there is a due process right to a suppression hearing. Both parties agree as to this core ingredient. It is also true that the Tribe has the right to establish the procedural parameters for the exercise of that right. It is a uniform rule at the federal, state, and tribal level that suppression of evidence is essentially a pretrial matter and absent the most extreme set of circumstances, it cannot be raised at trial. The trial judge was well within his discretion to deny the motion as untimely, when it was raised on the day of trial.

Defense counsel offered no explanation for his failure to raise the issue in a more timely manner. This failure clearly violated the Rosebud Sioux Tribal Rules of Criminal Procedure. *See*, for example, Rule Sec. 7, Art. IV(F) which provides:

> 1. The Court shall, upon motion of either party, or upon its own motion, hold a pretrial conference. The Court shall compel the attendance of the defendant and his counsel at the conference. The prosecution and defense may be required by the court to exchange discoverable information at the conference. *The Court shall at that time consider all pre-trial motions* and the Court may issue such orders as deemed proper to regulate the conduct of trial.
> 2. *Defenses or objections that are capable of determination other than at trial must be raised at the pretrial conference.* (emphasis added)

This error of counsel is particularly egregious in light of the fact that one of the charges, possession of a firearm while intoxicated, relied exclusively on physical evidence (*i.e.*, the firearm) seized without the benefit of either a search or arrest warrant. In addition, at the time of this occurrence, there existed no Tribal exceptions—statutory or decisional—that permitted the seizure of evidence without a warrant of some kind. In the case at bar, the Tribe did obtain a search warrant to seize evidence relative to whether the defendant was in possession of a firearm while under the "influence of marijuana." Indeed, defense counsel himself appeared to realize the necessity to deal with the issue of suppression by making a motion for suppression, even if it was done too late and in an untimely manner. The inescapable conclusion is that of attorney error.

b. Failure to Adequately Cross-Examine

Defendant/appellant also asserts that his attorney's cross-examination of the two law enforcement officers who testified at trial was deficient as a matter of law.[4] Officer Robert Sedlmayer was the first witness called by the Tribe. Officer Sedlmayer was the arresting officer and his direct testimony related largely to his observations of defendant's driving, which led him to conclude that there was probable cause to make a traffic stop, his concern (pursuant to a departmental dispatch) about the potential presence of firearms, his questions to the suspect about the presence of firearms, the perception of the smell of alcohol, the 'staggering' of the defendant, the subsequent administering of field sobriety tests to the defendant, and his ultimate conclusion that there was probable cause to arrest the defendant for DUI and the illegal possession of firearms.[5]

Defense counsel's cross-examination of Officer Sedlmayer focused largely on the training and competency of officers to administer and interpret the results of field sobriety tests, as well as whether Officer Sedlmayer at any point apprised the defendant of his *Miranda* rights. There was no cross-examination concerning probable cause or the seizure of the evidence.

The prosecution then called Officer Delta Anderson. The essence of Officer Anderson's testimony was directed to his observation of Officer Sedlmayer in possession of the weapons taken from the defendant's vehicle at the scene, his own subsequent securing and marking the evidence, and his role in the chain of custody in presenting the physical evidence to the Court as the lead-up to its offer in evidence. There was minimal cross-examination, relating to the chain of custody. The defense then rested and did not call any witnesses.

While defense counsel's cross-examination of the two law enforcement officers was not particularly probing, it was not deficient as a matter of law. Defense counsel did establish the failure to give *Miranda* warnings and did raise some essential questions relative to the field sobriety tests.

---

4. This assertion was not discussed in defendant/appellant's brief, but was presented for the first time in oral argument before this Court. Since there was no objection by counsel for the Tribe, any possible objection is deemed to have been waived.

5. Defense counsel did assert a number of objections—largely related to hearsay—to parts of this direct testimony.

2. Prejudice

Given our finding that there was deficient performance relative to the failure to timely request a suppression hearing, the question becomes whether such failure was prejudicial in the context of *Strickland*. The standard for prejudice is such that:

> The Defendant must show that there is a reasonable probability that, but for counsel's unprofessional errors, the result of the proceeding would have been different. A reasonable probability is a probability sufficient to undermine confidence in the outcome. 466 U.S. at 674.

In the context of suppression, the key inquiry revolves around the seizure of firearms, which was an absolute predicate to the conviction of the charge of possession of a firearm while intoxicated.[6] While there is no Tribal precedent on point, it is reasonable to conclude that the seizure of the firearms was *constitutionally* permissible under the (federal) plain-view, public safety, and automobile exceptions to the search warrant requirement. *See, e.g. Coolidge v. New Hampshire*, 405 U.S. 443 (1971); *New York v. Quarles*, 467 U.S. 649 (1984); and *Chambers v. Maroney*, 399 U.S. 42 (1970).

These exceptions also appear appropriate within the context of both the Indian Civil Rights Act of 1968 and the Rosebud Sioux Tribal Constitution. Since there is nothing in the record to suggest that plain view ought to be viewed differently in the Tribal context or that public safety is of a lesser concern or that automobiles should be considered differently, the Court adopts these exceptions to the United States Constitution search warrant requirement as permissible exceptions to the warrant requirement of both the Indian Civil Rights Act of 1968 and the Rosebud Sioux Tribal Constitution. Having adopted these exceptions, it is clear that seized firearms would have been admissible at trial and hence there was no prejudice that resulted from the failure of defense counsel to timely file a suppression motion.

B. *Miranda* Warnings

While it is clear that there was no *Miranda* violation in the federal constitutional sense because there was no "custodial interrogation," *Miranda v. Arizona*, 384 U.S. 436 (1966), a recent amendment to the Rosebud Sioux Tribal

6. The DUI conviction involves no suppression issues. Field sobriety tests involve no seizure of tangible or testimonial evidence, but, at best, evidence relative to the physiological impairment to the physical movement, including the ability to speak understandably. *See, e.g.*, Pennsylvania v. Muniz, 496 U.S. 582 (1990).

Constitution raises the question whether the new amendment is more exacting than the federal standard.

The place to begin is with the text of the new amendment to the Tribal Constitution. It reads in full that the Tribe shall not:

> Search or arrest any person without informing them of their right to remain silent, to have access to an attorney, to be informed that anything they say can be held against them in a court of law, to have their rights explained at the time of the search and arrest, and to ask them if they understand these rights. Art. X, Sec. 1(d).

This provision, while not identical, is very similar to the classic language that constitutes the *Miranda* warning established in the case with the same name:

> Prior to any questioning, the person must be warned that he has the right to remain silent, that any statement he does make may be used as evidence against him, and that he has the right to the presence of an attorney, either retained or appointed. 384 U.S. at 444.

The Fifth Amendment-like protections of *Miranda* are triggered by circumstances "stemming from custodial interrogations."[7] The remedy for the violation of *Miranda* requirements is the exclusion of the tainted statements, *Id.*, and any attendant fruit of the poisonous tree. *See, e.g., Wong Sun v. United States*, 371 U.S. 471 (1963).

The basic question before this Court is therefore whether the Tribal constitutional amendment reflects a basic Tribal intent to adopt *Miranda in toto* or to add additional requirements, or perhaps even subtract requirements. Despite the slight variation in text between the *Miranda* opinion and the Tribal constitutional amendment, no evidence was presented to suggest that there was any Tribal constitutional intent to have its amendment extend beyond *Miranda*. In the absence of such evidence, it is reasonable to conclude that Tribal intent was to adopt *Miranda* as its constitutional standard.

There are several other reasons that support such a reading. Given the sanction limitation of one year in jail or a $5000 fine or both in the Indian Civil Rights Act of 1968, 25 U.S.C. § 1302(1) and the Rosebud Sioux Law and Order Code, it would appear unlikely (especially with no evidence to the contrary) that the intent of the amendment was to exceed the federal contours of *Miranda*, where there is no sanction limitation whatsoever.

---

7. "By custodial interrogations, we mean questioning initiated by law enforcement officers after a person has been taken into custody or otherwise deprived of his freedom of action in any significant way." *Miranda*, 384 U.S. at 444.

It is further true that the relevant portion of the Tribal constitutional amendment mentions no express remedy whatsoever and this provides some additional support for our position. Such a view is bolstered by the section that precedes Art. X, Sec. 1(d). Sec. 1(c) largely mirrors the text of the Fourth Amendment[8] and the relevant section of the Indian Civil Rights Act,[9] but in a crucial way exceeds both by enumerating a *specific* remedy, which is not mentioned in either the Fourth Amendment or the Indian Civil Rights Act. Sec. 1(d) reads in whole that the government of the Tribe, including the community shall not:

> Violate the right of the people to be secure in the privacy of their persons, houses, papers, vehicles, and effects against unreasonable searches and seizures, nor issue warrants but upon probable cause, supported by oath or affirmation signed by a judge, and particularly describing the place, person, house, papers, vehicles, or effects to be searched, the object and scope of such search, and the person or thing to be seized, and *any search or seizure taken in violation of this provision shall be excluded.* (emphasis added)

An express remedy in the search and seizure context of Sec. 1(c) and no express remedy in the *Miranda* context of the very next section of 1(d) potentially suggests the lack of any intent to provide a remedy. While we do not accept such a reading, it does support the Court's basic conclusion that Sec. 1(d) does not exceed the core federal boundaries of *Miranda.*

In sum, the Court finds that Sec. 1(d) is the Tribal constitutional equivalent to the federal constitutional standard of *Miranda.*[10] And as a result, no exclusion of evidence is required, because there was no "custodial interrogation" that would trigger the *Miranda* remedy to suppress. Further, *Miranda* does not apply to roadside questioning of motorists detained pursuant to a routine traffic stop. *Berkemer v. McCarty*, 486 U.S. 420 (1984).

---

8. The Fourth Amendment states:

> The right of the people to be secure in their persons, houses, papers, and effects, against unreasonable searches and seizures, shall not be violated, and no Warrants shall issue, but upon probable cause, supported by Oath or affirmation, and particularly describing the place to be searched, and the persons or things to be seized.

9. The Indian Civil Rights Act states: "(2) violate the right of the people to be secure in their persons, houses, papers, and effects against unreasonable search and seizures, nor issue warrants, but upon probable cause, supported by oath or affirmation, and particularly describe the place to be searched and the person or thing to be seized. 1302(2)."

10. *Miranda* is a constitutional rule rather than some kind of a judicially created remedy. Indeed, *Miranda* warnings "have become part of our national culture." Dickinson v. United States, 530 U.S. 428, 430 (2000).

IV. Conclusion

For all the above-stated reasons, the conviction of the defendant is hereby affirmed. Despite upholding the conviction, it is important to restate the decision of the Court to adopt the standard articulated in *Strickland v. Washington*,[11] 466 U.S. 668 (1984), to determine whether there is ineffective assistance of counsel as a matter of Tribal constitutional law, as well as the determination that Sec. 1(d) of Art. X (Bill of Rights) of the Tribal Constitution is to be understood as identical to the rule(s) of *Miranda v. Arizona*, 384 U.S. 436 (1966) and its progeny.

IT IS SO ORDERED.

Dated this 30th day of October, 2009.

FOR THE COURT:

____

Frank Pommersheim
Chief Justice

Notes on *Rosebud Sioux Tribe v. Luxon* (2009)

Crime in Indian country—including Rosebud, Cheyenne River, and other places I have worked and continue to work—is persistent, culturally dysfunctional, and injurious to the basic need for public safety. The causes—according to many scholars and researchers—are manifold and not easily solved. They include such things as extensive poverty, alcohol and drug abuse, real and perceived lack of opportunity, lack of adequate law enforcement, and absence of criminal jurisdiction over non-Indians pursuant to *Oliphant v. Suquamish Indian Tribe*, 435 U.S. 191 (1978). Yet there is also a sense of emerging consensus about what needs to be done. This includes such things as increased and capable tribal law enforcement, better cooperation with federal and state partners, increased rehabilitative services, increased use of appropriate cultural approaches focusing on peace-making and restorative justice, increased tribal court infrastructure, and increased criminal jurisdiction over non-Indians.

To date, there have been fewer criminal appeals than civil appeals. Since the ICRA does not require appointed counsel for indigent criminal defendants in tribal court, most defendants are unrepresented and seldom capable of effective *pro se* appeal. In addition, this lack of representation leads to an extraor-

11. This includes the rule that extrinsic factors such as an extensive caseload do not dilute or revise downward the standard of effectiveness to which defense counsel is to be held. *See, e.g.*, United States v. Cronic, 466 U.S. 648 (1984).

dinary high rate of guilty pleas. ICRA also limits the permissible tribal sanction to one year in tribal jail, or a $5,000 fine, or both, and this also likely suppresses the inclination to appeal. Despite these factors, there has been a broad range of significant criminal appeals.

A. *Other Ineffective Assistance of Counsel Cases in Tribal Courts*

Other examples of tribal court ineffective assistance of counsel claims include the following cases. In a case of first impression, the Appellate Court of the Hopi Tribe addressed the issue of ineffective assistance of counsel in *Navasie v. Hopi Tribe*, 2 Am. Tribal Law 327 (App. Ct. Hopi Tribe 1999). The Court looked to federal law to help guide its decision on what standard the Court would use when evaluating this substantive issue. *Id.* at 332–33. Turning to guidance from *Strickland v. Washington,* 466 U.S. 668 (1984), the Court implemented the same two part standard where "[f]irst, the appellant must show that his counsel's actions were unreasonable under the circumstances in light of prevailing professional norms. Second, appellant must demonstrate a reasonable probability that, absent counsel's unprofessional errors, the result of the proceedings would have been different." *Id.* at 332 (citing *Strickland* 466 U.S. at 669–70). The Court also made a point to note the extremely deferential nature of the standard and the large burden of proof that the defendant bears in order to prove that his assistance fell outside of reasonable professional standards. *Id.* at 332–33. In the specific case, the lay advocate failed to address a pivotal piece of evidence that could have been used to the defendant's advantage in numerous ways. *Id.* at 333–34. The lay advocate also had severe hearing problems that resulted in the inability to properly hear or cross-examine witnesses. *Id.* Thus, the Court stated:

> The above errors meet the *Strickland* test for ineffective counsel. They are not merely strategic shortcomings; they are clear violations of the prevailing norms for professional conduct of defense counsel, and they likely affected the outcome of the trial. However, since this standard comes from a foreign jurisdiction, Hopi courts should consider whether it is suited to the Hopi community before adopting it. Representation by lay counsel has distinct advantages for Hopi litigants, including affordability and cultural familiarity, that merit preservation. Nonetheless, lay counsel should not be permitted to practice without basic competency in law and procedure. The *Strickland* test, in assessing the effectiveness of counsel by what is *reasonable under the circumstances,* allows competency to be evaluated in light of Hopi norms. It strikes an appropriate balance between the need to protect defendants from inept counsel and the need to take into account the

relevant cultural context, and thus can be applied to both lay advocates and attorneys. Since appellant's lay advocate provided ineffective counsel under the *Strickland* test, his conviction is reversed. *Id.* at 334.

The Court also addressed another issue that was grounds for reversal. *Id.* at 331. The Hopi Ordinance that addresses the defendant's right to counsel reads: " 'In all criminal prosecutions, the accused Indian shall have the right to defend himself in person or, at his own expense, by counsel.' " *Id.* (quoting Hopi Ordinance 21, §2.8.5). Although the ordinance does not guarantee a right to counsel, "the Hopi courts have interpreted it as requiring, at a minimum, that criminal defendants be informed of their options for counsel and choose knowingly amongst them. These options include retaining an attorney at the defendant's own expense, retaining a lay advocate at his own expense, or acting pro se." *Id.* (citing Harvey v. Hopi Tribe, 1259/88, 4, AP–001–89 (1997)). Along with options at the defendant's expense, the Tribe also offered a public defender program available to defendants that were indigent. *Id.* The defendant was not advised of these options, and because of this omission, neither part of the *Harvey* test was satisfied. He was not informed of his options for counsel, and there was no record of an active inquiry by the judge that the defendant understood the legal effect of waiving his right to counsel. *Id.* at 330–31. Thus, the Court found that he did not knowingly waive his rights to counsel. *Id.* at 331.

In another ineffective assistance of counsel case, *Hopi Tribe v. Chimerica*, 5 Am. Tribal Law 249 (App. Ct. Hopi Tribe 2004), the Appellate Court of the Hopi Tribe addressed the procedural requirements behind raising the claim. The Court held that the issue must first be raised in the trial court by post-trial motion and not via direct appeal. *Id.* at 252. The Court denied the petitioner's ineffective assistance of counsel claim as the petitioner did not follow the proper procedure of first having his post-trial motion rejected. *Id.* This ruling did not preclude relief for the defendant, as he could still file the proper motion and the trial court could then hold an evidentiary hearing where testimony from both sides would be heard on the merits of the claim of ineffective assistance of counsel. *Id.* Similarly, in *Duwala v. Hopi Tribe*, 6 Am. Tribal Law 389 (App. Ct. Hopi Tribe 2006), the Court remanded an ineffective assistance of counsel claim to the trial court to go through the proper hearing to determine the merits of the claim.

The Swinomish Tribal Court of Appeals also implemented the same *Strickland* two-prong standard for addressing ineffective assistance of counsel claims in its courts in *Edge v. Swinomish Indian Tribal Community*, 4 NICS Ap. 151, 156 (Swinomish Tribal Ct. App. 1996). In *Edge*, the appellant argued that her spokesman failed to move to suppress her statement that she was " 'having a bad day."' *Id.* However, the Court found that the statement "does not rise to the level of incrimination or intent to commit the crime. Taken in light of the other evidence presented at the trial court, this was an innocuous statement without probative value. Appellant failed to demonstrate that the statement affected the outcome or prejudiced the Appellant." *Id.* Although the appellant cited an additional three grounds for the claim, including "failure to advise Appellant of the issuance of a bench warrant, failure to sever offenses, and stipulation to validity of arrest warrant," the Court held:

> These issues are asserted without authority and do not rise to the level of ineffective assistance of counsel. Trial counsel must make a tactical, strategic decision at the time of trial as to their course of action to best represent their client. Although counsel in appellate proceedings may have used different tactics or strategy than the counsel in trial court proceedings, it is each attorney's determination as to how to proceed during trial. The Court is not in a position to second-guess trial counsel's decision without adequate evidence and authority. *Id.*

The Nevada Inter-Tribal Court of Appeals also used the *Strickland* standard in determining an ineffective assistance of counsel claim in the case *Plummer v. Walker River Paiute Tribal Court,* 2003 WL 25856878, 2 (Nev. Inter-Tribal C.A.). In this case, the defendant asserted that "his advocate failed to call a witness who the defendant believed would have presented testimony favorable to his defense." *Id.* The defendant averred that "on the day of his trial, prior to the start of the trial, his advocate refused to interview his witness … [and] that his advocate was only interested in urging him to accept a plea bargain." *Id.* The defendant also asserted that previous to the start of the trial "the witness again offered to testify and the advocate again refused to consider it…." *Id.* A transcript of the trial revealed the following interaction between the advocate and trial judge:

> Person from Audience: Yeah, I was there at that time, can I speak up?
>
> Judge: Only if one of the parties wants you to.
>
> [Advocate]: I have never had any contact with this individual, I'm not sure about putting her on the witness stand for the defendant.
>
> Judge: How about if you just step outside with her for two seconds and find out.
>
> [Advocate]: Well, I'm busy with a trial right now, I don't have time go over this thing with her. Mr. Plummer has had over two and a half months …
>
> Judge: Well, I'm not worried about that … step outside and find out if she's helpful to your case or not.

[Advocate]: I'm refusing to step outside with her.

In evaluating these facts in order to determine if the defendant had a valid ineffective assistance of counsel claim, the Court found that "[t]he witness' possible testimony is unknown." *Id.* However, the Court still found that "the advocate's refusal to confer privately with the witness to ascertain whether her testimony could be useful to the defendant to be conduct that falls below reasonable standards of professional conduct." *Id.* Although the Court found that prong one of the *Strickland* test was satisfied, it nonetheless held that the burden of proof was on the appellant to show that "the outcome of the trial would have been different." *Id.* This, however, was something the appellant was unable to accomplish. *Id.* Thus, since he failed to meet the prejudice prong of *Strickland*, his claim for ineffective assistance of counsel was unsuccessful. *Id. See also In re K.M.C.*, 1999 WL 34986349, 3 (Grand Traverse Band Tribal App. Ct.) (holding "a bare assertion of ineffective assistance of counsel without more will not support a decision to void" the decision of the tribal trial court); *Bullcoming v. Cheyenne Arapaho Tribes*, 9 Okla. Trib. 528 (Cheyenne and Arapaho Tribe Sup. Ct. 2006) (holding that the right to have lay counsel speak on behalf of the defendant was not a fundamental right, but was only discretionary and denial of lay counsel's request to speak for defendant was only harmless, not reversible, error).

B. Additional Criminal Procedure Issues Addressed by Tribal Courts

Tribal Courts have also addressed a wide variety of other criminal procedure issues. Some of these issues include the following: in *Eriacho v. Ramah District Court*, 6 Am. Tribal Law 624 (Nav. Sup. Ct. 2005), the Supreme Court of the Navajo Nation addressed the right to a jury trial. The defendant had waived her right to an arraignment, and by doing so, she was never informed that she had a right to a jury trial; a right which is statutorily required to be read to the defendant at the arraignment. *Id.* at 627. Although she received a form informing her of certain procedural rights when she waived her arraignment, no time limit was specified for requesting a jury trial. *Id.* As a result, by the time the defendant requested her jury trial, it was beyond the statutory requirement of fifteen days post-arraignment. *Id.* The Court held that the defendant, who was never informed that inaction would waive her right to a jury trial, did not provide a "knowing and intelligent" waiver of this right:

> For notice to be meaningful, and therefore a waiver to be effective, the Navajo government must explain to the defendant that the jury trial right is not absolute, as it may be waived by doing nothing within a certain time. Absent this explanation, the information received by a defendant is incomplete, as it appears the right is automatic and per-

> petual, like the federal constitutional right. Without this information, the waiver by inaction is not truly knowing and intelligent, and would violate the defendant's right to due process. As the description of the right to jury trial in the waiver of arraignment form does not include a statement that the right must be exercised within fifteen days, Eriacho's failure to request it within that time was not a knowing and intelligent waiver. *Id.* at 630–31 (footnotes omitted).

The right to confront a witness is discussed in several tribal court cases including *Eastern Band of Cherokee Indians v. Brady*, 2007 WL 7079614 (Eastern Cherokee Ct.) where the court held that the requirements of the federal Supreme Court case, *Crawford v. Washington*, 541 U.S. 36 (2004), were applicable to the Tribe's courts. *Brady*, 2007 WL at 4. In this case, the declarant, an alleged victim of domestic assault was unavailable, and the court found that her out of court statements to a detective dispatched to the scene were not admissible as they were testimonial in nature, similar to *Crawford*. *Id.* at 1–4. Although the Tribe requested that the court carve out a domestic violence exception in confrontation requirements in "consideration of Cherokee custom and tradition," ultimately the court did not find this persuasive, given the Tribe's history of allowing the confrontation of witnesses since at least 1827. *Id.* at 4. The decision of the court was also based, in part, on the fact that the Tribe had enacted a criminal procedure rule that required "the Magistrate to advise a criminal defendant in this jurisdiction upon his arrest 'that he or she has the right to confront the witnesses against him or her.'" *Id.* at 3.

In *Colville Confederated Tribes v. Marchand*, 33 I.L.R. 6036 (Colville Reservation Ct. App. 2006), the Colville Reservation Court of Appeals rejected *Crawford*'s requirement because it was not binding authority and was contrary to Tribal history. *Id.* at 6037. The Court ultimately decided to take an approach that balanced the rights of the community, victim, defendant, and tribe, instead of a hardline approach to the right of confrontation. *Id.* Taking a unique cultural approach, the Court requested the empanelment of a group of elders to "explain to the Court any traditions or customs as they related to the right to confront accusers" and stated that it would use the information obtained from the elder panel in order to determine the admissibility of statements that may create confrontation problems. *Id.* at 6037. The Court further noted, "Once the Court has heard from the elders, the Court will furnish a written statement of the standards the Court intends to apply in these domestic violence cases." *Id.*

In *Fort Peck Tribes v. DeCoteau*, 2 Am. Tribal Law 143 (Fort Peck Ct. App. 1999), the Court held that "the Tribal Court's unwritten policy of exacting recoupment of jury costs from convicted criminal defendants places an impermissible burden on those defendants' right to a trial by jury."

Tribal court cases have also addressed the issue of self-incrimination in the *Miranda* context. In *Gaddy v. Hopi Tribe*, 5 Am. Tribal Law 214 (Hopi Ct. App. 2004), an officer asked the defendant if he "had been using intoxicants" after the officer had performed field sobriety tests that the defendant failed. *Id.* at 217. The defendant responded that he had consumed two beers. *Id.* The Court looked to *Berkemer v. McCarty*, 468 U.S. 420 (1984), in making its decision that this preliminary questioning by the officer did not trigger the requirement to issue the defendant a *Miranda* warning. *Id.* at 217–18. *See also Fort Peck Tribes v. Bighorn*, 1997 WL 3467135 (Fort Peck Ct. App.) (holding that "the circumstances in this case indicate that Mr. Bighorn voluntarily disclosed that he had been drinking and that he was drunk and that these voluntary statements came prior to Mr. Bighorn being placed under formal arrest" so a *Miranda* warning was not required).

See also Swinomish Indian Tribal Community v. Reid, 11 Am. Tribal Law 179 (Swinomish Tribal Ct. 2011) (finding that "the Defendant made a clear and unambiguous request for a lawyer and all interrogation should have immediately ceased" but the officer "continued to engage the suspect in conversation, apparently intended to encourage the Defendant to continue the interview without the assistance of counsel." The court granted defendant's motion to suppress his subsequent statements); *Navajo Nation v. Rodriguez*, 5 Am. Tribal Law 473 (Nav. Sup. Ct. 2004) (holding that defendant did not voluntarily waive his *Miranda* rights and vacating the defendant's conviction).

Cases addressing search and seizure issues include the following: *Eastern Band of Cherokee Indians v. Rattler*, 2006 WL 6499919, 5–6 (Eastern Cherokee Ct.) where the court explained how search and seizure issues would be handled for the Tribe, pursuant to 25 U.S.C. § 1302(2), and with limitations "[i]dentical to those [i]mposed by the 4th Amendment." *Id.* at 5 (citing *United States v. Strong*, 778 F.2d 1393, 1397 (9th Cir.1985)). As the court declared: "The right to be free from unreasonable searches and seizures applies on Indian Reservations, including the Qualla Boundary...." *Id.* Although the defendant attempted to argue that the magistrate issuing the warrant to search his residence was not neutral, the court did not find this argument persuasive. *Id.* at 6.

The defendant also challenged the search of his residence, which resulted in finding firearms, marijuana, and paraphernalia, pursuant to *Franks v. Delaware*, 438 U.S. 154, 155–56 (1978). *Id.* at 2–3, 7. Arguing that the facially valid affidavit that was used as a basis for the search of his residence was not made in good faith but instead was intentionally misleading, the defendant failed to prevail. *Id.* at 7–8. The court did find the statements misleading. *Id.* at 8. The court stated, "Sgt. Nations admitted on the witness stand that he concocted portions of his application and falsified his Police Report to protect the confidentiality of his informant." *Id.* Given that the first prong of *Franks* was met, that the statements were made in reckless disregard of the truth, the court then turned to the second prong of the *Franks* analysis. *Id.* at 8–9. The court found that when the falsified information was excised, "[The] redaction removes the false information and leaves a facially valid core … [;] This evidence, redacted though it is, is sufficient to satisfy the requirements for probable cause, and therefore the Defendant's Motion to suppress should be denied." *Id.* at 9–10.

In the case of *Maho v. Hopi Tribe*, 1 Am. Tribal Law 278 (App. Ct. of Hopi Tribe 1997), the principal of a school requested police to perform a drug search, and the drug dog alerted on the backpack of the defendant. *Id.* at 279–80. The Court ruled that although the police were requested by the school to perform the search because of the belief of widespread drug use, the search constituted police action. *Id.* at 280. Since the search was police action, the police needed a warrant or an exception to the warrant, something which the prosecution was unable to provide. *Id.* at 281. Thus, the Court reversed the decision of the trial court. *Id.*

In the case of *Tulalip Tribe v. Johnny*, 2006 WL 6357124 (Tulalip Tribal Ct. App. 2006), the Tulalip Tribal Court of Appeals found an invalid search in a case where the defendant was aggressively pressured for ten minutes to grant permission to search his car when he had expressly denied permission several times. *Id.* at 1. The Chief of Police arrived after the ten minutes had passed and asked the defendant if the reason he denied permission for the search was because drugs were in the car, the defendant responded affirmatively. *Id.* The Court affirmed the trial court's decision to suppress the confession, finding that the continued detention and questioning of the defendant were not justified. As the Court stated, "Without the particularized suspicion required by §2.2.14, the continued detention was unlawful. Without a lawful stop, the contraband recovered from defendant must be suppressed." *Id.* at 2.

See also Tobey v. Reno-Sparks Indian Colony, 2006 WL 6358371 (Nevada Inter-Tribal Ct. App.) (holding that defendant who sat in a parked car in an open parking lot had no reasonable expectation of privacy when contraband seen by an officer was in "plain view"); *Fort Peck Tribes v. Vondall*, 2 Am. Tribal Law 139 (Fort Peck Ct. App. 1999) (finding that a tip from citizen informant about intoxicated driver lacked sufficient indicia of reliability to provide probable cause for an investigatory stop); *Swan v. Colville Confederated Tribes*, 9 CCAR 24

(Colville Confederated Ct. App. 2007) (finding that the warrant used for search lacked probable cause and thus a reversal of the conviction was required).

C. *Going Forward: The Tribal Law and Order Act and The Violence Against Women Reauthorization Act*

The rate of criminal appeals is likely to change in the near future. Two new federal laws make such appeals all the more likely. The Tribal Law and Order Act, 124 Stat. 2258 (2010), provides tribes with the opportunity to prosecute violations of tribal law and impose an enhanced sentence of up to *three* years and/or a fine of $15,000. The Violence Against Women Reauthorization Act, 127 Stat. 120 (2013), provides tribes with the option to have criminal jurisdiction over non-Indians in the area of domestic violence. Both of these statutes have (federal) conditions that must be satisfied before a tribe can opt in and implement these changes.

The key provisions of the Tribal Law and Order Act are:

1) The defendant must be prosecuted for an offense that a state or federal court would punish with more than one year in prison or have been previously convicted of a comparable offense by any jurisdiction in the United States, including tribal government;
2) Tribes must provide a right to counsel at least equal to that guaranteed by the United States Constitution;
3) The tribal (trial) judge must have sufficient legal training to conduct criminal proceedings and be licensed to practice law by any jurisdiction in the United States;
4) The tribe must make its criminal laws and procedures publicly available before charging the defendant and must keep an audio record of the criminal proceeding; and
5) Convicted defendants must serve their time in a tribal facility approved by the Bureau of Indian Affairs, in the facility of a state, local, or federal government, or in a tribal rehabilitation center.

President Obama signed the Violence Against Women Reauthorization Act, Pub. L. 113-4, Title IX § 904, 127 Stat. 120, on Mar. 7, 2013, and in so doing partially reversed the Supreme Court's decision in *Oliphant v. Suquamish Tribe*. Congress provided that:

> Notwithstanding any other provision of law, in addition to all powers of self-government recognized and affirmed by [the Indian Civil Rights Act, 25 U.S.C. §§ 1301 & 1303] the powers of self-government of a participating tribe include the inherent power of that tribe, which

> is hereby recognized and affirmed, to exercise special domestic violence criminal jurisdiction over all persons. 25 U.S.C. § 1304(b)(1).

The key provisions of the Violence Against Women Reauthorization Act are:

1) The statute applies to "dating violence" and "domestic abuse" as defined in the Act and is concurrent with any applicable federal or state jurisdiction over the same crimes. 25 U.S.C. § 1304(a) & (b);
2) The statute applies if either the defendant or the victim is an Indian and the crime or conduct giving rise to the civil protection order takes place in Indian country. 25 U.S.C. § 1304(c); and
3) If any jail time may be imposed, the tribe must provide the individual with a jury that constitutes a fair cross-section of the community, as well as the right to counsel and other protections. 25 U.S.C. § 1304(d).

There is little doubt that prosecutions under these two new federal statutes will result in many appeals, involving cases of first impression. The right to counsel, the right to jurors representing a cross-section of the community, and legal transparency are likely issues to crowd tribal court appellate dockets in the not so distant future.

There is also the issue of 'uncounseled' tribal court convictions and their potential federal court ramifications. Federal courts have generally refused to consider tribal court convictions for enhancement purposes under the Federal Sentencing Guidelines when the defendant was not represented by law-trained counsel. For example, *see, e.g.*, *United States v. Ant*, 882 F.2d 1389 (9th Cir. 1989); *United States v. Bryant*, 769 F.3d 671 (9th Cir. 2014). *State v. Watchman*, 809 P.2d 641 (N.M. Ct. App. 1991); *United States v. Lawrence*, 2006 WL 752920 (D. Minn. 2006). Two recent federal appellate court decisions may be calling into question previous federal precedent. In *United States v. Cavanaugh*, 643 F.3d 592 (8th Cir. 2011), *cert. denied*, 132 S. Ct. 1542 (2012) and *United States v. Shavanaux*, 647 F.3d 993 (10th Cir. 2011), *cert. denied*, 132 S. Ct. 1742 (2012), uncounseled tribal court convictions were allowed into evidence for habitual offender purposes.

In sum, there is an increasing tribal and federal concern about crime and criminal justice in Indian country, both inside and outside the courtroom. At least one result of these concerns will be a significant increase in the number of tribal court criminal appeals. Many will be watching and tabulating the results as a matter of craft, culture, and justice.

Criminal Law and Criminal Procedure—The Rights of Juveniles

In the Interest of R.K., minor child and concerning, M.K.

(Rosebud Sioux Tribe Supreme Court) (2011)

IN THE SUPREME COURT
OF THE
ROSEBUD SIOUX TRIBE

THE PEOPLE OF THE ROSEBUD SIOUX TRIBE IN THE INTEREST OF R.K., minor child and concerning M.K., Respondent.	MEMORANDUM OPINION AND ORDER

Per Curiam (Chief Justice Frank Pommersheim and Associate Justices Leroy Greaves and Cheryl Three Stars Valandra)

I. Introduction

On June 30, 2009, R.K., a minor child and member of the Rosebud Sioux Tribe, was charged with aggravated assault and the (illegal) purchase and possession of alcohol. Pursuant to a preliminary hearing on the same date and while being held at Wanbli Wiconi Tipi, the Tribe's juvenile detention center, the court services officer recommended that R.K. be sent to an alcohol treatment program. On or about August 7, 2009, R.K. left the treatment program without authorization and thus "escaped from custody." He subsequently turned himself in on or about December 9, 2009.

At the adjudicatory hearing on July 7, 2010, R.K. "pled" and admitted[1] to both the purchase and possession of alcohol and escape charges. He was sentenced to sixty days in the Tribe's juvenile detention center. The Tribe requested a continuance on the aggravated assault charge due to the state confinement of its sole eyewitness. Judge Steven Emery denied the motion and *sua sponte* dismissed the charge based on the failure to comply with the speedy trial requirement of Art. X § 1(f) of the Rosebud Sioux Tribe Constitution.[2]

---

1. R.K. was represented by the Tribe's law-trained public defender.
2. Article X § 1(f) of the Rosebud Sioux Tribe Constitution provides that:
The government of the Tribe including the community shall not ... [d]eny to any

This appeal followed. The sole issue briefed was whether the "speedy" trial guarantee of Art. X § 1(f) is tolled during the time a minor has "escaped from custody." However, at oral argument before this Court on November 5, 2010, it quickly became clear that there was a more basic question, that is whether Art. X § 1(f) even applies in juvenile proceedings and if not, whether there are other pertinent timing provisions within the Tribal Juvenile Code. The Court subsequently ordered the parties to file supplemental briefs on these questions.

II. Issues

This appeal raises four issues, namely the original tolling issue as well as supplemental questions identified in the Court's order of November 9, 2010:

(1) Whether the "speedy" trial guarantee of Art. X § 1(f) applies to juvenile proceedings;

(2) If not, whether there are pertinent provisions of the Tribal Juvenile Code that address "speedy" trial concerns; and

(3) If not, what rule, if any, should this Court adopt to provide judicial guidance in this matter.

Each issue will be discussed in turn.

III. Discussion

A. Tribal Constitution "Speedy" Trial Guarantee

Both parties—as well as the Court itself—agree that the Tribal Constitution guarantee of a "speedy trial" set out in Art. X § 1(f) does not apply to juvenile proceedings. This is so as a matter of text, intention, and federal analogy.

The text of Art. X § 1(f) makes no mention whatsoever of juvenile proceedings, which creates a not unreasonable inference that the constitutional text cannot be made to say what it does not say. This is especially so in light

---

person in a criminal or civil proceeding the right to a speedy and public trial which shall be initiated no more than six months from the time of criminal charges or a civil complaint and which shall be decided by the courts within one year, and in a criminal proceeding to be informed of the nature and cause of the accusation, to be presumed innocent until proven guilty, to be confronted with the witnesses against him or her, to have compulsory process for obtaining witnesses in his or her favor, to have the assistance of counsel for his or her defense including the right to have counsel provided subject to income guidelines; nor deprive any person of liberty or property without due process of law.

of the complete absence of any Tribal constitutional reference to the rights of juveniles.

The text of Art. X § 1(f) also includes language that is directly antithetical to the rights of juveniles as delineated elsewhere in the Rosebud Sioux Tribe Law and Order Code. Art. X § 1(f) speaks to a "speedy and *public* trial" (emphasis added). Under Tribal law, juvenile proceedings (including trial-like adjudications) are not open to the public. Sec. 3-3-20(D) of the Tribal Law and Order Code expressly provides:

> Hearings in children's cases shall be before the Court without a jury and may be conducted in an informal manner. The general public shall be excluded and only such persons shall be admitted whom the Judge finds have a direct and legitimate interest in the case or work of the Court. The child or one of his parents may be separately interviewed at any time at the discretion of the Court. The hearings may be continued from time to time at a date specified by the Court.

It would indeed be a rather strained and implausible interpretation to push the Tribal Constitutional text beyond its legitimate parameters. Federal analogy is also instructive. The phrase "speedy and public trial" also appears in the Sixth Amendment to the United States Constitution. The Sixth Amendment to the United States Constitution provides:

> In all criminal prosecutions, the accused shall enjoy the right to *speedy and public trial*, by an impartial jury of the State and district wherein the crime shall have been committed; which district shall have been previously ascertained by law, and to be informed of the nature and cause of the accusation; to be confronted with the witnesses against him; to have compulsory process for obtaining witnesses in his favor, and to have the assistance of counsel for his defence.[3] (emphasis added)

Given this likely borrowing of textual language, it is significant to note that while the United States Supreme Court has directly held that the Constitutional guarantee of "due process"[4] applies to juvenile hearings, it has never in-

3. Note the additional similarities of other Sixth Amendment language such as "to be informed of the matter and cause of the accusation," "confronted with the witnesses against them," "to have compulsory process for obtaining witnesses," and "to have the assistance of counsel," to language in the Rosebud Sioux Tribe Constitution at Article X § 1(f), *supra* note 2.

4. "Due process" appears in both the Fifth and Fourteenth Amendments to the United States Constitution.

The Fifth Amendment provides that:

> No person shall be held to answer for a capital, or otherwise infamous crime, unless on a presentment or indictment of a Grand Jury, except in cases arising in

cluded the "speedy trial" guarantee within the doctrinal reach of due process in juvenile matters. In *In Re Gault*, 387 U.S. 1 (1967), the Supreme Court found due process to apply to matters of adequate notice, the right to counsel, and the protection against self-incrimination. *See also* the express holding of *In re Winship*, 397 U.S. 358 (1970) that constitutional due process does *not* provide a juvenile with the right to a jury trial in the adjudication of a delinquency matter.

Tribal court jurisprudence is uniform in its recognition of a speedy trial guarantee (for adults). The source of such a right comes most obviously and consistently from the plain text of the Indian Civil Rights Act of 1968, 25 U.S.C. § 1302(6).[5] In addition, it is often found in such places as a Tribal constitution (such as the Rosebud Sioux Tribe), as well as the positive law enacted by various tribes. For example, both the Navajo Nation, at Navajo Nation Code, Title 1, § 1(7) and the Hopi Tribe, at Ordinance 21, § 2.8.5 have such guarantees.

The appellate courts of both these tribes have also adopted the multi-factor balancing test set out in *Barker v. Wingo*, 407 U.S. 514 (1972), to measure the reasonableness of delays in the context of the speedy trial guarantee. The fac-

---

> the land or naval forces, or in the Militia, when in actual service in time of War or public danger; nor shall any person be subject for the same offence to be twice put in jeopardy of life or limb, nor shall be compelled in any criminal case to be a witness against himself, nor be deprived of life, liberty, or property, without due process of law; nor shall private property be taken for public use without just compensation.

The Fourteenth Amendment (Section 1) provides that:

> All persons born or naturalized in the United States and subject to the jurisdiction thereof, are citizens of the United States and of the State wherein they reside. No State shall make or enforce any law which shall abridge the privileges or immunities of citizens of the United States; nor shall any State deprive any person of life, liberty, or property, without due process of law; nor deny to any person within the jurisdiction the equal protection of laws.

The due process guarantee also appears in the Indian Civil Rights Act of 25 U.S.C. § 1302(8): "No Indian tribe in exercising powers of self-government shall deny to any person within its jurisdiction the equal protection of its laws or deprive any person of liberty or property without due process of law."

It also appears in the Rosebud Sioux Tribe Constitution at Article X § 1(f), *supra* note 2.

5. 25 U.S.C. § 1302 (6) provides:

> No Indian tribe in exercising powers of self-government shall deny to any person in a criminal proceeding the right to a speedy and public trial, to be informed of the nature and cause of the accusation, to be confronted with the witnesses against him, to have compulsory process for obtaining witnesses in his favor, and at his own expense to have the assistance of counsel for his defense.

tors to consider are essentially fourfold, namely: the length of delay, the reason for the delay, the timeliness of the defendant's assertion of the right to a speedy trial, and the potential prejudice to the defendant. *Id.* at 530–33. The Hopi case applying this standard is *Komalestewa v. Hopi Tribe* (No. AP-004-90) (Hopi Court of Appeals, 1996). The Navajo Nation cases include *Navajo Nation v. Bedonie*, 2 Nav. R. 131 (1979) and *Yazzie v. Catron* (No. A-CV-13-91, 1992). *See also Fort Peck Assiniboine and Sioux Tribes v. Keiser* (No. 093, Fort Peck Court of Appeals) and *Coleman v. Colville Confederated Tribes*, 2 CCAR 1 (Colville Confederated Tribes Court of Appeals).

Only one tribal court case was found that even mentioned the speedy trial guarantee in the context of a juvenile delinquency proceeding. Though the issue was merely mentioned, but not resolved, the Hopi Court of Appeals noted in passing that the juvenile's counsel was waiving the *juvenile's* right to a speedy trial because he was seeking that the adjudicatory hearing be set in forty-five days, instead of the twenty days set out in the Hopi Children's Code. *M.P. v. Hopi Children's Court* (No. DoAC000009, Hopi Court of Appeals, 2001).

B. The Rosebud Sioux Tribe Juvenile Code and Adjudicatory Time Limits

Both parties agree that the Rosebud Sioux Tribe Juvenile Code contains no time framework for the adjudication of juvenile delinquency matters. There are time guidelines for dependency and neglect matters, but they clearly do not apply to juvenile delinquency cases. *See, e.g.*, Rosebud Sioux Tribe Law and Order Code—The Minor Child in Need of Care/Child in Need of Supervision Petition at § IV(A) which provides:

> The court will schedule an adjudication hearing to be held within thirty (30) days following the initial hearing. At the adjudication hearing, the Tribe will have the burden of proving by a preponderance of the evidence the allegations set forth in the petition. If the court finds that the Tribe has not proven the allegations in the petition, the petition will be dismissed and full legal and physical custody of the child will be returned to the parent. If the court finds that the Tribe has proven the allegations in the petition and rules that the child is a minor in need of care or a child in need of supervision, the court will schedule a disposition hearing. Pending the disposition hearing, the Court will enter appropriate orders concerning temporary custody of the child.

These timelines—specifically drawn and textually narrow—are clearly not meant to apply to juvenile delinquency proceedings and neither the Tribe nor the Public Defender's office argues to the contrary.

C. Other Legal Sources for an Appropriate "Speedy" Trial Rule for Juvenile Delinquency Proceedings

Both sides—as well as the Court itself—agree that some speedy trial like guarantee for juveniles is appropriate both as a matter of due process,[6] fairness, and essential Lakota respect for the dignity of all individuals, including juveniles. Potential sources identified include existing common practice within the Rosebud Juvenile Justice system, the Federal Juvenile Justice statute, 18 U.S.C. §5036, with guidance from the analytical balancing test set out in the seminal case of *Barker v. Wingo*, 407 U.S. 514 (1972).

The public defender's office asserts that it is "customary" practice within the juvenile offender proceedings to apply a 180 day speedy trial guarantee and that such practice does not distinguish between detained and non-detained juveniles.

The Tribe's brief makes no reference to this alleged "customary" practice, but instead argues for a thirty day speedy trial guarantee for detained juveniles in accordance with the (federal) Juvenile Delinquency Act, 18 U.S.C. §5036, which provides:

> If an alleged delinquent who is in detention pending trial is not brought to trial within thirty days from the date upon which such detention was begun, the information shall be dismissed on motion of the alleged delinquent or at the direction of the court, unless the Attorney General shows that additional delay was caused by the juvenile or his counsel, or consented to by the juvenile and his counsel, or would be in the interest of justice in the particular case. Delays attributable solely to court calendar congestion may not be considered in the interest of justice. Except in extraordinary circumstances, an information dismissed under this section may not be reinstituted.

The Tribe further argues for a seventy day speedy trial guarantee for non-detained juveniles, based on the basic federal speedy trial guarantee for adults set out in the Speedy Trial Act at 18 U.S.C. §3161.

While it is somewhat unusual for the prosecution to seek shorter time frames for implementation of a speedy trial than the public defender, the Court recognizes that both sides are advancing suggested rules that are within the rec-

---

6. Due process guarantees are recognized in both the Indian Civil Rights Act of 1968 at 25 U.S.C. §1302 (8), *supra* note 4 and the Rosebud Sioux Tribe Constitution at Article X §1(f), *supra* note 2.

ognized and legitimate sources of Rosebud Sioux Tribal law, which at §4-2-8,[7] provides that in the absence of direct Tribal law on point, the Court may look to such sources as federal law and/or the custom and practices of the Rosebud Sioux Tribe.

Within this Tribally-established framework and seeking to balance the rights and dignity of the juvenile and legitimate interests of the Tribe, the Court adopts the following rule. A detained juvenile shall be brought to trial within forty-five days of detention and a non-detained juvenile within seventy days of filing the information. Any failure to comply with these deadlines shall be evaluated within the analytical balancing test set out in *Barker v. Wingo*, 407 U.S. 514 (1972). This balancing test includes four factors, namely length of delay, reason for the delay, the juvenile's assertion of the right, and prejudice to the juvenile. *Id.* at 530.

In sum, the Court finds that there is a speedy trial guarantee for juveniles charged with acts of delinquency. Such right is grounded in the due process guarantee of the Rosebud Sioux Tribe Constitution and Lakota tradition and custom. The specific time frame for the guarantee is forty-five days if the juvenile is detained and seventy days if the juvenile is not detained. All delay beyond these time limits shall be evaluated in accordance with the four-part test set out in *Barker v. Wingo*. "Escape from custody," unless there are extenuating circumstances, tolls the running of these time limits.

IV. Conclusion

For all the above-stated reasons, the case is reversed and remanded to consider the delay in the adjudication of the "assault" charge in accordance with the above-stated principles.

IT IS SO ORDERED.

Dated this 11th day of February, 2011.

FOR THE COURT:

____

Frank Pommersheim
Chief Justice

---

7 Rosebud Law and Order Code §4-2-8 provides:

The Tribal Court shall apply the applicable laws of the Rosebud Sioux Tribe and the United States in actions before it. Any matter not covered by applicable tribal or federal laws shall be decided according to the customs and usages of the Tribe. Where doubt arises as to customs and usages of the Tribe, the Court may request the advise of persons generally recognized in the community as being familiar with such customs and usages. In any matter in which the rule of law is not supplied by any of the above, the Tribal Court may look to the law of any tribe or state which is consistent with the policies underlying tribal law, custom and usages.

Notes on *In the Interest of R.K., minor child and concerning M.K.* (2011)

Tribal appellate cases involving juveniles are more plentiful than expected. This is so despite the fact that there is no (automatic) right to counsel for indigent juveniles, most tribal juvenile proceedings are informal, not open to the public, and seek rehabilitation rather than adjudicative commitment.

Significant cases include the following: *In re C.T.* 8 Am. Tribal Law 386, 387–89 (Cherokee Ct. of Eastern Band of Cherokee Nation 2010), where the Cherokee Court of the Eastern Band of the Cherokee Nation addressed a situation where the Tribe failed to adhere to the jurisdictional filing deadline for the complaint, filing the petition in fifty-five days instead of the maximum statutory amount of thirty days. As a result, the court held that it did not have subject matter jurisdiction and could not adjudicate the case. *Id.* at 394. Similarly, the Supreme Court of the Navajo Nation held in the habeas case *L.R. v. Greyeyes*, 7 Am. Tribal Law 574, 577 (Nav. Sup. Ct. 2007), that "the juvenile was illegally detained when [the] petition [was] filed 31 days after a referral where the Children's Code requires dismissal with prejudice if it is not filed within 30 days from the date of referral." The Court vacated the charges for disorderly conduct and battery stating:

> Although this Court has previously held that the only relief it will grant upon a habeas corpus petition is release from illegal detention and that it will not grant dismissals of cases or the vacating of convictions, *In re H.M.*, No. SC–CV–63–04, 5 Am. Tribal Law 454, 457, 2004 WL 5658523 at *3 (Nav.Sup.Ct.2004), this Court makes an exception in this case. Under the circumstances of this case, the Court will vacate a conviction where the statute clearly mandates a dismissal with prejudice if the petition alleging delinquency is untimely filed. *Id.* at 577.

The Court also found that the juvenile's other charge of violating curfew should be dismissed as the child was "illegally detained" when the petition was filed and the child was not released within the time-frame that statutory requirements required. *Id.* at 578–79.

Another juvenile habeas corpus case, *In re N.B. v. Greyeyes*, 7 Am. Tribal Law 615 (Nav. Sup. Ct. 2008), addressed the issue of "whether a minor is illegally detained when a Family Court revokes probation and reinstates an original sentence of 180 days in detention for a statutory offense that does not authorize incarceration when committed by an adult." *Id.* at 617. Specifically, "Petitioner argued that the statutory provisions of disorderly conduct do not provide for incarceration as a sentencing option and therefore asserts he is being held unlawfully." *Id.* at 619. However, the Supreme Court of the Navajo Nation noted that, "[r]ather than cite statutory authority that specifically allows the incarceration of a *minor* for disorderly conduct, Respondent justified Petitioner's detention by simply citing the Family Court's order, and argued she was simply following the instructions of the court." *Id.* The Supreme Court of the Navajo Nation ultimately agreed with the juvenile's argument and released him from incarceration. *Id.*

The Appellate Court of the Hopi Tribe addressed the burden of proof in a juvenile homicide in the case of *In re J.P.*, 10 Am. Tribal Law 331 (App. Ct. of the Hopi Tribe 2010). In this case, a juvenile was playing around with his best friend, and aimed a gun at the friend. *Id.* at 334. The gun discharged, killing the friend. *Id.* The Tribe failed to introduce any evidence about the cause of death other than a photograph of the body, and no direct evidence of the medical cause of death was presented. *Id.* Moreover, the Tribe did not introduce evidence that the defendant himself was the cause of the death, and that the discharge of the weapon was not a defect or accident. *Id.* at 336–37. No evidence that the defendant-juvenile knew the gun was loaded was introduced by the Tribe, or that the aiming of the gun at the friend was deliberate. *Id.* at 337–38. The Court held that the Tribe had failed to meet the burden of proof of beyond a reasonable doubt on two issues, namely: proving causation and proving negligence. *Id.* at 336–38. Because the burden of proof was not met for each of the elements of homicide, the Court granted the defendant's motion for a directed verdict. *Id.* at 338.

Addressing the due process rights of juveniles, the Fort Peck Court of Appeals held in *In re Bell*, 3 Am. Tribal Law 305 (Fort Peck Ct. of App. 2001), that although the juvenile and his mother were orally alerted at the initial hearing about certain Tribal constitutional protections including the right to counsel, the failure to strictly adhere to the written notice requirement about these protections justified the Court in reversing the judgment of the juvenile court. The Supreme Court of the Navajo Nation addressed the rights of a non-Indian juvenile excluded from the reservation in *In re A.P. v. Tuba City Family Court*, 6 Am. Tribal Law 660 (Nav. Sup. Ct. 2005), where it held that it was a violation of a non-Indian juvenile's due process rights when an exclusion order was issued without first holding a dispositional hearing.

The Inter-Tribal Court of Appeals of Nevada addressed a simple due process issue in a juvenile case, *McCahill v. Pyramid Lake Paiute Tribe*, 2006 WL 6358355 (Nev. Inter-Tribal C.A.), where the Court held that when the probation of a juvenile was revoked after the juvenile had pled guilty to the violation of probation, it was not a violation of due process. Another juvenile case addressing due process, but with the focus on the Tribal Prosecutor being afforded due process of law, is the case of *In re L.T.*, 5 Am. Tribal Law 142 (Fort Peck Ct. App. 2004). In this case, the complaint was withdrawn by the affidavit of the aunt of the juvenile a day before he was scheduled to appear. *Id.* at 143. Although the affidavit was signed in front of a Court Clerk, it was not given to the judge before the hearing. *Id.* A second affidavit by the juvenile's aunt alleged that because the first affidavit was not given to the judge, the juvenile was denied due process as the Tribal Court had accepted guilty pleas from the juvenile and sentenced him to time in a detention center. *Id.* at 143. Subsequently, a guardian of the juvenile brought this matter to the attention of the judge who presided over the hearing, and the judge ordered a release of the juvenile. *Id.* The Prosecutor appealed the release alleging that the release was made *ex parte* and because of the gravity of the matter, the prosecution would not support a dismissal. *Id.* at 144. The Fort Peck Court of Appeals held that it was error for the Tribal Court to order the release of the juvenile without first notifying the Tribal Prosecutor. *Id.* at 144. Moreover, the court held that "the *ex parte* ruling denied the Tribal Prosecutor due process of law, therefore the order must be set aside." *Id.* The Court was not using the phrase "due process" in its usual meaning, involving the obligation of the government to private individuals, but rather in a more basic sense of essential fairness to all participants in the judicial process. *Id.*

In the case of *Simmons v. Colville Confederated Tribes*, 2002 WL 34540594 (Colville Tribal Ct. App.), the tribal court addressed the procedural and jurisdictional question of "[w]ho has jurisdiction over a defendant who is alleged to have committed an offense as a minor and who has turned [into] an adult over the age of eighteen (18) years within the time of the statute of limitations for the offenses alleged?" *Id.* at 2. The Court held that the right court for the case was not the juvenile court, but instead the adult court basing its decision on the Washington state rule that jurisdiction attaches when the complaint is filed. *Id.* at 5.

In *H.M. v. Greyeyes*, 5 Am. Tribal Law 454, 455–56 (Sup. Ct. Navajo Nation 2004), the Navajo Supreme Court addressed the extent of habeas corpus relief in juvenile cases by holding:

> We clarify here, for juvenile cases, and generally in other habeas cases, that the only relief we will grant is release from illegal detention. We will not grant dismissals of cases or the vacating of convictions. Those types of relief are appropriately dealt with by other writs, such as mandamus, prohibition, or superintending control, where the trial court is an actual party and is allowed to respond to the petition. Such relief may also be appropriate through the regular appeals process, when a full record is submitted and the parties are allowed more time to

prepare their arguments on the merits of the underlying case. *Id.* at 457–58.

Based upon that reasoning, the court released the child, but did not dismiss the pending child in need of supervision and delinquency cases. *Id.* at 458.

In a separate case, the Navajo Supreme Court addressed a certified question from family court concerning conflicting portions of the Children's Code. *In re Certified Question from Crownpoint Family Court*, 8 Am. Tribal Law 377 (Sup. Ct. Navajo Nation 2010). In this case, where criminal charges were brought against a juvenile, the Court addressed the following question:

> [H]ow should courts of the Navajo Nation resolve the conflict between the two following provisions of the Children's Code; 9 N.N.C. § 1055(C)(1) which states that "[j]urisdiction obtained by a Family Court over a child is retained until terminated by [t]he child becom[ing] an adult, except where a child becomes an adult during the pendency of proceedings in the Family Court" and 9 N.N.C. § 1156(H) which states that "[w]hen a child reaches 18 years of age all judgments affecting the child then in force automatically terminate."
> *Id.* at 379.

The Court found that the two statutes were clearly contradictory. *Id.* The Court resolved the dispute by holding: "[B]oth statutes are to be read that the jurisdiction of family courts terminate[s] by the child becoming an adult. By enacting Section 1156(H), the legislature obviously decided that the laudatory purpose of the Code that our young people be provided treatment and rehabilitation stops when the young person becomes an adult." *Id.* at 381–82. The Prosecutor was not without options and could have charged the juvenile with a violation of 9 N.N.C. 1121(A), which mandates the exclusive jurisdiction of the district court over a minor who is over fifteen years old. *Id.* at 382. Moreover, the case could have also been brought originally in district court as the child was over fifteen at the time of the incident and the case could have been transferred to district court before the child reached the age of eighteen. *Id.* at 382.

In the Matter of C.S., 1999 WL 34995925 (Nev. Inter-Tribal C.A. 1999), the Inter-Tribal Court of Appeals of Nevada held that the tribal court was required to meet the ten-day notice requirement for a juvenile to be transferred to adult court. *Id.* at 2. However, the juvenile in this case was transferred to adult court, found to be guilty, and sentenced all on the same day. *Id.* Moreover, the juvenile had no conversation with a parent or counsel about "the rights he was giving up in regard to transfer of his case from juvenile to adult court." *Id.* Thus, the matter was remanded for a proceeding consistent with the notice requirement. *Id.*

Addressing the extent of the tribal court's jurisdiction over a juvenile's family, the Fort Peck Court of Appeals held in *M.P.M. v. Fort Peck Tribes*, 11 Am. Tribal Law 334 (Fort Peck Ct App. 2013), that the authority of the Tribal Court did not extend to an order requiring the juvenile's mother to obtain counseling and a mental health assessment. *Id.* at 335. Thus, the appellate court reversed the trial court order. *Id.* The juvenile in this case had been charged with felony theft and had previously tried to accept a plea agreement, which the trial court rejected as not in the youth's best interests before issuing its order. *Id.* Also addressing the responsibility of parents for the offense of a juvenile, the Appellate Court of the Hopi Tribe held in *In re E.S.*, 3 Am. Tribal Law 446 (App. Ct. Hopi Tribe 2001), that the mother of a juvenile was not responsible for the restitution payments of the juvenile for his various offenses, as the Tribal Council had passed a statute that explicitly stated that the responsibility for payments rests on the minor and not on the minor's parents. The Grand Traverse Band of Ottawa and Chippewa Indians Tribal Court addressed the question whether a juvenile's trust fund should pay for required residential facility treatment ordered by the court in *Ocean County v. Chippewa*, 2001 WL 36194127 (Grand Traverse Tribal Ct.). The court stated:

> This Court finds that significant intervention in Savannah Chippewa's life was required for her health and welfare. This Court finds that without the commitment of access to her trust fund, Savannah Chippewa would not have received the care she needed. This Court finds that it was and is in the best interest of Savannah Chippewa to access her minor trust fund to pay for the care she received at Fort Rosa Parks. This Court further finds that it is not repugnant to the public policy of the Grand Traverse Band to invade minor per capita trust funds to provide for the minor's health and welfare. *Id.* at 4.

In *M.C. v. Greyeyes*, 10 Am. Tribal Law 385 (Nav. Sup. Ct. 2012), the Navajo Supreme Court addressed the right to counsel for a juvenile. The court held that it was error for the court to proceed with a preliminary hearing when a juvenile, through his guardian, asserted his right to counsel. *Id.* at 387. A detention hearing was held at the same time, and the court granted the Navajo Nation's request to further detain the child. *Id.* The juvenile filed a petition for Writ of Habeas Corpus. *Id.* The Supreme Court of the Navajo Nation made a point to explain that a detention hearing should be held before a preliminary hearing; and although the right to counsel applied to preliminary hearings, it did not statutorily apply to a detention hearing. *Id.* at 390–91.

In *In re M.G. v. Greyeyes*, 7 Am. Tribal Law 514 (Nav. Sup. Ct. 2007), the Navajo Supreme Court addressed the issue of "whether a family court may incarcerate a juvenile adjudicated a child in need of supervision under its contempt powers for violation of a child in need of supervision order." *Id.* at 515. The Court answered this question by holding:

> The Court holds a family court cannot use contempt to accomplish the incarceration of a CHINS child when it could not have incarcerated that child in the original CHINS order. The Children's Code reflects the clear intent of the Navajo Nation Council that CHINS children are a distinct group from juvenile delinquents and require a different type of treatment. *Id.* at 516.

See also In re C.M., 5 Am. Tribal Law 144 (Fort Peck Ct. App. 2004) (holding that an order dismissing the delinquency charge against a juvenile for failure to prosecute could not stand given the factual circumstances of this case, where the juvenile did not appear and the prosecutor was told that the hearing would be at a different time); *Fort Peck Tribes v. T.M.*, 11 Am. Tribal Law 239 (Fort Peck Ct. App. 2009) (holding that the decision by the trial court to allow a juvenile to withdraw his plea of guilty to a drug offense with a 180 day sentence in the Juvenile Detention Center was a proper exercise of discretion of that court). *Swinomish Indian Tribal Community v. T.T.*, 2009 WL 9125778, 4 (Swinomish Tribal Ct.) (holding that juvenile's right to a speedy trial was not "substantially prejudiced by the delay" where the "delay was at least partially attributable to the Defendant's own earlier requests for a continuance"); *Hopi Tribe v. Q.T.*, 4 Am. Tribal Law (Ap. Ct. Hopi Tribe 2002) (upholding trial court's ruling and dismissing juvenile's motion to vacate possession or distribution of a controlled substance sentence because there was no separate showing that marijuana qualifies as a controlled substance as this was not required by the ordinance); *In re M.F.H.* 5 Am. Tribal Law 147 (Fort Peck Court of App. 2004) (holding that no abuse of discretion occurred when the Tribal Court released the juvenile who was adjudged guilty and gave him the sentence of "Release to mother (name)—Time served."); *Fort Peck Tribes v. M.L.*, 4 Am. Tribal Law 273 (Fort Peck Ct. App. 2002) (holding that the tribal court's denial of the prosecution's motion for a continuance based upon a failure to summons prosecution's witness was not an abuse of discretion).

Tradition and Custom

In the Matter of the Probate of Tasunke Witko a.k.a. Crazy Horse

(Rosebud Sioux Tribe Supreme Court) (2007)

IN THE SUPREME COURT
OF THE
ROSEBUD SIOUX TRIBE

IN THE MATTER OF THE PROBATE OF: TASUNKE WITKO, a.k.a CRAZY HORSE, Deceased,	NO. CA2006-09
SETH BIG CROW, SR., and HARVEY WHITE WOMAN, Co-Administrators, Appellants, vs. FLOYD CLOWN, Co-Administrator, Appellee.	MEMORANDUM OPINION AND ORDER

Per Curiam (Chief Justice Frank Pommersheim and Associate Justices Patrick Lee and Cheryl Three Stars Valandra)

I. Introduction

Appellants Seth Big Crow, Sr. and Harvey White Woman, Co-Administrators of the Estate of Tasunke Witko, a.k.a. Crazy Horse, appeal the Findings of Fact and Conclusions of Law dated July 21, 2006 by the Honorable Stanley E. Whiting, Special Probate Court Judge for the Rosebud Sioux Tribal Court. The trial court concluded, primarily based upon the testimony of Appellants' expert witness, that Lakota society was patriarchal in nature and bloodlines were more patrilineal in descent, exclusive only to the father of the decedent if there were no surviving children.

II. Issue

The issue in this appeal is whether the findings of fact and conclusions of law of the trial court provide sufficient clarification of the applicable traditional Lakota inheritance law in order to determine who the rightful heirs of Tasunke Witko are and what property of his should be distributed.

III. Discussion

The appropriate standard of review for questions of law or an erroneous application or interpretation of substantive law by a tribal court is *de novo* review. *See In the Matter of the Commitment of Lawrence Lee, Jr.*, CA 99-03, p. 5, RS Sup.Ct. (2000) and *First Computer Concepts, Inc. v. Rosebud Sioux Tribe*, CA 89-02, p. 5, RS Sup.Ct. (1990). This Court is, therefore, reviewing *de novo* the trial court's determination of what the applicable traditional Lakota inheritance law was in 1877, the year of Crazy Horse's death.

The findings and conclusions of the trial court, which found that Lakota society was patriarchal in nature and bloodlines were more patrilineal in descent, do not appear to take into account any transitional developments of the Lakota kinship system that may have occurred. For instance, the expert witness testified that the Lakota kinship system changed over time from a matrilineal clan system to a bilateral descent system, which allowed for both patrilineal and matrilineal bloodline to inherit and that eventually a patrilineal system developed during the reservation period.

The findings and conclusions of the trial court, further, do not clearly specify what the Lakota traditional inheritance law was in the year 1877, what was considered "property" that could be inherited during that period of time and how such property should be distributed at the present time. Although it may be difficult to ascertain with complete certainty what the Lakota traditional inheritance laws and customs were at the time of Tasunke Witko's death, such a determination must be made by those who are qualified and well-versed in Lakota tradition and custom.

The Rosebud Sioux Tribe Law and Order Code, Section 4-2-8, provides:

> The Court shall apply the applicable laws of the Rosebud Sioux Tribe and the United State in actions before it. Any matter not covered by applicable tribal or federal laws shall be decided according to the customs and usages of the Tribe. Where doubt arises as to custom and usages of the Tribe, the Court may request the advice of persons generally recognized in the community as being familiar with such customs and usages. In any matter in which the rule of law is not supplied by any of the above, the Court may look to the law of any Tribe or state which is consistent with the policies under tribal law, custom and usages.

This section of the code allows for the Court to apply Lakota customary law and where there is doubt as to what the law is, the Court may request the advice of persons recognized in the community as knowledgeable in that area of law. As is evident in this case, there remains doubt as to what the applicable customary laws pertaining to inheritance would have been during the year 1877.

IV. Conclusion

To resolve the issue before this Court requires use of a more traditional process, including following a consensus approach rather than an adversarial approach in making a decision of what the traditional inheritance laws were and how they should be applied to determine the rightful heirs of Tasunke Witko. This process further requires the assistance of recognized experts with knowledge of Lakota traditional law. The Rosebud Sioux Tribal Law Order Code allows the Court to request such advice. RST Law and Order Code, Sec. 4-2-8.

For all of the above reasons, this case is remanded to the trial court to administer a mediation process involving qualified experts who are well-versed in Lakota tradition and custom during the year 1877 and who have no interest in this case. The Chief Judge of the Rosebud Sioux Tribal Court shall administer the mediation process, including making decisions regarding expenses to be reimbursed and other special requests made by the mediation panel.

There shall be three (3) experts in Lakota tradition and custom selected to serve as mediators. The appellants and appellee in this case shall each select a mediator and those two (2) mediators shall, in turn, choose the third. The names and qualifications of the selected mediators shall be submitted to the Chief Judge who shall present such to the Supreme Court for certification.

The questions to be considered by the mediation panel shall include, but are not limited to, the following:

1. Who would have been the eligible heirs of Tasunke Witko in 1877 and who would be the eligible heirs today?
2. How was it determined who would have inherited the property of Tasunke Witko?
    - A. Was there a process involved in making this determination?
    - B. If there was dispute or disagreement, how were such disputes handled?
3. What would have been considered "property" during that period?
    - A. What were the types or categories of property that could have been inherited in 1877 Lakota society? For example, were there distinctions made as to real, personal, spiritual, ceremonial, or intellectual property?

B. Was the name of a person considered property that could be passed on or inherited by another person? If so, what was the process or law in determining who was eligible to receive the name?

C. Similar to the above question, were there certain types of property that passed on to a particular person or persons? For example, were there specific individuals entitled to inherit certain property, such a decedent's ceremonial items or clothing?

A final written report containing the findings of the mediation panel shall be submitted to this Court for review by May 15, 2008. If the final report is not submitted by the deadline and absent an extension granted by the Court, the above questions shall be referred back to this Court for consideration.

The Court shall give deference to the expert knowledge of the mediators involved in this process as much as possible. However, the Supreme Court shall have the final review of all findings and conclusions made by the mediation panel, including any research, literature, or interviews relied upon by the mediators.

IT IS SO ORDERED.

For the Court:

____

Cheryl Three Stars Valandra
Associate Justice

Dated: November 9, 2007
ATTEST:

____

Chief Clerk of Courts

Notes on *In the Probate of the Estate of Tasunke Witko* (2007)

The Continuing Journey

As noted elsewhere, I am not the author of this opinion. It was authored by Associate Justice Three Stars Valandra. I was, however, a member of the deciding panel and joined the unanimous decision. The Rosebud Sioux Supreme Court is one of the few, if not the only, tribal supreme court that has six members, but only three members hear and participate in a given case. Recall in the original *Crazy Horse Malt Liquor* opinion reprinted *supra* pp. 30–60, was heard *en banc* with all six justices participating. *See* Rule 20 of the Rosebud Sioux Supreme Court Rules of Appellate Procedure.

This case is included in the section on tradition and custom as the necessary complement to its predecessor, the *Crazy Horse Malt Liquor* case. These two cases demonstrate the powerful arc of a cutting edge 'modern' case about tribal court jurisdiction over a non-Indian brewery that found its way into federal court and finally returned to tribal court as a straightforward probate case seeking to determine the heirs of Crazy Horse according to 1877 rules of Lakota tradition and custom. The legal and cultural distance between these two cases is extensive, almost beyond the imagination.

On remand, it became clear that the contending potential heirs fell into three groups—those from the Pine Ridge Sioux Reservation (Oglala Sioux Tribe), those from the Rosebud Sioux Reservation, and those from the Cheyenne River Sioux Reservation. In light of this configuration, Chief Judge Sherman Marshall authorized each of the three groups to name its own "qualified expert."

This process—for numerous reasons—has taken a great deal of time.[8] Regardless, all three "qualified experts" or "mediators" were finally named in late 2009.[9] This group, under the direction of Chief Judge Sherman Marshall, began to meet in December 2010.

These various "mediation" sessions were moderated and facilitated by Judge Marshall and were largely conducted in Lakota. Judge Marshall, who is bilingual and was raised in accordance with traditional cultural ways, is particularly well-suited to assist in this attempt to bridge two worlds, with due respect for each.

Judge Marshall also used additional methods to enhance the body of relevant cultural information. He recruited a University of South Dakota law student[10] to write a research memorandum response to the "specific questions" addressed to the traditional mediation panel. Judge Marshall has indicated that the research memorandum was quite helpful and appears to support and to converge with the ongoing discussions of the traditional mediators.

---

8. Time itself is a cultural variable. Three years for a mediation process to take hold may indeed seem (too) long from a legal docket perspective, but from a cultural perspective of respect, continuation, and survival, such a time frame would cause little or no concern. Indeed, none of the parties have registered a complaint concerning the length of time taken to date. The Court originally envisioned the submission of a report by May 15, 2008. This was far too optimistic. It is now more than *three* years later (February 2012). Yet time is *not* a critical factor; substance is.

9. These individuals are Karen Lone Hill of the Oglala Sioux Tribe; Marilyn Circle Eagle of the Cheyenne River Sioux Tribe; and Webster Two Hawk of the Rosebud Sioux Tribe.

10. Bradley Richardson, Class of 2013.

Given the enormity of this undertaking as a matter of both (traditional) culture and law, the "experts" have moved forward with extreme care and due commitment. Chief Judge Sherman Marshall has informally communicated to the justices of the Rosebud Sioux Supreme Court that progress is being made—however slowly—and that he remains cautiously optimistic that the "experts" will produce the written report identified in the Rosebud Sioux Supreme Court's opinion.

In 2012, the traditional mediators submitted their oral findings to Chief Judge Sherman Marshall. In turn, Judge Marshall prepared the written Findings of the Mediation Panel.[11] On the key questions posed by the Rosebud Sioux Supreme Court, Judge Marshall's Findings of the Mediation Panel noted that the traditional, customary practice of determining heirs was a matter completely within the control of the extended family or *tiyospaye*.[12] It was further understood that inheritable, personal property of a man included clothing, weapons, tools, horses, spiritual property, and a person's name.[13] Perhaps, most critically, the Findings note that a Lakota person's name could be passed on, but that Crazy Horse's name was never passed on.[14]

The Rosebud Supreme Court subsequently 'adopted' Judge Marshall's Findings on the questions posed to the traditional experts appointed in the *Crazy Horse Estate* case. The Court then remanded the case back to Judge Marshall for the difficult task of taking additional evidence—both documentary and testimonial—and making a final determination of who the heirs of Crazy Horse are and what is the nature of his inheritable estate.

While these findings and processes are obviously not precise or final in the conventional language and the ordinary procedure of law, they speak with dignity and continuity across a long historical and cultural journey. Indeed, this is a journey that is likely to continue as part of the mapping of the contem-

11. Findings of the Mediation Panel, *In the Matter of the Probate of Crazy Horse* (Rosebud Sioux Tr. Ct. Feb. 22, 2012).

12. *Id.* at 2.

13. *Id.* at 3.

14. *Id.* at 4. Judge Marshall also indicated how this traditional practice took place in his own family life; how he received the Lakota name "Otakutepi" (Many Shot Him) as a young child in honor of his father who served in the U.S. Army in World War II in Europe. He was also given the name "Oyakapi" (They Tell Him) as the result of a ceremony put on by his grandmother before he went to Vietnam. In addition, he and his wife, Marilyn, gave traditional Lakota family names to their two sons in traditional public naming ceremonies sponsored by the family. The two names were "Mato Wahancanka" (Bear Shield) and "Hoiyekiyapi" (They Called Him). *Id.* at 5.

porary legacy of Crazy Horse within both the modern and traditional worlds of Lakota law and custom. This is the way of time, patience, and commitment.

Additional Examples of Tradition and Custom in Tribal Court Cases

There are many tribal court cases that raise issues about the use of tradition and custom. These cases cover a wide breadth of topics, some of which are exemplified in the following cases: In *Smith v. Colville Confederated Tribes*, 1998 WL 35315070, 3 (Colville Tribal Ct. App.) the Colville Tribal Court of Appeals addressed how the Court views tradition and custom arguments:

> We believe that incorporating our customs into our written law is very important. It is what will set us apart from the state and federal courts. Our courts must approach this carefully, however. Customs and traditions are viable, living doctrines that grow with the community and the time. They are not static, frozen in the past of tepees and buckskin clothing.
>
> A good analysis of the applicability of custom and tradition in a case must be able to trace a current practice back to its roots in our society. It will not necessarily have the same complexion, but it should have the same foundation. Our customs and traditions define our uniqueness not only from the non-Indian society, but from other Indian tribes, too. To define a custom or tradition in our current Tribal Court system is an important task which should not be taken lightly by the courts or the parties.

The appellant in this case argued that the Tribe had a custom of sentencing individuals to community service rather than imprisonment, but the Court noted that the argument was "without any factual support." *Id.* The Court stated, "The person asserting custom and tradition should have an initial burden of producing *some* evidence that may support the claim, *i.e.* affidavits, articles, etc., so the trial judge could base his decision to call a panel of Tribal elders or members on something more credible than just someone's assumption that it should be a tradition or custom." *Id.* Because the appellant failed to meet his evidentiary burden at the trial level, the Court found for the Tribe on the issue. *Id.*

Addressing what type of tradition and custom issues are justiciable, the court, in *Redman v. Birdshead*, 2003 WL 25783118 (Cheyenne-Arapaho D. Ct.), stated:

> The Tribal Court can hear cases and use custom and tradition in areas where the Tribal Court already has written tribal law. Custom and tradition may help to explain an area of law. But if there is no written area of law, *i.e.*, spiritual practices, then custom and tradition will dic-

tate if the Tribal Court or some other forum is appropriate for making decisions. *Id.* at 4.

The plaintiffs sought injunctive relief from a Business Committee resolution forbidding defendants from advertising, promoting, or conducting a Sun Dance on tribal land. *Id.* at 1–4. The Court held that it lacked jurisdiction to decide the case because there was no written Tribal law on point. Interestingly, the Court also noted that "there is a proper procedure to spiritual ways, and the parties are directed to submit this matter for the proper traditional way of resolving these types of disputes" and that "the Court will give recognition and 'full faith and credit' to the decisions of the traditional leaders in this dispute." *Id.*

Addressing tradition and custom in a contracts context, in *Ho-Chunk Nation v. Olsen,* 2 Am. Tribal Law 299, 304–05 (Ho-Chunk Trial Ct. 2000), the Ho-Chunk Nation trial court evaluated a claim for breach of contract where the Nation paid a substantial payment for delivery of cigarettes that was never made. The breaching party refused to pay the payment back or deliver the cigarettes. *Id.* As the court noted, "[T]he plaintiff provided the defendant with an $87,120.00 down payment. This payment was made pursuant to the defendant's assurances ... The plaintiff has yet to receive the cigarettes." *Id.* at 308. Specifically speaking to the potential cause of action through tradition and custom, the court announced: "[U]nder the traditions and customs of the Ho-Chunk Nation, the defendant has violated a binding agreement by retaining the benefit of the down payment without providing the agreed upon compensation." *Id.* In this example, tradition and custom reflected black letter contract law. The court ordered that the monetary payment be returned to the Tribe. *Id.*

Although the Ho-Chunk Nation trial court acknowledged a cause of action for a breach of contract claim through tradition and custom in *Olsen,* the court later refused to find a cause of action for fraudulent inducement or concealment and conversion in *Ho-Chunk Nation v. Money Centers of Am., Inc.* 9 Am. Tribal Law 308 (Ho-Chunk Nation Trial Ct. 2008). The court explained: "To date, the HCN Legislature has not passed any laws conferring jurisdiction on this Court over the tort claims of fraudulent inducement, fraudulent concealment, or conversion. The Traditional Court has never articulated such claims as arising from tradition and custom and therefore the Supreme Court and Trial Court have not adopted them as such." *Id.* at 315.

One area of law that seems to be frequently addressed in tribal court opinions involving tradition and custom is family law. For example, in the case *In re Marriage of Napyer,* 19 I.L.R. 6078 (Yakima Nation Tribal Ct. 1992), the Yakima Nation Tribal Court addressed a portion of the Tribal code that conflicted with the way that traditional marriage ceremonies were often performed within the Tribe. *Id.* at 6078–79. Specifically, Mr. and Mrs. Napyer were married in a traditional ceremony complete with family representatives from both sides and a traditional Yakima "wedding trade." *Id.* at 6078. The Court, striking a middle ground, decided not to invalidate the law, but upheld the marriage as valid and noted that the questioned code provision conflicted with the Indian Civil Rights Act, the American Indian Religious Freedom Act, and the 1977 Yakima Nation Code. *Id.* at 6079.

In the case of *Rosario v. Arneach*, 2006 WL 6500567 (Eastern Cherokee Ct.), the Cherokee Court of the Eastern Band of Cherokee Indians addressed the issue whether the court would recognize a cause of action for alienation of affection and conversion in a case where the defendant was a mistress of the plaintiff's husband and he had a brief affair with her before returning to his marital home. Specifically, the court went through a long historical analysis of how women were traditionally treated in European societies as contrasted with their role in Cherokee society. *Id.* at 4–5. As the court summarized:

> The parties agree that in Cherokee culture and tradition the roles of females and males were very different than in European society. The parties stipulate that, in Cherokee culture and tradition, Cherokee wives were never considered the property of their husbands. Rather, Cherokee women held an amount of societal power that was stunning to Europeans. *Id.* at 4.

Ultimately, the Court granted summary judgment for the defendant, finding that:

> [O]verwhelming evidence, agreed to by the Plaintiff, is that in the culture and tradition of the Cherokee people no such property rights in spouses existed. Thus, although Cherokee law recognizes the tort of injury to property, neither party to marriage in this culture has ever been considered property. No historical antecedents support application of these torts on the Qualla Boundary …
>
> In common law jurisdictions, a great policy debate exists on the continued social viability of these "heart balm torts." The Plaintiff invites the Court to enter Into that debate so as not to deprive her or future plaintiffs rights of recovery for these alleged indignities to the marital bed.
>
> But legislating from the bench is not the Court's role. There being no support in either the Cherokee Code or the culture and traditions of the Cherokee people for such actions as these, the Court must enter judgment as a matter of law, just as the Louisiana Supreme Court in *Moulin*. The debate is for the common law jurisdictions where the ac-

> tions already exist, or for the Tribal Council. If it is the will of the Council to create a cause of action for alienation of affection and/or criminal conversation, that is a simple matter for the political branches. *Id.* at 5 (citations omitted).

One particularly interesting tradition and custom case addressing the federal standing doctrine and political question doctrine is *Village of Mishongnovi v. Humeyestewa,* 1 Am. Tribal Law 295 (Hopi App. Ct. 1998). Factually, the case presented the issue of whether these two federal doctrines should apply in a case involving a dispute over which alleged governing body should rightfully control a bank account that was held in the name of the Village. *Id.* at 297, 303–04. Although the appellate court did not ultimately rule on the merits of the case and remanded the case to the trial court, it decided that neither of these two federal doctrines should preclude the case from being adjudicated.

As to standing, the Court said:

> [The] narrow federal standing doctrine, developed to restrict litigants' access to federal courts of limited jurisdiction, is inconsistent with Hopi customs of open and consensual dispute resolution and inappropriate given the Hopi tribal court's general jurisdictional authority.
>
> Given the institutional and philosophical foundations of federal standing doctrine, it is not surprising that transplanting its elements into the body of Hopi common law poses substantial risk of rejection. The exclusionary and highly formalistic operation of federal standing doctrine is a poor fit in the Hopi tribal court system, which exists in a radically different cultural and institutional context.
>
> First, the Hopi tribal court system operates squarely within a custom and tradition of open and consensual dispute resolution. Hopi traditions of discussion and consensus decision-making emphasize maximizing opportunities to air grievances and encouraging participation by clan and village members. Imposing a restrictive standing regime on Hopi tribal courts would deny tribal members access to an important neutral arena for adjudication of disputes. *Id.* at 299–302.

Describing its approach to standing, the Court noted, "[s]tanding doctrine should be simple and flexible and should not pose an impenetrable barrier for tribal members to challenge the actions of their village and tribal officials." *Id.* at 303. The Court ultimately announced a rule for how it would view standing in Hopi Tribal Court, stating, "in order to have standing in Hopi Tribal Court, a party need only assert some actual or threatened injury that is logically related to the legal claims it seeks to present to the court." *Id.*

Addressing the political question doctrine, the Court insightfully stated:

> The conceptual foundation for political question doctrine is the importance of preserving the separation of powers. This principle is only imperfectly applied to the Hopi system of government. Unlike the U.S. Constitution, the Hopi constitution does not establish a tripartite system of government that depends on the separation of executive, legislative and judicial functions to provide checks and balances …
>
> Although the concern for separation of powers may not have the same resonance in the Hopi Tribal Court system as in the federal judiciary, political question doctrine may nonetheless be useful in determining whether the Tribal Court should refrain from deciding certain disputes. However, the factors enumerated in Baker v. Carr, must be modified to reflect the distinct institutional framework of Hopi government. Federal political question doctrine very specifically evolved out of a constitutional scheme that granted the federal judiciary only limited jurisdiction. In contrast, Hopi courts are courts of general jurisdiction and have been empowered by the Tribal Council to exercise broad authority to resolve disputes … Within this distinct institutional context, political question doctrine may restrain the Tribal Court's authority to resolve disputes only when the "textually demonstrable constitutional commitment" of the issue is made to another branch in the Hopi Constitution. *Id.* at 304–05.

For a nuanced discussion about how tradition and custom has shaped evidentiary and confrontation requirements for different tribes in regard to the *Crawford* standards for domestic abuse cases *see supra* p. 216. *See also* Matthew L.M. Fletcher, *Rethinking Customary Law in Tribal Court Jurisprudence,* Indigenous Law & Policy Center Occasional Paper Series, *available at* https://www.law.msu.edu/indigenous/papers/2006-04.pdf (discussing the role of customary law in tribal court jurisprudence and discussing how tribal court judges should apply it).

Due Process—Law and Culture from Both Worlds

If one would do a Google word search for the most common phrase that appears in federal and tribal appellate decisions, it would surely be the term "due process." This phrase appears in the Fifth and Fourteenth Amendments to the United States Constitution, in the Indian Civil Rights Act at 25 U.S.C. §1302 (8), and in many tribal constitutions such as Art. X of the Rosebud Sioux Tribe Constitution. Its prevalence is not difficult to understand. Its core meaning of essential fairness has become a widespread judicial norm across the spectrum. While there may be disagreements about its nuances, its foundation remains inviolate, a product of evolving federal and tribal jurisprudence; an anchor amidst the vicissitudes of politics and much contemporary law. Because of how frequently due process issues arise in cases, examples involving this issue can be found in all the previous sections. However, this additional section exists to provide a more focused discussion of this important jurisprudential bedrock.

Given this history, it is not surprising that due process has found a home in evolving tribal court jurisprudence. Due process is also culturally resonant for many tribes. For example, as noted by the Oglala Sioux Supreme Court in the case of *Bloomberg v. Dreamer*:

> It should not be for the Congress of the United States or the federal courts of appeal to tell us when to give due process. *Due process is a concept that has always been with us.* Although it is a legal phrase and has a legal meaning, due process means nothing more than being fair and honest in our dealings with each other. We are allowed to disagree ... what must be remembered is that we must allow the other side the opportunity to be heard. *Bloomberg v. Dreamer*, Oglala Sioux Civ. Ap. 90-348 (1991) (emphasis added).

This cultural resonance is further complemented by the relative flexibility of due process in its application to any particular set of circumstances. It does not have to mimic the *exact* details of federal jurisprudence, but rather remain true to the core of respect and essential fairness. This quintessential legal and traditional norm easily migrates between cultures in both directions.

For example, in *Cheyenne River Sioux Tribe Housing Authority v. Howard*, No. 04-008A (Chey. R. Sx. Ct. App. 1988), the Court discussed the due process requirements for an eviction action. Both federal and tribal court precedent were discussed by the Court when it reaffirmed how due process would be evaluated in the Tribe's courts:

> This Court has long recognized that basic Lakota concepts of fairness and respect as well as the federal Indian Civil Rights Act, 25 U.S.C

> §1302(8), clearly guarantee all parties who appear before the courts of the Cheyenne River Sioux Tribe due process of law. E.g., *Dupree v. Cheyenne River Housing Authority*, 16 Ind. L. Rep. 6106 (Chey. R. Sx. Ct. App.1988). Basic to any concept of due process of law in a civil proceeding, such as this eviction case, is receipt of timely notice and the opportunity to be heard and present evidence at a hearing in support of one's case. *Mullane v. Central Hanover Bank*, 339 U.S. 306 (1950). The basic requirements of notice and hearing, which lie at the core of civil due process of law, do not constitute mere formal requirements or hoops that must be surmounted before judgment. Rather, due process involves functional procedural prerequisites designed to assure that every party has a realistic opportunity to be heard in any case affecting their legal rights. *Id.*

These due process requirements were upheld in a subsequent case involving garnishment and attachment, *High Elk v. Veit*, 6 Am. Tribal Law 73 (Chey. R. Sx. Ct. App. 1988), where notice was not provided in a timely manner. Notice occurred after the attachment and garnishment order were filed with the Court. The Court held that, "[f]or the reasons stated in this Opinion entry of the attachment/garnishment order at issue here constituted a departure from Lakota traditions of respect and honor, was contrary to law, and violated the guarantees of due process of law found in the federal Indian Civil Rights Act of 1968, 25 U.S.C. §1302(8)." *Id.* at 80.

With similar focus on the unique cultural context of due process, the Appellate Court of the Hopi Tribe in *Nevayaktewa v. Hopi Tribe*, 1 Am. Tribal Law 306 (Hopi App. Ct. 1998), held that "at a minimum, fundamental fairness required notice and an opportunity to be heard. Because of its basis in Hopi custom and tradition, fundamental fairness must always be determined within the context of Hopi values." *Id.* at 320 (citations omitted). The Court further explained what fundamental fairness means when it stated:

> "Fundamental fairness" has never acquired a precise definition. Fundamental fairness requires adherence to those "principles of liberty and justice" that are "implicit in the concept of ordered liberty." that are "so rooted in the traditions and conscience of our people as to be ranked as fundamental." and that "lie at the base of all our civil and political institutions." Moreover, it prohibits actions that "offend those canons of decency and fairness which express the notions of justice of English-speaking peoples even toward those charged with the most heinous offenses" and that are "repugnant to the conscience of mankind." *Id.* at 321 (footnotes omitted).

The Navajo Supreme Court held that due process rights attach to public housing eviction cases in *Atcitty v. District Court for the Judicial District of Window Rock*, 7 Nav. R. 227 (Nav. Sup. Ct. 1985), and expressed this same sentiment in the eviction case of *Fort Defiance Hous. Corp. v. Lowe*, 5 Am. Tribal Law 394 (Nav. Sup. Ct. 2004):

> [W]e have also held that Navajo due process encompasses a wider range of interests than due process under the United States Constitution. The centrality of a home to Navajo life means that a tenant's interest in a home, whether a rental unit or not, cannot be taken away without due process. Also, independent of this interest, we have recognized a due process right of access to the courts, including appeals. That right requires that our Court give appellants meaningful notice and an opportunity to be heard. It also means that the right of access to the courts should not be denied on technical grounds. *Id.* at 398–99 (citations omitted).

Part of this reasoning was based on the centrality and importance of the home in Navajo culture: "The home in Navajo thinking is not a mere piece of property in which one holds an equity interest, but *hooghan* rises to a level of spiritual centrality." *Id.* at 398. The Court explicitly held, "Given the importance of a home to Navajos, a tenant has an absolute right to due process in eviction proceedings." *Id.* The Court further explained what this would mean logistically for appellate purposes:

> We therefore hold that in order to assure due process, a district court's eviction order must give tenants notice of the appeal bond requirement, the timing requirements, and the specific conditions for the bond set by the court. We also interpret the five days in the statute to be five working days from receipt of the order, to give tenants additional time to comply with the judge's conditions. *Id.* at 400.

For a focused discussion on how due process has evolved in the Navajo tribal courts, *see* Paul Spruhan, *The Meaning of Due Process in the Navajo Nation* in THE INDIAN CIVIL RIGHTS ACT AT FORTY 119–130 (Kristen A. Carpenter, Matthew L.M. Fletcher & Angela R. Riley, eds. 2012).

The breadth of other tribal court due process cases is immense, as the following cases illustrate. In the case of *In re Constitutional Question re: Voting*, 1998 NASR 0000001(Saint Regis Mohawk Tribal Ct. 1998), the Saint Regis Mohawk Tribal Court addressed a due process question involving voting. Specifically, the court held that timelines and requirements for voter registration and challenges of being left off the voting list did not violate due process. *Id.* These requirements, as the court noted, did not create a burden upon the right to vote which was impermissible. *Id.* Addressing a different election issue, specifically the right to challenge primary election results, in *Jacobs v. Zimmer*, 9 Okla. Trib. 410 (Cheyenne-Arapaho Tribal Ct. 2006), the Cheyenne-Arapaho Tribal Court held that "[a] key component of elections that deals with due process are the challenges to candidates and to the election results. At the primary election there was no opportunity to challenge either. This is a due process violation." *Id.* at 410.

An *ex parte* order to disqualify a judge was addressed in *Fort Peck Tribes v. Azure*, No. 081 (Fort Peck Ct. App. 1989) where the Tribe was the appellant and argued due process violations. The Fort Peck Court of Appeals held that the *ex parte* order disqualifying a judge was indeed a violation of due process as notice and the right to be heard were denied. *Id.*

In *In re D.H.*, 8 Am. Tribal Law 164 (Grand Traverse Tribal Ct. 2009), the Grand Traverse Band of Ottawa and Chippewa Indians Tribal Court addressed a due process question in relation to the Indian Child Welfare Act (ICWA). Specifically, the Court addressed whether a parent should be entitled to a jury trial in an ICWA proceeding. *Id.* Even though Michigan state law required a jury trial, the court made it clear that it was not bound by state precedent and instead held:

> Respondent is entitled to fundamental due process in this proceeding. The Court is not persuaded that a jury trial is a component of that due process requirement in this type of proceeding. Nor is the Court persuaded that a judge cannot adequately protect Respondent's due process rights or reach a determination while also recognizing and acknowledging tribal customs and traditions of the Grand Traverse Band regarding child rearing as required under the Children's Code.
>
> The Court agrees with Respondent that Tribal Council *could* adopt a provision in the Children's Code providing for a right to a jury trial, and that the Tribal Court *could* adopt a court rule providing for the right to a jury trial in this type of proceeding. However, neither has done so to date. 10 GTBC § 107(a) states that "The procedures in the Children's Court shall be governed by the rules of procedure for the Tribal Court, not in conflict with this Code. In the absence of Tribal Court promulgated rules of procedure, the Michigan Rules of Civil Procedure shall be utilized *as a guide*." (emphasis added). This Court reads this provision to provide that the Court will look to Michigan law for guidance, but the use of Michigan procedure (including the right to a jury trial) is discretionary, not mandatory. Again, the Court is not persuaded that a jury trial was intended by the Tribal Council

> in adopting the Children's Code, nor that the Tribal Judiciary has intended to provide for a jury trial in Children's Code proceedings. *Id.* at 166–67.

Due process in the tribal court context has also been employed in cases involving non-Indian defendants, and occasionally non-Indian plaintiffs. For example, the Hopi Court of Appeals addressed this very issue in *Monestersky v. The Hopi Tribe*, 01AP000015 (Hopi Ct. App. 2002), where a non-Indian asserted that her due process rights under Indian Civil Rights Act (ICRA) were violated when the Chairman of the Tribe issued an order of exclusion. However, the Court did not find this argument compelling and held that the appellant had received both proper notice and had an administrative hearing, thus she both received notice and had her opportunity to be heard. *Id.* Even though those grounds were sufficient, the Court made the further point that because the appellant suffered no loss of property or deprivation of liberty interest, her (substantive) due process rights were not triggered. *Id.*

In *Monette v. Schlenvogt*, 32 IRL 6074 (Turtle Mtn. Tr. Ct. App. 2005), the Turtle Mountain Tribal Court of Appeals decided the due process claim of a defendant tribal member in an eviction action initiated by a non-Indian landlord. *Id.* The Court held for the defendant Tribal member stating, "Ms. Monette's due process rights were violated because of the lack of adequate notice.... [the] trial court order granting forcible eviction and back rent ... are hereby vacated." *Id.* at 6075. The Court also noted that the Tribe's Constitution directly incorporated the Indian Civil Rights Act at Art. 14, Sec. 3(a). *Id. See also In re A.P. v. Tuba City Family Court*, 6 Am. Tribal Law 660 (Nav. Sup. Ct. 2005) (discussing how the due process rights of a non-Indian juvenile were violated when an exclusion order was issued without a hearing).

Finally, a non-member Indian, was found to be subject to the criminal jurisdiction of the Navajo Nation through a *hadane* (in-law) relationship in *Means v. District Court of the Chinle Judicial District*, 2 Am. Tribal Law 439 (Nav. Sup. Ct. 1999). The Navajo Supreme Court found that none of the non-member Indian's ICRA rights, including the right to counsel, due process, and equal protection were at risk. In fact, the Court indicated that the rights of Mr. Means under Navajo law were equivalent to any rights he would have in state or federal court:

> The petitioner's attorney was asked whether Navajo Nation law affords criminal defendants all the rights guaranteed by the sixth amendment to the United States Constitution during oral argument, and he evaded the question. Although such is not required by the Indian Civil Rights Act of 1968, criminal defendants in the Navajo Nation court

> system are entitled to the appointment of counsel if they are indigent, and they are entitled to a jury composed of a fair cross-section of Navajo Nation population, including non-Indians and nonmember Indians. The petitioner has all the rights he would have in a state or federal court. *Id.* at 446 n.11.

This decision was affirmed by the Ninth Circuit in *Means v. Navajo Nation*, 432 F.3d 924 (9th Cir. 2005).

Conclusion

Accomplishment and the Continuing Challenge of Justice, Tradition, and Respect

There is no doubt in my mind that the past twenty-five years reflect a period of tremendous growth in the breadth and depth of tribal court appellate jurisprudence. This is certainly true in my own judicial experience, but it is equally true across Indian country as these materials and notes attest to. A growing sense of justice, cultural integrity, and fair play animates the core of these positive developments.

These advances also reflect certain growing pains that must be attended to in order to prevent stagnation and the loss of encouraging momentum. Some of these growing pains involve the issues of resources, infrastructure, and transparency. Many tribal courts across Indian country, but particularly here in South Dakota, continue to face serious funding challenges. These financial challenges often effect both professional and non-professional staffing levels, training opportunities, and operating costs. For example, several years ago, I attended the grand opening of the impressive three and one-half million dollar Mississippi Band of Choctaw judicial complex. When I returned home to South Dakota, I contacted the Clerk of the Rosebud Sioux Supreme Court to set up a conference call with the other justices to discuss a pending case. The Clerk, somewhat embarrassingly, informed me that that would not be possible as the Court had not been able to pay its phone bill. This 'crisis' was subsequently overcome, but funding remains precarious for many tribal courts. While we often prefer not to think about it, it remains a truism that the level of financial resources plays a considerable role in matters of judicial efficiency, legal competence, and advancing the docket. Justice delayed—whether on or off the reservation—is justice denied.

Closely related to resources is the issue of infrastructure. Infrastructure involves such things as the physical nature of the tribal courthouse, the adequacy of the tribal jail, the level of computer and technical support, and the ready availability of court records and transcripts. For example, I have participated in several appellate cases that have led to a summary reversal in favor of the appellant because of the absence of any reliable recording or transcript of the trial court proceedings. Such failures often constitute a violation of due process under the ICRA, 25 U.S.C. § 1302 (8), and the tribe's constitution.

The enhancement of infrastructure also includes such things as the continued development and growth of tribal bar associations and the implementation and administration of tribal bar examinations. Tribal bar associations are key to establishing a legal community—Native and non-Native, law-trained and not—of individuals, who practice in tribal court and are committed to advancing recognition and respect for their common endeavors. Tribal bar examinations are also significant markers of legitimacy in establishing basic threshold requirements to practice in tribal court. These associational and legal practice elements of infrastructure need not simply mimic mainstream legal institutions, but rather strike the necessary balance between the outside and the inside, the dominant and the indigenous.

There is also a growing focus on the issue of transparency, which reflects renewed popular concern with government secrecy and the withholding of information. Transparency is the basic notion that such things as a tribe's constitution, substantive and procedural law, and its judicial decisions should be published and readily available to the public. In fact, these matters of transparency are express conditions that must be satisfied in order for a tribe to opt into enhanced opportunities available under the Tribal Law and Order Act and the Violence Against Women Reauthorization Act. See discussion, *supra* pp. 219–20.

Transparency is not only a matter of cost and infrastructure, but it is also a matter of a tribe's 'will' to be transparent. While it is hard to quibble with the benefits of transparency, many tribes are hesitant to comply because of a lingering historically based fear that they will somehow become victims of this federal 'benevolence.' For example, there is the failed 'benevolence' of the late nineteenth century federal policy of allotment. The alleged benefit of individual Indian ownership of land never materialized, but instead resulted in a staggering reduction in the Native land base. The result of this federal 'benevolence' was the loss of ninety million acres between 1889 and 1934. In this view, tribal sovereignty will be potentially compromised even further if its transparency efforts are deemed incomplete or inadequate. The taint of the federal past often infects the possibilities of the tribal present. Despite such legitimate concerns and suspicions about the federal and state motives for requiring increased tribal transparency, improved transparency is the order of the day. In fact, it is often voiced most strongly by tribal members themselves.

Lastly, there must be continuous growth in the reporting of tribal court opinions and developing reliable research tools to find them. As tribal jurisprudence grows and evolves, it must be readily available to judges and practitioners so that they may refine and build on this foundational body of law. Without such availability, the orderly development of tribal court jurisprudence will be slowed and compromised. This book and accompanying Libguide are a modest attempt to enhance this process of foundational growth and development.

The ongoing legitimacy of tribal court decision-making cannot and should not be taken for granted. There are certainly still pockets of resistance to tribal court decisions within and especially outside the reservation. It only takes one poorly decided or inflammatory case to potentially upset gains already made.

Legitimacy is largely incremental and cumulative. Each and every tribal court decision adds to (or subtracts from) this ongoing process. Fragility, in many ways, is still the order of the day. The foundation is still being poured. Potential threats to this foundation are likely to come from two primary sources. The first is the treatment of non-Indians (as plaintiff or defendant) in civil cases or in criminal cases under the Violence Against Women Reauthorization Act. Such cases are and will continue to be closely watched by the powers that be. Many states and non-native interests are posed to cut tribal sovereignty down to size. Any failure to treat non-Indians with due process, fairness, and respect will surely draw ire and calls for Congressional and Supreme Court adjustment.

The second source of threat is internal and one that flows from any growing political turmoil that unduly interferes with tribal government or cultural stability. For example, prolonged struggle between competing groups as the legitimate tribal governing body or issues involving the painful and divisive issues of enrollment and disenrollment can often rock and destabilize tribes. If tribal courts fail to perform with competency and legitimacy in any of these areas, the losers are likely to vigorously seek redress elsewhere, such as within Congress, state and federal courts, or the Bureau of Indian Affairs. Such non-tribal court approaches can only undermine the integrity of tribal sovereignty and self-governance. As the cases in this book indicate, such alternative methods have been largely unsuccessful and rejected because of the essential thoughtfulness, persuasiveness, and cultural respect reflected in the tribal court opinions.

As tribal citizens develop more sophisticated expectations of their tribal governments, the bar of tribal court competence and persuasion is also set higher. Tribal courts must not fail to take this into account. Growing local political participation by tribal citizens must not devolve into political chaos or fractious dissension because of any failure of tribal courts to craft convincing and robust decisions.

In this vein, it is fruitful to recall that the United States Supreme Court at its inception had no courtroom, staff, budget, or inherent legitimacy. In fact, the Court's very existence was rattled by the *Cherokee* cases of 1831 and 1832. The state of Georgia refused to appear in either case and President Jackson (supposedly) stated with regard to *Worcester v. Georgia*, 31 U.S. 515 (1832), "Chief Justice Marshall made his decision, now let him enforce it!" Fortunately, Georgia's truculence subsided and President Jackson successfully convinced the Governor of Georgia to pardon the defendants in the *Worcester* case.[1] The salient lesson is that the rule of law can never be taken for granted. Respect is earned day by day and case by case. It accumulates into tradition through *daily* attentiveness.

The arc of justice gathers and deepens with the continuing commitment to thoughtfulness, tradition, and fair play. Justice is never automatic or guaranteed. Wisdom comes from what has gone before and what is added in the present to create a just and enduring legal order. Such an order is the gateway to a meaningful judicial future across Indian country. That is the (red) road. Way beyond any search engine, any keystroke.

There are no guarantees in the development of tribal (appellate) jurisprudence. Each opinion must be fully informed by a proper mix of reason, understanding, and legal analysis. Each opinion undergirded by a persuasive blend of history, culture, and understanding of practical consequences. All done in such a way that any reader, whether lay or professional, whether Native or not, would immediately note the grounding of respect and the commitment to justice and fair play. From many strands, one strong braid. Daily effort, ample and committed.

1. *See* the discussion in GETCHES ET AL., FEDERAL INDIAN LAW 122–25 (6th ed. 2011).

Table of Cases

Principal cases are in bold type.

Nevayaktewa v. Hopi Tribe, 1 Am. Tribal Law 306 (Hopi App. Ct. 1998), 246

Ocean County v. Chippewa, 2001 WL 36194127 (Grand Traverse Tribal Ct.), 232

Oliphant v. Suquamish Indian Tribe, 435 U.S. 191 (1978), 211, 219

Ordinance 59 Ass'n v. U.S. Dep't of Interior Sec'y, 163 F.3d 1150 (10th Cir. 1998), 130

Paul v. Southern Ute Indian Tribe, 24 I.L.R. 6038 (S.W. Intertr. Ct. App. 1997), 128

Pearce ex rel. Gen. Council v. Nuckolls, ASSC-99-01, 1999 WL 33589156 (Ab. Shawnee Tribe Sup. Ct.), 199

Plains Commerce Bank v. Long Family Land and Cattle Company, Inc., 32 I.L. R. 6001 (2004) (Cheyenne River Sioux Tribal Court of Appeals) (2004), 61, 77

Plains Commerce Bank v. Long Family Land and Cattle Co., Inc., 440 F. Supp. 2d 1070 (D.S.D. 2006), 103

Plains Commerce Bank v. Long Family Land and Cattle Co., Inc., 491 F.3d 878 (8th Cir. 2007), 79, 87–88, 103

Plains Commerce Bank v. Long Family Land and Cattle Co., 554 U.S. 316 (2008), 25, 77–78, 91, 97–99, 103

Plummer v. Walker River Paiute Tribal Court, 2003 WL 25856878 (Nev. Inter-Tribal C.A.), 214

Redman v. Birdshead, 2003 WL 25783118 (Cheyenne-Arapaho D. Ct.), 240

Rosario v. Arneach, 2006 WL 6500567 (Eastern Cherokee Ct.), 242

Rosebud Sioux Tribe v. Luxon (Rosebud Sioux Supreme Court) (2009). This case is not available in the Indian Law Reporter and has not been reported elsewhere. 108, 203, 211

Ruhrgas AG v. Marathon Oil Co., 526 U.S. 574 (1999), 55, 56

Sac & Fox Tribe of Mississippi In Iowa Election Bd. v. Bureau of Indian Affairs, 439 F.3d 832 (8th Cir. 2006), 174

Santa Clara Pueblo v. Martinez, 436 U.S. 49 (1978), 89, 105, 106, 107, 125, 129, 130, 131, 178

Seminole Nation of Oklahoma v. Norton, 223 F. Supp. 2d 122 (D.D.C. 2002), 131

Sherman v. Enbridge Energy LLC, 9 Am. Tribal Law 462 (Leech Lake Band of Ojibwe Tribal Ct. 2010), 200

Simmons v. Colville Confederated Tribes, 2002 WL 34540594 (Colville Tribal Ct. App.), 230

Index